HOUSE IN
THE COUNTRY

ALSO BY SIMON MATTHEWS

PSYCHEDELIC CELLULOID
LOOKING FOR A NEW ENGLAND

HOUSE IN THE COUNTRY

Where Our Suburbs and Garden Cities Came From and Why it's Time to Leave Them Behind

SIMON MATTHEWS

Oldcastle Books

First published in 2022 by
Oldcastle Books Ltd,
Harpenden,
Herts, UK
oldcastlebooks.co.uk
@noexitpress
Editor: Nick Rennison
© Simon Matthews, 2022

A CIP catalogue record for this book is available from the British Library.

ISBN
978-0-85730-495-7 (Print)
978-0-85730-496-4 (Epub)

2 4 6 8 10 9 7 5 3 1

Typeset in 11.75 on 14.6pt Goudy Old Style
by Avocet Typeset, Bideford, Devon, EX39 2BP
Printed and bound by TJ Books Limited, Padstow, Cornwall

CONTENTS

FOREWORD

Anyone interested in the challenges of housing policy will want to read this methodical analysis of what went well and what did not over much of the last century. The most depressing conclusion arises from the inconsistency of policy. It is as though new ministers felt they had to make changes as a sort of virility symbol of their competence.

The last words of the book conclude the story with the question as to whether subsequent generations will hold us to account for the inadequacy of their inheritance. We are shown a projection of housing demand to meet the increasing population, the consequences of global warming on coastal communities and the imbalance between public and private housing to name just some of tomorrow's certainties.

The private sector cannot meet the cost of social housing. Land supply and the cost of acquisition together with all the planning constraints and nimby pressures militate against any radical and comprehensive answers. There are people living in conditions that will be increasingly unacceptable as the years pass. I am all too familiar with the reality of this background having wrestled with its pressures for six years as Secretary of State for the Environment.

A first step, which I would recommend if we are to offer a positive answer to that question, would be the establishment of an independent enquiry to recommend what policies are needed now to provide the all too predictable scale of both public and private housing in the future. Members of the enquiry would be well advised to commence their homework by reading this book.

Lord Heseltine, April 2022

PREFACE

Unless you're very lucky indeed – and most of us today are not – you will have had at least one, and usually many more, conversations about how expensive it is to buy a house, or how little truly affordable housing now seems to exist. This book arose out of one such conversation.

What it attempts to do is explain why housing is an issue in the UK today, and to highlight the various choices the country has made in the recent past that have produced the present predicament. It also suggests solutions to our difficulties. Too many books present the reader with a narrative that comes across as an opinionated fault-finding exercise. Given the fraught politics of the last couple of decades in the UK, and given too the challenges the country faces in the future, this seemed to me to be an inadequate approach. It's easy to say what is wrong: it isn't so easy to fix it.

What the book isn't is a list of every piece of parliamentary legislation affecting housing, every architect of significance, every major estate or building, every significant public figure linked to housing or every song, novel, play or film with some sort of housing connection. Instead, it offers a narrative threading through the key events, locations and personalities that have affected UK housing policy since the mid-nineteenth century. In doing so it concentrates on the enormous influence that the garden city/garden suburb movement, via its originator Ebenezer Howard, has had (and continues to have) on what kind of housing is built, for whom and where. It suggests that, by default, the UK follows two different models: high-density urban living vs low-density suburban living, with the latter generally preferred. And it argues that whatever the reader's personal views, the onset of significant climate change demands that we change this.

Thanks are due to publisher Ion Mills and his team at Oldcastle Books, particularly Nick Rennison, without whose largesse none of this would have been possible. I am also grateful for the time given by Lord Heseltine, Joint Leader of the Green Party Councillor Carla Denyer, Councillor Guy Nicholson, Aman Dalvi, Sunand Prasad, Richard Morton, Jonathan Schifferes, Gareth Crawford, David D'Arcy, Andrew Bosi, Tom Bolton, Mazhar Ali and Robin Ramsay all of whom offered advice and opinions about various elements of the text.

Finally – full disclosure here – I served as a local councillor in London between 1987 and 1998. During this time, I chaired a planning committee, a housing committee and sat on a City Challenge board. As well as this my day job for many years involved working as a housing assessment officer for another London local authority. Later, from 2001, I ran my own housing consultancy, buying land and property, advising on land use and carrying out resident surveys across the UK for a client group drawn from local authorities, housing associations and private sector developers. Inevitably, my personal experiences in this field colour the narrative and affect the arguments made, but the positions taken, and the conclusions reached are not partisan, and the aim of the book is to both entertain and inform.

Simon Matthews, February 2022

1

EARLY STIRRINGS

Not everyone in England was pleased by the outcome of the Battle of Waterloo. After 23 years of war, funded by a deeply unpopular income tax, and with the UK dependent on obviously illiberal allies to do most of the fighting on the European mainland, there were many who wanted to withdraw from further conflict, abolish income tax, forswear continental entanglements with Russia, Prussia and Austria, and concentrate on an expansion of trade to deliver the prosperity that the country needed. Among those making this case were Lord Grey, an opposition politician, formerly Foreign Secretary between September 1806 and March 1807, and Robert Wilson, an army officer and radical who had served alongside Wellington in Spain. Both were speaking on the morning of 22 June 1815, at Brooks Club in St James, about the inevitability of Napoleon's victory when news arrived of his defeat at Waterloo. Thus, instead of gloomy prognostications in Parliament about British-German-Prussian-Dutch reversals, the Secretary of State for War, Earl Bathurst, moved a vote of thanks to Wellington, Field Marshal Blücher and the soldiers of the allied armies.[1] Like many, Grey and Wilson had been prepared to fight France when it was a case of resisting revolution and social upheaval. But neither wanted a Bourbon restoration. When it became clear that this was the alternative preferred by the various kings and emperors of Europe, both had changed their minds about Napoleon. Similar views were shared by the critic and essayist William Hazlitt, Samuel Whitbread, Whig MP for Bedford (who committed suicide in despair), many nonconformist Protestants and even Lord Byron, whose poem *The*

Age of Bronze (1823) portrayed everything that had happened since Waterloo as a triumph for the selfish, profiteering aristocracy at the expense of the poor.

Nor were such opinions wrong. In the expectation that Napoleon's 1814 abdication and exile to Elba had brought an end to the cycle of wars that had raged for more than two decades, Parliament had already passed, in April 1815, an Act which forbade any importing of foreign grain until prices reached 80 shillings a quarter, roughly £1,000 a ton. This was a tremendously high level, and one picked to guarantee the profits of landowners even when harvests were poor. Then, with the war against France finally ended at the Treaty of Paris (November 1815), the clamour for the abolition of income tax became impossible to resist, and duly took place in March 1816, after a series of government defeats. Nicholas Vansittart, Chancellor of the Exchequer and MP for Harwich, actually wanted to maintain it, recognising that it was an effective and simple revenue-raising tool. But the tax was so unpopular that Parliament, flexing its muscles and opting for a decisive illustration of its power, ordered the destruction of all documents connected with it.[2] A desire to revert to the *status quo ante bellum* was also behind the government decision, made in 1819, to return to the gold standard by 1823, a task it completed two years earlier than envisaged. In theory, these arrangements reflected the liberal economics of the time: low taxes, sound money, low expenditure and a balanced budget, all underpinned by free trade. It was considered axiomatic that government spending should be as low as possible, with little made available for education and virtually nothing for health.[3] In practice, despite dramatic cuts in government spending, particularly with the demobilisation of much of the armed forces after 1815, the national debt continued to grow, and the government continued to borrow. Nor was the government against spending large amounts of money on projects that it considered worthy, provided extra taxes were not required.[4] In 1818, it voted to allocate £1m (about £560m in 2020 money) to the Church Building Society as thanksgiving for victory at Waterloo. This was invested in building new Anglican churches, church halls and vicarages, and was specifically targeted at competing with the growing nonconformist and evangelical congregations.

The speed of this enforced transition led to mass protests by the unemployed, exacerbated by a series of poor harvests. The early stages of a national famine occurred in 1816, "the year without a summer", with extensive rioting taking place in Ely and Spa Fields (London). This was followed in 1817 by an attempted march from Manchester to London by unemployed blanket-carrying textile workers in Manchester and a failed uprising in Derbyshire. The infamous Peterloo massacre, when a gathering in favour of political reform was attacked by heavily armed cavalry, followed in 1819. Many of the participants in these events believed they could favourably petition the Prince Regent and obtain redress for their grievances, or some kind of favourable national settlement. The unrest culminated in the Cato Street Conspiracy, an unsuccessful plan to assassinate the entire cabinet in February 1820, shortly after the death of George III and the accession of the Prince Regent as George IV.

Thus, after 1815, the UK returned to a world where the wealthy lived in some opulence, with scant provision for the rest of the population. Due to the operation of the franchise, most adults (more than 90%, including most of the middle classes) could not vote, and, because boundary changes had not reflected where people lived for hundreds of years, entire towns, particularly recently established manufacturing centres in the midlands and north, had no representation of their own in Parliament.

* * * * * *

In 1820 poet Percy Shelley, then living in semi-exile in Italy, would write in *Peter Bell the Third*:

Hell is a city much like London—
A populous and a smoky city;
There are all sorts of people undone,
And there is little or no fun done;
Small justice shown, and still less pity.

The poem, a savage satire on the London-based ruling class, followed his political verses *The Masque of Anarchy* and *England in 1819* (both 1819) and extended prose essay *A Philosophical View of Reform*, which would not be published until 100 years later. It portrays a crowded and expanding metropolis at a time when the population of the UK was already drifting from its villages and small market towns to the larger towns and cities. Between 1811 and 1821 the population rose from 18 million to 21 million, and that of London, which grew steadily, comfortably exceeded 1 million. The capital was large, but proportionally smaller than it is now in relation to the rest of the country, and the UK still remained a land of long-established boroughs and small, compact and ancient cities. London and its many crowded streets were considered to be crime-ridden, particularly by gangs of delinquent children (though the extent of this is debated) and there were very few rules governing what could, or couldn't, be built. Anyone proposing a scheme merely had to ensure that the vestry – the bureaucratic section of the local Anglican parish that dealt with such matters – didn't object to their plan. For many it was just a question of buying land and starting work.

The growth of towns and cities largely followed an organic process – tendrils of ribbon development slowly advancing along the roads emanating from an old inner core (usually the mediaeval town centre) with, as the development crossed them, rivers and streams culverted into sewers to facilitate drainage. A typical example might be the gradual creeping northward along Ermine Street (now the A10) between Bishopsgate, in the City of London, and Kingsland, in Dalston, then part of Middlesex, of houses, terraces and small streets, the building of which took approximately 250 years. Within cities and towns themselves something quicker was often attempted, and the laying out of a traditional square surrounded with townhouses was particularly popular. This feature first appeared in London in the 1630s, with Inigo Jones a notable exponent, and had been copied from France where Henri IV built the Place des Vosges in 1605. Building around a square or courtyard had, of course, existed in England for centuries prior to this, with many examples of traditional northern European market places to be found across the country, usually where dense networks of buildings faced onto an open space, used for commercial purposes, at an intersection of numerous alleyways and roads. The difference with the Place des Vosges, Covent Garden and its successors, though, was that the properties built as part of these schemes were intended for the very well off, whereas in the older mediaeval "market square" layouts, various social classes tended to live jumbled up together.

Houses were thought of as having an organic life too: they were built, stayed in use for their purpose, went into decline and were often sub-divided into multiple occupancy, with individual rooms separately rented out, before they collapsed into disrepair and were demolished. Most large-scale (by the standards of the time) building was sponsored by wealthy landowners as a means of maximising their return on their estates. From 1800 the Duke of Bedford developed Bloomsbury, where Thomas Cubitt completed Woburn Walk, the first street specifically designed for shopping in 1822. Cubitt also undertook the development of Belgravia, from 1826, for the Duke of Westminster. Promoted as *"a stuccoed rival to Mayfair"*, its streets featured classical facades and decoration both internally and externally and the scheme as a whole took over 30 years to complete. The greatest exponent of this type of development was John Nash who came to prominence in the 1790s and whose style wobbled between anachronistic Gothic and faux-classical. By 1806 he was personal architect to the Prince Regent, and engaged on the design and building of Regent Street and the massive terraces encircling Regent's Park, the latter creating an extremely exclusive new residential area of London. Nash's career was a confirmation that architects were an elite profession, only engaged by the very wealthy. Their training was part of the fine arts, including as it did drawing, an awareness of light, perspective and proportion, and they were heavily steeped in classicism, being deployed on the construction of country houses with landscaped grounds. Appointed to oversee the rebuilding of Buckingham Palace, for which he designed the Marble Arch in 1827, Nash was also a director of the Regent's Canal Company, which aimed to open up areas adjoining London to commercial development, but would lose his influence after the death of George IV.

Outside London, and with less elevated social connections, James Gillespie Graham designed 150 houses for upper middle-class occupants on the Moray Estate in Edinburgh. Construction of these began in 1822, and the scheme was only finally built out in 1858. Long, drawn-out completions of this type were common then (as now) and reflected the fact that developers building for sale, especially if building an expensive product, would only build at the rate that they could sell. Grainger Town, in Newcastle, was developed for mixed use – shops, public houses, a theatre and houses – by Richard Grainger, John Dobson and Thomas Oliver from 1834 (though adjoining areas were being worked on from 1824). It finally completed in 1841. Similarly, the gated suburb of Victoria Park, Manchester, built by Richard Lane from 1836, took decades to come to fruition. Somewhat less exclusive and dating from the 1830s were Hoxton New Town and De Beauvoir Town. Both were part of the gradual filling in of land along the Ermine Street-A10 corridor and were designed and built by the architects Lewis Roumieu and Alexander Gough. But, again, neither was quick. Although pleasant, clean and well proportioned (compared to many of the surrounding properties) both took until 1850 to complete.[5]

The majority of the "streetscape" created by these schemes, particularly in London, and especially in Belgravia, consisted of houses, built to a density that was typical in European cities, although never quite as high as that found in Paris. In Belgravia, and later in the development of Ladbroke Grove, Kensington during the 1840s, density in selected areas would reach 1067 habitable rooms per hectare, implying a population of 345,000 per square mile if applied consistently: similar to locations like Kowloon today. This reflected how essential it was at the time to compress developments within a small area, reflecting the fact that most people walked everywhere, particularly to and from work.

In terms of what was actually built, the ideal was individual family houses. Apartments (flats) would have been regarded as almost shockingly alien, notwithstanding the historic tendency for many families to live above a shop.[6] The only buildings that resembled flatted blocks were workhouses, and eventually a number of eminent architects did model workhouse designs, including William Adams Nicholson. There was almost nothing, though, that might be called "social housing", with the arguable exception of almshouses. This was a concept that dated back to mediaeval times, and most towns and cities had a tiny terrace or courtyard of them which were provided almost exclusively by either churches or livery companies, and intended to "relieve" poverty affecting pious, and usually well-connected, elderly residents. Efforts were made to bring the design of such properties up-to-date throughout the nineteenth century, notably by Henry Seward (in Camden for St Martin-in-the-Fields, 1817) and George Porter (in Penge for the Watermen and Lightermen of the City of London, 1840). But their numbers remained tiny, and none was intended for families.

* * * * * *

When victory at Waterloo was being celebrated the idea of building a "new town" barely existed, and density itself in the networks of streets and terraces that spread out from cities was not particularly an issue. But, in the hard, unremitting and largely uncaring years that followed, with cities and towns expanding and exhibiting appalling levels of overcrowding, pollution and generally insanitary conditions, some efforts to address these issues were started.

Anthony Ashley-Cooper, 7th Earl of Shaftesbury established the Labourer's Friend Society in 1830, to improve the conditions of the labouring classes in rural areas, principally by allotting them land for "cottage husbandry" ie, providing them with space to grow a useful proportion of their own food.[7] This action came after widespread rioting caused by poor wages and impoverishment, much of which occurred a month prior to the July 1830 revolution in France. The English aristocracy required little reminding of how revolutions in France tended to end. Shaftesbury's action was thus timely, though we might note today, rather curiously, that his grandfather (the 4th Earl) had been one of the founders of the Colony of Georgia in 1733. Here, throughout the 1740s, the Oglethorpe Plan was promoted for building a model capital city at Savannah: an interlocking series of geometric street blocks and squares, where white settler families were given 5-acre kitchen gardens. One wonders to what extent he was aware of this prior involvement of one of his ancestors in creating an ideal living environment. In promoting "cottage husbandry", he was certainly not following the precedent set by David Dale and Richard Arkwright when they started the settlement of New Lanark in 1785. Here homes had been built to house the workforce of nearby cotton mills. The settlement eventually accommodated 2,500 people in blocks of property spread, mainly due to topography, across 360 acres. However, New Lanark was not widely emulated, possibly because of its location in Scotland or because it provided housing to facilitate industrial production in a country that was still coming to terms with the practicalities of the industrial revolution.[8]

The Labourer's Friend Society was definitely harking back to a safer, nicer living environment that was supposed to have existed in the recent past, and this theme would become constant through the nineteenth and twentieth centuries as visionaries – and many of the public – sought to avoid the stress of city living. By itself, such sentimentality, or nostalgia, no matter how well intentioned or apposite, might not have amounted to much in terms of social change. But, two things helped. Firstly, a significant cholera pandemic occurred in the UK in 1832, killing 55,000 people nationally, and claiming 6,536 victims in London alone. With so many living in filth and poverty, and nothing approaching a safe water supply available, this was hardly surprising. Secondly, and largely due to the efforts of Prime Minister Lord Grey, whose dismay at Bonaparte's defeat in 1815 had been at variance with the emotions of so many of his parliamentary contemporaries, 1832 also saw the passing of a Reform Act. This increased the electoral franchise, which rose, in England and Wales, from 400,000 to

650,000, an increase of 37.5%. All remained male and under these arrangements it was still the case that only about 10% of the adult population could vote in parliamentary elections.[9] A very limited form of participatory democracy, Grey's legislation ushered in an era where the country was ruled by middle-class men whose education, background and interests were somewhat different from the previous aristocracy-dominated electorate with its numerous anomalies. It became easier to pass legislation with a social purpose.

Thus, in the aftermath of 1832, Parliament agreed a year later to spend £20,000 (approximately £7m in 2020 money) on providing facilities to educate the poor. The money was distributed – as was the default position then – to the Anglican Church, for onward transmission to the National Society for Promoting Religious Education. This was followed by the Poor Law Amendment Act, 1834, which established local Poor Law Guardians, funded from a rate paid by local land and property owners. The combination of the education grant, the rate paid to the Poor Law Guardians (who were elected in each parish) and the 1818 donation to the Church Building Society produced three areas of building work – schools, workhouses and churches – where funds, no matter how inadequate, could be accessed to complete projects, and helps to explain why so many nineteenth-century architects specialised in work of this type.

The Municipal Corporations Act of 1835 went further, introducing a uniform system of local government, funded once more by ratepayers, the majority of whom were also electors in the same district. This quickly produced a spate of significant buildings – town halls, libraries, baths, concert halls – but, in terms of expenditure, barely ventured beyond such "public works". On a grand scale the early 1830s saw the planning of Trafalgar Square and the start of a grandiose Gothic rebuilding of the Houses of Parliament, both involving Sir Charles Barry, assisted on the latter by Augustus Pugin. London also got two new bridges across the River Thames, a Metropolitan police force and the introduction of horse-drawn buses and taxis.

But there was nothing for housing.

Notes

(1) The battle took place on 18 June 1815, and was conclusively decided late that day (after 6.30pm) by the arrival of Marshal Blücher's Prussian army. Wellington's account of the battle was written on 19 June, reached London on 21 June and was officially published in the *London Gazette* on 22 June. In holding their views about a likely French victory, Grey and Wilson may have been relying on news of Napoleon's initial defeat of Blucher at Ligny on 16 June, or possibly of accounts that had reached London of the earlier stages of the fighting at Waterloo.

(2) An empty gesture, as the King's Remembrancer, an official in the Exchequer with a legal duty to keep records of "such things as were to be called upon and dealt with for the benefit of the Crown", had copies made.

(3) Average life expectancy at the time was 41 years, and few, even amongst the middle classes, could afford medical fees.

(4) The Public Works Loans Board was established in 1817, originally to fund mines and turnpike trusts. An independent body it loaned money to properly accountable bodies at a rate of interest slightly below market level.

(5) Development of De Beauvoir Town actually began in 1821 when William Rhodes, a wealthy local farmer, acquired a lease on 150 acres immediately adjoining the Regents Canal. A court case later concluded that Rhodes had acquired his lease unfairly, and control of the scheme passed back in 1834 to the landowner, Peter Benyon de Beauvoir. (Rhodes's grandson, Cecil, was responsible for the extension, in the 1890s, of British rule into current day Zimbabwe and Zambia, an area five times the size of the UK, during which tribal-owned land was passed on to white settlers in ways that were widely regarded, then and now, as illegal).

(6) In this respect, note that most of the residential dwellings built in Grainger Town, Newcastle were maisonettes above shops.

(7) Because of the continued growth, from the eighteenth century onwards, of "enclosures" – the asserting of private ownership over what had once been open land – people progressively lost their historic rights to take reasonable amounts of firewood, and game from such areas. It is instructive to remember that much of the diet of the rural population had been "foraged" as we would now say: hence Shaftesbury's attempts to address this by the granting of plots of land where they might grow their own food and graze a few livestock.

(8) New Lanark passed into the ownership of philanthropist Robert Owen in 1799 and was managed by him according to early cooperative and socialist principles. The homes at New Lanark, though, were not self-contained: as they were built, families occupied a room or rooms and shared various facilities. Owen later visited the US, where in the 1820s he established a number of "Owenite" settlements, none of which survived longer than a few years. Their failure was attributed to most of the residents failing to embrace Owen's notions of community living and property sharing.

(9) The Act directly linked voting rights to property ownership and also specifically stated that voters in parliamentary elections could only be male, disenfranchising the small number of women voters who existed up to 1832. The qualification required in a borough (ie a town) was to be the male head of a household that lived in a property worth £10 a year (£3s 8d per week) in rent: a reasonably high sum, for the time. In rural areas ("counties") the arrangements were more complex and covered male freeholders of homes worth £2 per annum (an ancient mediaeval qualification – but there were few such cases), those who owned land or had long leases on land worth £10 per annum and those with short leases or

tenancies worth £50 per annum. In Scotland, these arrangements increased the electorate by a factor of thirteen. (From 5,000 to 65,000). In Ireland, though, relatively few people met the criteria and the size of the rural electorate barely changed.

2

PIECEMEAL IMPROVEMENTS

The bits of legislation passed between 1832 and 1835 were soon overwhelmed by events in the real world. They proved wholly inadequate to deal with the challenges that arose in the ensuing decade. A truly miserable period, the 1840s were marked by hunger, famine, pestilence and political upheaval. Further reforms were enacted, as a result of which the British state moved very slightly closer to having a government policy on housing – its provision, where it should be built, by whom, and for whom.

The driving force for this came from hunger, poverty and the threat of political turmoil. There were bad grain harvests every year, from 1839 onwards. The impact of these was felt most by those crowded into the UK's growing towns and cities. The poor were denied the possibility of using grain imported from abroad, and the months of July andAugust 1842 brought extensive hunger riots with 2,000 troops (and 6 field guns) sent to Manchester to face down political opposition led by the Chartists and the Anti-Corn Law League. Manchester had been the birthplace of Edwin Chadwick, who, following an outbreak of cholera in 1838, began preparing, at his own expense, his *Report on the Sanitary Condition of the Labouring Population of Great Britain*. This appeared in July 1842 and became one of the best-selling publications of its day. The Prime Minister, Sir Robert Peel, set up a Royal Commission on the Health of Towns, chaired by Chadwick, the following year. The work of this body, and the impact of Chadwick's original report eventually produced the Public Health Act 1848, the first instance of a British government taking responsibility for the health of the population.[1]

The turmoil of the time, and the problems that ordinary people experienced as they tried to survive in such circumstances, were fruitful material too for novelists, as well as politicians and the authors of official reports. Those who enjoyed Charles Dickens would have noted his switch from the Henry Fielding-type picaresque adventures of *The Pickwick Papers* (1836) to *Oliver Twist* (1837) with its setting in a squalid London of criminal infested "rookeries". Later works such as *A Christmas Carol* (1843), *David Copperfield* (1849) and *Hard Times* (1854), featured a gallery of heartless businessmen, oppressed families, cripples and orphans forced to live and work in a London where they endure a lack of proper living accommodation, crime, illness and poverty. *Hard Times* was also partly set in an industrial (and continually industrialising) metropolis in the north of England. The early to mid-Victorian state-of-the-nation novels included *Sybil* (1845) written by Benjamin Disraeli, whilst MP for Shrewsbury. Set in a northern town, with horrific living conditions, it reflected his belief that "two nations" existed within the UK, and showed some sympathy for some of the aims of the Chartists.[2] Disraeli's book prefigured Elizabeth Gaskell's *Mary Barton* (1848) and Charles Kingsley's *Alton Locke* (1849) and may have been an influence on Dickens's *Hard Times*. All explored similar political and social themes. Mrs Gaskell set *Mary Barton* in Manchester and showed her main characters emigrating to Canada. Her later work, *North and South* (1854), like *Sybil*, argued that society was split, in this case by a difference in the social problems affecting the north of England as opposed to the south.

But, for all the awareness that the novelists of the time demonstrated, Disraeli only sold 3,000 copies of *Sybil* and Friedrich Engels's *The Condition of the Working Class in England*, which appeared the same year in Germany, was not even published in the UK at the time. A minutely researched account of working people's lives and circumstances in Manchester, it showed that industrialisation, and the way it forced people to live, had shortened life expectancy in comparison with how the same people had lived and worked a decade or so earlier.[3] Outselling everyone, including Dickens, was

George W M Reynolds whose *The Mysteries of London* (1844) used urban squalor to provide lurid, almost gothic, entertainment set in a dirty city inhabited by a starving, ragged working-class and a small, corrupt aristocracy. A Chartist, and an ardent republican, Reynolds emphasised poverty, crime and violence, and, from 1850, ran *Reynolds's Weekly Newspaper*, which, owned by the Co-operative Party lasted, as *Reynolds's News*, until the 1960s.

As to what ought to be done, and how it should be paid for, the means to implement even the modest provisions of Chadwick's Act only existed because Peel, Prime Minister after 1841, and much frustrated by the lack of a significant and reliable source of raising revenue, reintroduced income tax. Effective from May 1842, this was initially set at a rate of 7d in the £ for incomes above £150, and only applied to the relatively wealthy and above.[4] In an era when almost all politicians were independently wealthy, this appears as an interesting example of politicians voting against their own interests and agreeing to do what was best for the country. But, setting the tax at such a low rate only raised a limited amount, and initiatives aimed at improving conditions still tended for many years afterwards to come mainly from private or voluntary sources.[5] Typical of these were the Rochdale Pioneers, a group of artisans who decided to band together in 1843 to open their own store, which they accomplished a year later, selling food items, as a "co-operative", that they could not otherwise afford as individuals. Similarly, the terrible living conditions faced by many who were forced to migrate to London in search of employment led to the founding of the Young Men's Christian Association in 1844 by George Williams, who had arrived in the city from Dulverton in Somerset three years earlier. In Lord Shaftesbury they found a willing patron of the organisation.

The notion that something ought to be done was picked up too at the highest level. In 1845, Victoria Park was opened for the recreational use of those crammed into the teeming slums of the East End. Its origin lay in a mass petition to the Queen, asking that support be given to recommendations from epidemiologist William Farr, who argued that ill-health was determined by poor environment. The Queen acted: via the Crown Estate, 218 acres of derelict land, mainly spoil left over after gravel and clay had been extracted to make bricks used in the construction of the thousands of houses creeping out from London, was purchased and a large new park – Victoria Park – laid out.[6]

Finally, efforts were made, if only on a tiny scale, to build homes for those who couldn't afford to buy the properties erected by private builders. In 1844, Shaftesbury's Labourer's Friend Society became the Society for Improving the Condition of the Working Classes, with Prince Albert, no less, as President. They engaged Henry Roberts as their architect and, within a few months, had built in Lower Road, Pentonville two narrow terraces designed to house "23 *families and 30 aged women*" in shared accommodation, different households occupying separate floors within each property.[7] Although an improvement on whatever the residents would have had as an alternative, this quickly turned out to be a far from ideal arrangement. A better plan was devised by Roberts, for the similarly named Metropolitan Association for Improving the Dwellings of the Industrious Classes. Run by Thomas Southwood Smith, a doctor, sanitary inspector and ally of Edwin Chadwick, the Metropolitan Association's management board was extremely well connected politically, with a membership that included George Hamilton-Gordon (son of Lord Aberdeen, the Foreign Secretary), Viscount Ebrington (a former Lord Lieutenant of Ireland) and George Howard (a former Chief Secretary for Ireland) as well as Thomas Gibson, a merchant and member of the Anti-Corn Law League. Founded in 1841, the Association took some while to prepare and build its first scheme, Metropolitan Buildings, Old Pancras Road. Opened in 1848, this was superior in every respect to Lower Road and contained 21 one- and 90 two-bedroom self-contained flats (each complete with their own flushing lavatories – a huge improvement in itself) in a five-floor block that by virtue of its shape quickly became known as Pancras Square. Solidly built, with pitched roofs, stairwells and long common balconies on each floor that gave access to the front doors of individual flats, it became, with few exceptions, the template for all subsequent blocks of British social housing. Rents were set at 3s 6d (17.5p) per week for a one-bedroom flat and 6s 6d (32.5p) per week for a two-bedroom flat. At a time when a labourer might earn £20 per year (7s-8s per week) this indicates that living in the Metropolitan Buildings either meant spending a very high proportion of one's income on housing costs, or required one to be a highly paid artisan. But, in the complete absence of government subsidy of any type, it is hard to see what else Southwood Smith and his colleagues could have done. In every other respect they, and Henry Roberts, got the basics right and their development deserves to be better known and appreciated – had it not been destroyed by bombing in 1941, it probably would be.[8]

Slowly, prodded by the emergence of these self-help societies and the influence exerted by a small number of wealthy aristocratic figures, a cadre of architects was appearing who specialised in solving the dilemmas of rapid urban growth.[9] As to what new buildings and blocks should look like, it was clear that visual innovation was frowned on by some of the intelligentsia, and in terms of design, the preferences of many remained backward looking. The same year that Metropolitan Buildings opened, John Ruskin pronounced "...We want no new style of architecture...the forms of architecture already known to us are good enough for us..." Only 29 years old at the time, Ruskin expanded on this view a year later, after a tour of the continent, in The Seven Lamps of Architecture, in which he argued that the designs executed in the thirteenth century (the "Gothic" style) were truer and more certain than anything subsequently produced. In doing so he was reinforcing the pre-eminence of Augustus Pugin, the leading exponent of what became known as "Victorian Gothic", and a prolific designer of churches, colleges, presbyteries and country houses through the 1840s. Not content with these commissions, Pugin decried the functional appearance of many of the new workhouses of the time, advocating that such buildings should resemble instead mediaeval monasteries.[10] The views held by Ruskin and Pugin had influence by virtue of their connection to a wider artistic and cultural movement. Ruskin was heavily involved with the Pre-Raphaelite

Brotherhood (a group of painters and critics inspired by the clarity and beauty of the art produced before 1500, ie, before Raphael) whilst Pugin, a convert to Catholicism, something which resulted in a plethora of work for him in Ireland, advocated *"a return to the faith and the social structures of the Middle Ages"*.[11]

Ruskin's essentially conservative opinions were not necessarily at variance with those held by significant figures within progressive politics, some of whom saw little to be gained by improving urban conditions, and much better prospects to be had by avoiding towns and cities altogether. Feargus O'Connor, formerly MP for Cork (1832-1835) and latterly as the Leeds representative of the London Working Men's Association, promoted the idea that people should leave heavily overcrowded and insanitary industrial areas and live instead in a properly planned, low-density, rural setting growing their own food.[12] Essentially, people should revert to how they might have lived 50 or so years earlier. To facilitate this, he established the Chartist Co-Operative Land Society in 1845, which bought various pieces of land. One of these, near Rickmansworth, Hertfordshire, covered 100 acres, on which 35 detached houses, with adjoining plots of land were provided. It was called O'Connorville, later renamed Heronsgate, and members of the cooperative "won" their homes through a prizedraw, carried out whenever there were properties available. O'Connor was re-elected to Parliament in 1847, for Nottingham, only to have his plan declared illegal by Parliament a year later on the grounds that it was a lottery and he could never, because of this, reward all those who joined the Chartist Co-Operative Land Society.

It is difficult to understate the unfairness of this attack on the scheme. Parliament involved itself in investigating the National Land Company (as the Chartist Co-Operative Land Society became known) on the basis that complaints were made about how it operated, whilst at the same time a petition containing nearly two million signatures requesting that it be registered as a friendly society was rejected out of hand. Of course, it was true that at any one time there would be a queue of people waiting to win one of O'Connor's lotteries, and that the only way that queue would "lessen" would be whenever another site was developed. But, on that basis, the Epsom Derby should have been declared illegal too, as it was only held once a year and not everyone who placed a bet could win it. The same predicament affected the early building societies too: the Leeds Permanent Building Society, formed in 1846, was originally intended to wind itself up once it had housed all its subscribers. It continued only because it became clear that people were opening accounts faster than the organisation could build houses.

Perhaps O'Connor should have been more adroit and allocated most of the properties according to housing need, only holding back a few for the prize draw. It is hard not to conclude that the reason his fellow MPs moved rapidly against his scheme was that none of them wanted politically aware (and radical) households rehoused in miniature towns, some of which might well have been in their constituencies. The notion that the Chartists might run their own house-building company, moving educated working men and their families into purpose-built developments was clearly something that alarmed them. O'Connor oversaw the development of six small schemes, one of which, at Dodford in Worcestershire, became relatively successful and proved to be an inspiration 40 years later to another generation of political radicals searching for a solution to urban overcrowding.[13]

* * * * * *

By the time the House of Commons rounded on O'Connor, Peel had departed as Prime Minister. As conditions worsened during his tenure, particularly in Ireland where, from 1845, the potato famine resulted in people being driven off the land, Peel decided, in response, that he had no alternative other than to repeal the Corn Laws. His party refused to back him and split, but the measure was carried out anyway in May 1846, after which his government collapsed. What replaced it was an administration led by Lord John Russell, and the new Chancellor of the Exchequer, Sir Charles Wood, refused any further assistance to Ireland.

Russell and his colleagues promoted a kind of aristocratic, bombastic nationalism. There was a noisy attempt to outlaw the establishment of a Roman Catholic religious hierarchy in England, the dispersing, by force, of the last major Chartist demonstration and an attempted uprising in Ireland, together with various overseas adventures, including the annexation of the Punjab and a blockade of Greece.[14] Very little money was available for domestic improvement. Successive cholera epidemics killed 14,000 and 10,000 people respectively in London in 1849 and 1854, during a period in which the population of the city rose to 2.3 million. It continued to rise in the country too, albeit at a slower rate due to the famine in Ireland (which killed a million people) and increasing migration. The drift off the land and into towns and cities continued.

With the government far from engaged in dealing with the problems posed by rapid urbanisation, Prince Albert, the Prince Consort, now emerged as a key sponsor of better housing. Unlike many of his ministers, he was aware that urban overcrowding, poverty, together with hunger and land shortages in rural areas, had provoked uprisings across Europe. Starting in Sicily in January, revolutionary upheavals moved across the continent via Paris, where Louis Philippe I abdicated in February, to Austria and much of Germany by March. Fearing that similar events could happen in the UK (and being related to some of the heads of state facing this turbulence on the other side of the Channel), Albert gave a speech on 18 May 1848 as President of the Society for the Improvement of the Condition of the Labouring Classes, stating his *"sympathy and interest for that class of our community who have most of the toil and fewest of the enjoyments of this world"* and declaring that it was the *"duty of those who, under the blessings of Divine Providence, enjoy station, wealth, and education"* to help those who would otherwise struggle.

His chosen method of doing so was via a *"Great Exhibition of the Works of Industry of All Nations"*, organised by the Royal Society for the Encouragement of Arts, Manufactures and Commerce, of which he was also President.[15] Bitterly opposed by many in Russell's government, it opened in Hyde Park in May 1851, accommodated inside a gigantic iron and glass structure weighing nearly 10,000 tons, designed by Joseph Paxton, an eminent landscape architect and director of the Midland Railway.[16] Among the programme of works visitors could inspect was an example of a tiny block of model dwellings, known as Prince Albert's Model Cottages, erected immediately outside Paxton's huge glasshouse. Containing four, three-bedroom self-contained flats, it was designed by Henry Roberts, *by command of his Royal Highness, the Prince Consort*. At the conclusion of the Great Exhibition the small block was dismantled and re-erected (where it remains today) on the edge of Kennington Park – an ironic choice, as this had been the rallying point in April 1848 of the Chartist demonstration demanding electoral and constitutional reform. Anyone in Hyde Park curious about seeing another example of this type of housing could have visited Streatham Street Buildings (known now as Parnell House), also by Roberts and built in 1849-1850 on land leased from the Duke of Bedford, as part of a small-scale slum clearance project in an area of Bloomsbury then known as the St Giles "rookery". Solidly built of brick with a pitched roof, it had five floors, with stairwells and access balconies to each, and provided 48 self-contained flats with self-contained kitchens and water closets. As with Metropolitan Buildings and Prince Albert's Model Cottages it was built for the Society for the Improvement of the Condition of the Labouring Classes.

All this was welcome, but was only a tiny level of provision in comparison to actual housing need. Another modest attempt at speeding development and producing homes with better light and ventilation came in 1851 with the abolition of the Window Tax.[17] It remained the case throughout this period, however, that the preferred method of providing housing remained via private builder-developers, notably the Cubitt brothers whose streets, echoing their earlier Belgravia scheme, marched across Finsbury, Canonbury, Highbury and Barnsbury, culminating in their completion, in 1852, of King's Cross Station, then the largest in the world.

Few would look back on the 1840s with any sentiment, but, during that justly maligned decade, viable designs emerged for both high-density city and suburban homes.

Notes

(1) In this context it is useful to remember that the Prime Minister, Sir Robert Peel was from an industrial and manufacturing background in Lancashire, and familiar with the conditions described by Chadwick.

(2) Disraeli's own preference was for an alliance between enlightened members of the aristocracy and the working classes against the merchants and industrialists. In 1852, when Chancellor of the Exchequer and Leader of the House of Commons in the minority Lord Derby administration, he had unsuccessful discussions with John Bright, the radical Liberal MP for Manchester toward this end.

(3) Engels's family were wealthy textile manufacturers and owned a large mill in Salford (where disturbances among the workforce were recorded in 1842) to which they sent their son as manager. An English translation of *The Condition of the Working Class in England* only appeared in 1887.

(4) 7d in the £ was equal to a tax rate of 2.9%, or only a seventh, approximately, of what it is now.

(5) Income tax was reintroduced by Henry Goulburn, Chancellor of the Exchequer. One of only 5 members out of a cabinet of 14 who sat in the House of Commons, Goulburn was a former slave owner with extensive sugar plantations in Jamaica.

(6) The land had been previously owned by the Church Commissioners, as part of the grounds of Bishop's Hall, the residence of the Bishop of Stepney. The purchase by the Crown, was, therefore, a moving of an asset between government departments rather than any expenditure on privately owned land.

(7) The site is now occupied by the Action for Children play centre, in Cubitt Street WC1. It appears that the land for the project became available when the River Fleet, which passes directly beneath, was culverted.

(8) It was located at what is now the north side of Chenies Place NW1. Again, in development terms, this was marginal land, with both the culverted River Fleet and the St Pancras Gasworks (opened 1823) only a short distance away. Metropolitan Buildings later had the extensive Midland Railway Somers Town Goods Yard built against its southern boundary in 1877.

(9) Typical of these was Edmund Sharpe, later a significant figure in municipal affairs in Lancaster. A church architect, railway architect and sanitary engineer, Sharpe had been a childhood friend of Mrs Gaskell.

(10) Pugin, whose work can be seen as a revolt against English utilitarianism, also carried out extensive alterations and extensions to Alton Towers, the country house of the Earl of Shrewsbury. (Now in use as a theme park).

(11) Pugin often expressed libellous views of his contemporaries, and, after his death, was disowned by Ruskin.

(12) One of O'Connor's successors as MP for Cork was Daniel O'Connell. Both were part of the Repeal Association: they advocated repealing the 1800 Act of Union between Great Britain and Ireland with the restoration of an independent Irish Parliament. O'Connell, who held a rally at Clontarf in 1843 that attracted a million supporters, died whilst on a pilgrimage to Rome in 1847.

(13) The National Land Company owned each of the settlements. Those allocated

plots paid rent for them and could, in time, purchase them. However, in a poor year (or if the plot owner was less than competent at managing their holding) they fell into arrears and some were uninterested from the start in paying any rent at all: they wanted to own their own freeholds. There were, therefore, problems with both plot management and rent arrears on all the sites. Essentially a large and early version of a housing cooperative, the fact that such difficulties arose would come as little surprise to anyone familiar with the workings of some such bodies in later years.

(14) The Young Ireland movement, under William Smith O'Brien, took forward their objectives via an armed rising, which was easily suppressed in July 1848, a few months after O'Connor's campaign for political reform via Chartism was abandoned following a gigantic demonstration on Kennington Common.

(15) The inspiration for such an event appears to have been the Great Exhibition of Products of French Industry, held regularly in Paris from 1798 to 1849.

(16) Paxton's building was dismantled and re-erected in Sydenham in 1854 where it remained until destroyed by fire in 1936.

(17) Introduced in 1696, and related to the beginning of a national debt and establishment of the Bank of England, the Window Tax was an ineffectual revenue-raising device that the government fell back upon when the notion of an income tax was held to be an intrusion into the privacy of the public. It mainly applied to houses with 10 or more windows: to avoid payment builders simply completed houses with less than that number, or with bricked up spaces where windows could be reinstated at a later date, whenever the tax was repealed.

3

THE DRIVE TO ESCAPE THE CITY

After the immense spectacle generated by the Great Exhibition of 1851, Paxton, with the support of Prince Albert, presented another grand scheme, the Great Victorian Way, to the Parliamentary Select Committee on Metropolitan Communications in June 1855. This proposed an enormous iron and glass arcade, 108 feet high and 72 feet wide, that would surround central London in a loop ten miles in length. Similar in appearance to "the Crystal Palace", and in reality, a gigantic version of Leadenhall Market, it featured a central road, with shops to either side. Above the shops were residential apartments, and behind the housing and shops, on both sides of the structure, "atmospheric railways". The Parliamentary Select Committee also considered a smaller version of this – an "inner circle" to Paxton's "outer circle" – from Manchester-based architect William Moseley. Named "the Crystal Way", this had a similar wrought iron arcade with shops and residential above, but substituted a twin-track railway for the central roadway. The adoption by both Paxton and Moseley of an "atmospheric railway" as their preferred method of transport, reflected the mid-Victorian recognition that steam trains polluted the air within cities at a time when electric traction had not yet been developed. Alas, as a viable method of transport, atmospheric railways proved to be a dead-end.[1]

Paxton, who estimated that his scheme would cost £34m (or about £16.5bn today, not much less than the current cost of Crossrail) explained his choice of route, which avoided anything east of Aldgate, by stating *"towards Whitechapel there are people who do not go about so much*". In the event neither Paxton's project nor Moseley's was built, and cheaper and quicker options were pursued. In transport terms, sub-surface railways were driven through central London, beginning with the route from Paddington to Farringdon in 1863. Like the projects pursued by Paxton and Moseley this was a response to attempts to find a solution to the continued and quite extraordinary growth of London. Through the 1850s the city's population was rising by 44,000 a year, with the number of dwellings increasing by approximately 5,700 annually to accommodate this.[2] To try and cope with this, the Metropolis Management Act (1855) established the Metropolitan Board of Works, under the chairmanship of John Thwaites, a nonconformist businessman in Southwark. Its first significant challenge occurred when the Great Stink (July 1858) flooded most of the riverside and its immediate surroundings with untreated sewage, an event caused by an order made in 1847 by London's Metropolitan Commission of Sewers that all cesspits should be closed and house drains connected instead to sewers, usually culverted rivers and streams, that emptied into the Thames. This decision led to cholera epidemics in both 1848 and 1853 that between them killed 25,000 people.

By 1858 the stink and disease reached the point where Parliament, based as it was beside the river, could no longer function. Without an effective sewage system that could handle its rapid expansion as a city, the Metropolitan Board of Works contracted civil engineer Joseph Bazalgette to provide a comprehensive drainage and sewage disposal system for London. He did this between 1862 and 1875, also embanking the Thames as it passed through the city. Nor did the Great Stink solely result in the construction of sewers. Mindful of the origin of the problem – inadequate housing provision and a sharply rising population – Parliament finally started to take active measures to facilitate the improvement of urban homes. Between 1866 and 1868 William Torrens, Liberal MP for Finsbury, introduced and had passed the Artisans' and Labourers' Dwellings Act during the period Lord Derby and Benjamin Disraeli were running a minority government. The legislation required local authorities to ensure that landlords kept their homes habitable and in good repair. If they did not do so, the local authority would act following a report from the local Medical Officer, and, in theory, recover the costs from the owner. By this method it was hoped that the worst housing would be either repaired or eliminated. In practice, however, many owners did not have the money to improve their property (a common feature even today) and the local authorities were either obliged to expend their limited funds on dealing with slum housing in the knowledge that they might not be reimbursed, or avoided the issue.[3]

Torrens's legislation was imperfect, but it was a start, and it reflected the fact that noticeable action was already being taken. In 1867, for instance, Shoreditch Vestry demolished 650 dwellings. On one of the sites created by this the Improved Industrial Dwellings Company built Langbourne Buildings, containing 90 self-contained flats, in Luke Street EC2. Founded in 1863 by Sir Sydney Waterlow, a significant businessman and Liberal politician, the company paid investors a 5% dividend, achieved by charging rents that were often beyond the means of those displaced by slum clearance in the first place. But a demand clearly existed for the schemes they developed. From 1869 they built an estate that eventually totalled 797 flats in Bethnal Green and in 1872 they erected 112 flats at Leopold Buildings, again in Shoreditch, on land made available by Baroness Burdett-Coutts.[4] The wealthiest heiress in the UK, Baroness Burdett-Coutts had, prior to this, built her own model dwellings estate at Columbia Square, Bethnal Green. Completed in 1862, it was joined seven years later by Columbia Market, her pièce de résistance, an immensely ornate and hugely expensive covered food market, with space for 400 stall holders, built in the style of a French gothic cathedral. It cost £200,000 (approximately £110m today) and struggled to remain open, with most of the local traders preferring to sell their goods in the surrounding streets.

Both Waterlow and Burdett-Coutts were extremely wealthy benefactors who chose to use part of their personal fortunes on the provision of better housing, and other related facilities, for the poor. They were joined by George Peabody, a US banker and philanthropist, who launched the Peabody Donation Fund in March 1862 with an initial capital of £150,000, subsequently increased in 1869 to £500,000 (£82.5m and £275m respectively in current values). The first Peabody Estate appeared in 1863, in Commercial Street, Spitalfields, and remains standing today.

That same year, at the suggestion of Sir Sydney Waterlow, the City of London Corporation addressed the problem of rehousing many of the households made homeless by the construction of the Metropolitan Railway through Farringdon. It did so by building a local authority-owned housing estate, the very first in the UK, at Corporation Buildings, on Farringdon Road. Completed in 1865, it contained 168 tenements, arranged in 5 floors above shops. As with Metropolitan Buildings, access to each of the self-contained flats was via a stairwell and balconies.[5] The City of London Corporation, then as now, was the wealthiest local authority in the UK and in a position, as few others were, to spend money on housing projects. As with the various companies building model dwellings, though, the rents charged were high (today we would say sub-market) and reflected the fact that there was no subsidy available to offset the cost of provision, management and maintenance of the properties. It was not the only such scheme in the area. Not quite opposite could be found Farringdon Road Buildings, built by the Metropolitan Association for Improving the Dwellings of the Industrious Classes. A very dense development of 260 flats over shops it was opened by the Home Secretary, Richard Cross MP, in 1874 and was joined a decade later, on a site just to the south, by Peabody's Clerkenwell Estate.[6]

The driving of railways through densely built and populated urban areas also led directly to the availability of a third stream of social housing provision. Those displaced were provided, either via the railway companies themselves, or indirectly via companies like those run by Waterlow, Shaftesbury and Burdett-Coutts, with a new home in a block of model dwellings somewhere along the route. When the Dalston to Broad Street railway was built in

1865, for instance, hundreds of houses occupied by 4,500 people (an average of 7 per house, indicating that virtually all of the properties were in multi-occupancy) were demolished. The railway companies proved adept, though, at minimising their liabilities to rehouse those affected by their work, and in most cases only a limited amount of replacement housing was provided by them.

* * * * * *

The mid-nineteenth century also produced a statutory basis for the establishment and operating of the various companies that sought to offer rented housing to the more prosperous members of the working class. The Friendly Societies Act (1855) produced a regulatory framework for these, whilst the Limited Liability Act (also 1855) safeguarded investors, particularly in bodies incorporated as companies. The period also saw the formation of the Building Societies Association in 1860, a trade body for those who lent money to enable the purchase of new homes.

But with clearly insanitary conditions continuing to be a feature of most towns and cities, the view also took root that it was better to leave high-density urban environments and reside in properly planned semi-rural (or suburban) locations. This sentiment was endorsed by many of the intellectuals of the time, notably John Ruskin, who in 1865 referred to *"the great foul city of London...rattling, growling, smoking, stinking – a ghastly heap of fermenting brickwork, pouring out poison at every pore– a cricket ground without the turf, a huge billiard table without the cloth, and with pockets as deep as the bottomless pit..."* Equally prominent were the views of William Morris, who looked back to a largely mediaeval (and fantasy) past. After a spell at Oxford in the early 1850s, where he encountered "the Birmingham Set" of undergraduates, none of whom regarded the evolution of Birmingham into a great manufacturing metropolis as an attractive development, he moved with Edward Burne-Jones to Bloomsbury, London as an apprentice to the architect, George Edmund Street. He abhorred the city (*"the spreading sore"*) and, as early as 1859, hired architect

Philip Webb, who also worked with Street, to design and build the Red House. Set in extensive grounds at Bexleyheath, then a straggling village spread along Watling Street in a decidedly rural setting in Kent, it was very much the prototype of the Victorian gothic house. Morris was also an anti-elitist, believing that all craftsmen were as good as professionally qualified artists and architects, and attempted a synthesis of art, architecture, design and politics in a way that would later be replicated in Germany, 60 years later by Walter Gropius and his Bauhaus collective, as well as influencing more local adherents like Charles Voysey, from the 1890s. By the 1870s Morris would write in *The Earthly Paradise. Prologue – The Wanderers* "...*Forget the spreading of the hideous town; think rather of the pack-horse on the down, and dream of London, small and white and clean, the clear Thames bordered by its gardens green...*" His vision, unlike that of Gropius, remained backward-looking and he subsequently founded the Society for the Protection of Ancient Buildings in 1877.

This outlook was perfectly reasonable, but as an approach that could be widely replicated it proved impractical. Both Morris and Philip Webb owed much to Street, a significant figure in the Gothic Revival in the UK, whose masterpiece was the Royal Courts of Justice on the Strand. Other major "gothic" architects included George Gilbert Scott who worked as an assistant to Henry Roberts on some of the early "model dwellings" schemes, but who took a very different view of how housing should be provided for those higher up the social scale. His major achievement was St Pancras Hotel 1865-1868, for the Midland Railway. Over time, the legacy of the gothic-mediaevalist style amounted to not much more than a limited array of houses, often commissioned by the wealthy, some important public buildings, and via James Brooks, a number of churches built between 1865 and 1890. In practical terms, the style was too expensive for widespread application as a house type and could only be built for those with significant means.

By the mid-1860s, then, two different, and competing, approaches had emerged in the UK to the question of how best to house people. On the one hand: high-density urban streets lined with houses or model dwellings. And on the other: smaller numbers of low-density private residences designed in a way that (a) provided a spacious, well-built and healthy, almost utopian, home, and (b) harked back to a mythologised version of how (some) people had lived in the past.

For many, the second of these became the most attractive, and a number of early prototype versions of what would later be called "the garden suburb" began to appear from the 1870s. At the same time, in the public eye, insofar as the public noted such matters, the choice about what was built and how it was argued for, also lay between the two competing models of society represented by emerging political figures like Joseph Chamberlain and cultural ambassadors such as Morris. Chamberlain, a Unitarian from London later related via marriage to the Peabody family, became Mayor of Birmingham in 1873. Unlike Morris, who saw cities as something to escape from, he pursued an agenda of making a large conurbation pleasant to live in for its rapidly growing number of inhabitants. Presiding over the purchase by Birmingham of private power companies and private water companies, his reputation was such that he was consulted by Richard Cross MP, during the drafting of the Artisans' and Labourers' Dwellings Improvement Act in 1875. Passed early in Disraeli's majority administration, its failing was that the high compensation cost it relied upon for compulsory purchase limited its effect. The same government also established the cabinet position of President of the Local Government Board, a role with specific responsibility for housing.[7]

There was in fact, a small-scale, but significant, movement beyond London that sought, like Morris, to escape the overcrowded and insanitary conditions of the UK's rapidly expanding cities. This predated Chamberlain, and found an early expression in Bradford where Titus Salt (Mayor of Bradford in 1848, and MP 1859-1861) built Saltaire 3 miles north-west of the city in 1851. Set across 25 acres, it contained schools, churches, shops and 850 homes housing over 4,000 residents, most of whom worked in Salt's woollen mill. It was emulated, on a smaller and much more limited scale by Ripley Ville, where 196 houses were erected by

Sir Henry Ripley (MP for Bradford 1868-1869, 1874-1880).[8] Both
Saltaire and Ripley Ville were, though, quite compact "urban"
developments. By contrast, an early example of a spacious "garden
suburb" laid out in conformity with Morris's outlook came with
The Avenues, Hull, built from 1875 and designed, in part, by
George Gilbert Scott Jnr. Here gothic emulation competed with
mock Queen Anne style. The estate, which benefitted at the time
from proximity to Hull Botanical Gardens Station, took until
1910 to be completed, demonstrating once more that private
builders move only as fast as the market allows them to sell their
produce. Queen Anne style was also adopted by Norman Shaw,
who designed Bedford Park, regarded as the first true UK "garden
suburb". Developed by city merchant Jonathan Carr, it was spread
across 24 acres of what was then open countryside on the outskirts
of Ealing and Hounslow, and adjoined Turnham Green Station
which then, as now, had a regular train service into the City and
West End. As with The Avenues, proximity to public transport
was an important factor in selecting sites where middle-class
housing could be provided.

Like Morris and Webb, Shaw had also trained at Street's
practice and the relatively small circle from which these
pioneering architects and developers were drawn was confirmed
when Matthew Allen, a Quaker philanthropist, who had worked
for Waterlow's Improved Industrial Dwellings Company, built
Allen's Gardens. Nothing like as ambitious as Bedford Park, this
consisted of ten small 3-floor blocks of flats (44 in total) that
looked, externally, like houses. Built in 1873, on land that became
available after the construction of the Bethnal Green-Edmonton
railway, they were described as "Middle-Class Dwellings" and were
rented by their occupants at figures ranging between £20 to £60
per annum (7s 9d to 23s 6d per week). This was quite expensive
(at a time when a reasonable salary was £2 per week) but the
scheme came with substantial communal grounds managed by a
resident committee.[9] Commuting to London was via the recently
opened Stoke Newington Station in what was then a select outer
suburb.

A far larger provider of housing, than any of these, was the Artizans, Labourers and General Dwellings Company Ltd. Founded in 1867 by William Austin, a drain-laying contractor, it aimed to meet the demand for housing in London for the "industrious poor" by building low-rise housing in open countryside alongside existing railway lines, thus allowing residents to live in pleasant surroundings and commute to work by train. Workmen employed on its various construction projects did so on a cooperative basis, receiving a share of the profits, and initially houses were resold to recoup working capital. These arrangements attracted the support of the Earl of Shaftesbury, who served as its President until 1875. A particular feature of their schemes was the absence of licensed premises, something replicated by many developers private, charitable and social at the time.[10]

Their first development, in Battersea, was sold on completion to its occupants and the money raised was used to buy land at Salford, on which 78 houses were built by 1879. Through the 1870s Austin's company purchased sites in Liverpool, Birmingham, Gosport and Leeds, and established offices, for raising money via membership subscriptions, in Manchester, Oldham, Huddersfield and Plymouth, Devon. Unusually then, for a "dwellings" company, Austin's concern was truly national. A further 40 acres were purchased in Battersea – making it a bigger project than Bedford Park – this being the prototype of four estates (the others being in Queens Park, Wood Green and Streatham) which would make a notable contribution to London's housing needs.[11]

What emerged in Battersea was Shaftesbury Park, conceived as a 'Workmen's City' by Austin and consisting of 1,200 two-storey houses with gardens, in terraces along newly laid tree-lined streets. They came in four basic types and were sold where possible on 99-year leases at between £170 and £310. At a time when average earnings for artisans and labourers were about £1 4s per week (£1.20p) this represented in 2020 prices of between £84,000 and £130,000, depending on the size of the property. Repayments were made over 21 years. Alternatively, the homes

were rented at between 5s 9d and 10s a week, £139 per week
to £240 a week today. Easily dwarfing Bedford Park or Allen's
Gardens, Shaftesbury Park was opened by Benjamin Disraeli,
the first time a Prime Minister opened a working-class housing
project, following his victory at the January 1874 general election,
an event that also saw two MPs elected on a Liberal-Labour ticket:
Alexander Macdonald (Stafford) and Thomas Burt (Morpeth),
both of whom were members of the Miners' Union.[12] Austin
followed Shaftesbury Park with a 2,000-home development on 80
acres in the Queens Park area of Westminster. Here the architect
was Rowland Plumbe, who would also design their next scheme
in Wood Green.

The number of homes provided by the Artizans, Labourers
and General Dwellings Company in Battersea and Queens Park
(3,200) made it easily the largest landlord of housing for working-
class families in London, albeit their homes were located in what
were then regarded as suburbs. Elsewhere, by 1875, 6,800 similar
dwellings (mostly flats) existed within inner London, a distance,
say, a mile either way of the City. The largest providers here were
the Improved Industrial Dwellings Company (1,900) followed by
Peabody (1,400) and the Metropolitan Association for Improving
the Dwellings of the Industrious Classes (1,100). In the context of
the population of London, reaching 3.9 million by 1871 (of which
3.3 million were in inner London), and the population of the
UK rising to 31 million at the same time, the provision of 10,000
"affordable" homes (as we would now say) may seem slight and
inadequate. But, having started from a zero base a few decades
earlier, and being entirely bereft of state funding, one can only be
impressed by the energy and precision with which these various
projects came to fruition.

Nor were the various companies, bequests and charities
that provided dwellings for the working classes alone. There
were other providers too. Much of the development to do with
housing and health that occurred in the nineteenth century
was either directly due to Industrial and Provident Societies,
or the indirect consequence of their existence (such as savings

accounts, loans, mortgages etc). By the 1870s membership of Friendly Societies had reached four million, which assuming most of these were typically heads of households, meant their membership "covered" approximately 20m people...nearly 50% of the population. As a phenomenon their impact, then and for some years afterwards, was far greater than that of trade unions, though many trade unions (and employers) also ran insurance and sickness schemes. In terms of building property, mention should be made of the National Penny Bank, formed in 1875, which provided homes above its banking premises in London and other cities.[13] Similarly, the Royal London Friendly Society for Granting Policies of Insurance to the Working Classes, formed in 1861, built flats over their offices from 1871, allocating these to their salesmen, rather as railway and mining companies did to (some of) their employees.[14]

Thus, as the last quarter of the nineteenth century arrived, three funding mechanisms were in existence to provide good quality rented housing for those who could not afford to buy their own home: friendly societies, local government and charitable benefactors. Rent levels in all of these tended to be high, albeit slightly lower than market levels and were set at a level that allowed for a dividend to be paid to investors. Politically as well, progress had been made to get the government to "own" housing as an issue.

Finally, the design of these homes is still recognisable now: self-contained flats in blocks and small terraced houses in streets, built in locations that adjoined transport and shops. Today, many remain extant and in use for the purpose for which they were built 150 years, or more, after their construction.

Notes

(1) Atmospheric traction was adopted by the railway that was built between New Cross and Croydon over the infilled Croydon Canal in 1844. It proved impractical and the route had reverted to conventional steam haulage by 1847.
(2) Information found in *Cruchley's London in 1865: A Handbook for Strangers* (1865).
(3) The term local authority is used here to refer to the Vestries that administered a network of 15,600 Church of England parishes. Elected by male ratepayers they

dealt with local government business in their area until superseded by a much smaller number of local borough councils in 1894 (outside London) and 1900 (inside London).

(4) Both passed into the ownership of the London Borough of Tower Hamlets and both survive today. Waterlow Buildings, in Bethnal Green, was acquired by Barratt Homes in the 1980s and modernised as housing for sale whilst Ujima Housing Association acquired Leopold Buildings in Columbia Road as part of the Bethnal Green City Challenge project in the 1990s.

(5) Waterlow's wealth derived from the fact that his family were printers to HM Government. He was an Alderman of the City of London Corporation from 1863 and a Liberal MP from 1868. Metropolitan Buildings, like much of the housing subsequently built by the City of London Corporation, was located outside its boundaries. The block was demolished in 1970 and the site sold to *The Guardian* newspaper whose offices remained there until 2008.

(6) Farringdon Road Buildings cost £39,000 to build (approximately £19m today). Declared unfit for human habitation by the GLC in 1968, they were demolished in 1976 and replaced by an NCP car park. The Peabody Estate survives.

(7) Cross, from Preston, was MP for South West Lancashire, having defeated Gladstone in that seat in the 1868 general election. The Local Government Board remained in situ until replaced by the Ministry of Health in 1919.

(8) Salt and Ripley, like Howard and several others in this narrative were Congregationalists. Ripley was also a friend of Edward Akroyd (see below).

(9) As with Farringdon, this was marginal land. Allen's Gardens was built on a site that became available after the construction of the Bethnal Green-Edmonton railway through a shallow valley containing the drained and stopped-up course of a tributary of the Hackney Brook.

(10) Notably in Stamford Hill, where Lord Amherst of Hackney sold off land to building companies from the early 1870s. No public houses were provided anywhere in the network of new streets lined by large, spacious residences. In consequence the area was popular with respectable nonconformist middle-class families, including that of Ebenezer Howard.

(11) As with Bedford Park, all were built on agricultural land on the city edge with immediate proximity to a railway station.

(12) Prices given in this text are adjusted for inflation, relative to average earnings then and now. Throughout the nineteenth century houses were ranked in much the same way as warships ie, 1st rate, 2nd rate and so on. In 1855 a 700 square foot/70 square metre 3-bedroom house (classed as 4th rate) cost £300 to build, approximately £100,000 today. When making these comparisons one is struck by how much higher prices are today, compared with what they "ought" to be if house prices had followed the same inflationary trend as other economic items. However, since the early 1970s and the growth of consumer credit, they have clearly accelerated at a much greater rate.

(13) The encouragement of thrift and saving was a feature of the nineteenth century, characterised by the establishment of the Post Office Savings Bank in 1861, and, just prior to that, the West Riding Penny Savings Bank of 1859. The latter, founded by Edward Akroyd, a prominent textile manufacturer, survives today as part of the Yorkshire Bank. (Akroyd also funded a model housing development, Akroydon, near Halifax, where 90 gothic houses designed by George Gilbert Scott were built in the 1860s). The National Penny Bank, established by George Bartley, formerly a colleague of Lord Shaftesbury and later MP for Islington North, opened in London in 1875 and provided a network of branches, on main roads, that were open in the evening and which took deposits from

working people. Examples of their blocks, which provided artisan's dwellings above commercial ground-floor premises, survive in Great Eastern Street and Clerkenwell Road, both in London.

(14) Examples of these survive in Junction Road, Islington, Old Kent Road and Mare Street, Hackney.

4

EBENEZER HOWARD

Whilst Leopold Buildings were under construction, and the various dwellings companies were gearing up to produce a series of major schemes, a 21-year-old man emigrated from the UK to the US. If he was taking to heart the views of Ruskin and Morris isn't known. More likely, like many others then, he was looking for better career opportunities abroad. Throughout the 1870s an average of 194,000 people per annum left the UK, with half going to the US and the majority of the remainder to Canada, South Africa, Australia and New Zealand, the old, white, Dominions.

Ebenezer Howard was born in Fore Street, Moorgate in 1850 to a prosperous, nonconformist shopkeeper. His father, also Ebenezer, had been born in Harwich and had moved to London circa 1830, slowly building up his business and eventually owning several different premises in and directly adjoining the City of London. The Howard family moved to Postern Row, by the Tower, a year after Ebenezer's birth and was later living at 97 London Wall. Like many then, their horizons were small, with each of these addresses within a few hundred yards of the other. In the mid-nineteenth century, London, as the writings of Dickens bear witness, remained a heavily congested, sprawling mass of buildings, many of which were in poor repair and occupied by a multitude of different tenants. Coal, the main source of power domestically and industrially, produced dirty air and many fatal respiratory illnesses whilst the population as a whole lived in a world where poverty and malnutrition were commonplace and highly visible.

At the age of 4, Ebenezer was despatched by his family to a nonconformist boarding school in Sudbury, Suffolk where he remained, with occasional trips home during the school's holidays, for the next 11 years. Such arrangements were common then: middle-class families could not afford public school fees and would not wish their children to mix with the offspring of the working classes in the "National Schools" that had operated from 1833. More to the point, the Howards, whose income came from a string of confectionery shops, wished their children to have a conventional, nonconformist education away from the noise and temptations of London.

By 1865, Ebenezer was back with his family and working as a clerk. He taught himself shorthand, and around 1869 met Joseph Parker, one of the significant preachers of the Victorian era. Self-educated and bombastic, Parker had arrived in London from the north east in 1852 and was originally based at Whitefield's Tabernacle in Moorfields.[1] His speaking style was described by contemporaries as "energetic, theatrical and impressive" and avoided detailed theological exposition. Chapelgoers of the day were impressed by his passion and, on 19 September 1869, Parker, after an interlude in Manchester, began a ministry at the prestigious Poultry Chapel, in the City. This had been in existence since at least 1640, and after 1819 became one of the principal places of worship for Congregationalists, the offshoot of Anglicanism to which the Howard family adhered. The intention of those who sought Parker's appointment was to increase attendance at the Chapel, and raise sufficient funds, to enable it to vacate its small, cramped, site 100 yards or so from the Bank of England, and relocate to bigger premises in Holborn.

At the point Howard came across Parker he was working in a solicitor's office (*"where my skill in shorthand was very useful"*) and he may have been one of the crowds of office workers who attended Parker's weekday noon services which commenced on 23 September 1869. Up to a thousand attended these at any one time and Parker also began publishing his sermons in a pamphlet – *The City Temple* – that sold 4,000 copies each week. In fact, the Poultry

Chapel and its minister thrived so much that Howard was briefly employed, after demonstrating his short-hand prowess in taking down an extemporised sermon, as Parker's personal secretary. It seems that Parker had an interest in phrenology (which had been largely discredited on medical grounds nearly 30 years earlier) and carried out a "reading" of Howard's head concluding after he had done so, *"...I think you should have been a preacher. I would rather see you in a pulpit than any young man I have met..."*

This spell in Howard's life did not last long. In 1871, on doctor's orders following an examination that showed his lungs had been weakened by the poor air in London, Howard emigrated to the US, with two friends. Their journey took them to Des Moines, Iowa, then a thriving and expanding town at the centre of a newly opened coalfield. From here, following the advice of some Irish-Canadians, they headed to Nebraska, arriving in 1872, where they acquired a smallholding of 160 acres, and attempted to live off the land.

There was certainly a lot of land available in Nebraska, and it was easy, then, for incoming immigrants to acquire property. With an area of 77,000 square miles (roughly the size of England and Scotland combined) its population amounted to no more than 190,000. Of these a mere 5,000 were displaced Native Americans, who had ceased resisting the westward march of white settlers in 1865.[2] Nebraska was declared a State of the Union in 1867, and settlement and railway construction were proceeding at a rapid pace. It is easy – on paper – to see why Howard and his colleagues thought they might prosper but they reckoned without the difficulties caused by the harsh climate. This had an immense temperature range, with winters sinking to -10F and summers averaging 90F. As well as this, the area was prone, in spring and summer, to tornadoes, with up to 40 occurring annually.

In 1873, Howard gave up and moved to Chicago where he found employment as a shorthand stenographer, with Ely, Burnham and Bartlett, 93 Washington Street. His work involved recording cases at the law courts. It was an immensely significant period for the city of Chicago, a large part of which (3 square miles, nearly 5 times that destroyed in London in 1666) had been burnt down in a massive fire in 1871.

Reconstruction work, initially co-ordinated from the First Congregational Church[3], was visible everywhere, as measures to rehouse and provide for 112,000 homeless people were undertaken. As part of this, the city gained national attention during Howard's stay for its measures to improve public health, much of which were in the hands of Dr John H Rauch, Sanitary Superintendent. One feature which was apparent was the establishment of many large, well-landscaped municipal parks, so many of which existed that Chicago was known, at the time, as "the garden city". There was also the plan, in abeyance in the aftermath of the fire, but still being discussed during Howard's period in Chicago, to build a large low-density community in rural surroundings at Riverside, two miles outside the city limits. Designed by Frederick L Olmsted, this eventually housed 8,000 people in an area of two square miles. Although Howard did not discuss possible origins for his later ideas, it is highly unlikely that he was not aware of Olmsted's scheme.

In 1876, Howard was assigned by *The Chicago Times* to record an address by Mrs Cora Tappan, a spiritualist and medium. A prominent figure in US society, with connections at the White House, Tappan was pastor of the First Spiritualist Church of Chicago, which had many wealthy adherents, and she gave numerous, and on the face of it, persuasive, audiences in which she appeared to be channelling the thoughts, and views, of the recently deceased. As such she reflected the Victorian era preoccupation with the supernatural, science and religion. This was a period, right through to the 1920s, when many public figures took an interest in the occult and the likes of Thomas Edison would spend time trying to devise a telephone that could speak to the dead. Tappan also had an international reputation. Prior to returning to the US, she had toured Europe and the UK, where she spoke regularly at Cleveland Hall, 54 Cleveland Street, the centre of the British secularist movement.[4] The evening made an impression on Howard. In an encounter with Tappan, part of a process where she gave her insights into the lives of her audience members, she pronounced of him, *"...I see you in the centre of a series of circles working at something which will be of great service to humanity..."*

This, and the earlier experience with Joseph Parker seem to have given him the notion that he was ordained to achieve something, and he would later state *"...My stay in Chicago had great influence on my life – giving me a fuller and wider outlook on religious and social questions than I should have gained in England..."* His period in the US, though, was brief. By the end of 1876 he had returned to London.[5] In the years that followed, Chicago, whilst remaining a city of broad streets and large municipal parks, opted for high-rise buildings when it redeveloped its fire-damaged areas. From the cleared sites, previously occupied by combustible wooden structures, arose replacement buildings in steel and stone. These set many precedents for construction, including the completion of the world's first skyscraper, the Home Insurance Building, at the junction of South LaSalle Street and West Adams Street in 1885, complete with steel framing and much use of concrete.[6]

* * * * * *

The UK to which Howard returned was in the midst of a great depression. Rural areas were being depopulated as people left the land and landowners were, for once, in distress as their rents declined. Ironically, the 25% decline in agricultural productivity that the UK experienced between 1875 and 1900 was caused by cheap grain flooding into the country from the US Midwest, precisely the area where Howard had tried, and failed, to make a living only a few years earlier.

Because of these economic and geopolitical factors, the population of London rose by 900,000 in the 1870s as people poured into it from the surrounding countryside. This in turn brought about an accelerated mass migration by the middle classes to the suburbs, where much cheap, and formerly cultivated land, was available. Among those in this exodus were the Howard family, who purchased a newly built house at 127 Evering Road in 1877 as builders advanced steadily across what had once been Middlesex countryside. Midway between Stoke Newington and Clapton, it was handily positioned for access to the Rectory Road Congregational Church as well as being in a considerably cleaner and more respectable locale than their previous residences in and around the old City area.

Howard found employment as a shorthand writer in the House of Commons, and via that got to know many MPs and other major public figures. He married and joined The Zetetical Society in 1879. A free-thinking club founded in London the previous year as a forum for debate of social, political, and scientific matters, its fellow members included Sidney Webb and George Bernard Shaw, with Shaw, like Howard, nominated for membership by a civil servant who knew them both.

In the decade that followed, Howard assembled the theories upon which he would base his garden city idyll. To begin with, from Henry Hyndman, leader from 1881 of the Social Democratic Federation (the UK's first Marxist political party) he acquired views on land nationalisation and rent income, which Hyndman took in turn from Thomas Spence. Prominent in the 1790s, Spence had been radicalised by the threatened enclosure of the common land known as the Town Moor in Newcastle in 1771. In 1775 he published *Property in Land: Every One's Right*, which owed much to the writings of his close friend, economist Charles Hall.[7] The key features of Spence's plan were: the ownership of land by the aristocracy and landlords should be brought to an end; replacing this all land should be publicly owned by self-governing democratic parishes; all the rents collected within these areas should, after expenses had been deducted, be shared equally among the population as a social dividend; universal suffrage (including female suffrage) would be adopted and the parishes would send deputies to a national senate; there would be a guaranteed income for those unable to work; children would have rights to free them from abuse and poverty. Spence's book went through many editions and was republished, with notes, by Hyndman in 1882 as *The Nationalization of the Land*.

Then, there is the question of how much Howard was influenced by the efforts of Joseph Chamberlain and Jesse Collings who campaigned on land reform using the slogan "*3 acres and a cow*" from 1885. This originated with Collings, who like Chamberlain served as Mayor of Birmingham and was impressed by the (relative) success of the 1845 Chartist settlement at Dodford, Worcestershire. (The expression itself was copied from John Stuart Mill, writing about Flemish husbandry in the 1840s: "*When the land is cultivated entirely by the spade and no horses are kept, a cow is kept for every three acres of land*"). The idea that the preferred option was a smallholding, with a detached cottage, was in contradiction to the urbanisation of Birmingham, where both Chamberlain and Collings started their political careers. In its practicalities too, their programme was flawed. Had it been applied logically, and the entire UK population had land allocated to it on that basis, it would have meant 50,000 square miles of the useable land in the UK, more than half the land in the country, being distributed to the people as smallholdings.[8]

It is also relevant that Chamberlain and Collings were both well-known MPs at a time when Howard was working in the House of Commons and both were famous for their nonconformist connections. It is hardly a great leap to conclude they were an influence on Howard. Less certain, but more intriguing, is whether he borrowed his ideas from Robert Pemberton. A disciple of Robert Owen, Pemberton published *The Happy Colony* in 1854, and dedicated it to "the workman of Great Britain". In his 60s when it appeared, he wrote prolifically on social matters, and recommended organised migration to New Zealand where new purpose-built towns, planned down to the last detail, could be built. Limited to 100,000 people, each of them would consist of concentric rings of ten smaller settlements of 10,000, connected by circular roads and containing a self-supporting mixture of agricultural, manufacturing and educational uses. His drawings of this do indeed look very similar to the plans Howard would produce 30 years later. Pemberton's chosen site for the first settlement, which he proposed to name Queen Victoria Town, was near New Plymouth, a trading post in North Island and specifically in the foothills of Mount Egmont, a volcano that was active at the time he wrote. Pemberton spotted that land there would be cheap in a country that had a population in 1854 of 32,000 settlers and 60,000 indigenous people, who like the Native Americans in Howard's Nebraska didn't feature in the narrative. For various reasons, Pemberton's scheme failed. Attempts to buy land from the Maori chiefs near New Plymouth led to a war between them and the white settlers that lasted through to 1869. In any case New Zealand was a very long way from the UK, and building a large new town on the slopes of a volcano possibly had less appeal than he imagined.

Howard would also at this time have been aware of the views of James Keir Hardie, a prominent figure in the Scottish miners' union and the Scottish Land Restoration League, who wanted the unemployed settled in new towns around the UK. Like Howard, Hardie followed the theories of Henry George, a US political economist and journalist, prominent in the last quarter of the nineteenth century.[9] Another influence was Prince Peter Kropotkin, whom Howard heard speak in London in the 1880s. Kropotkin was invited to Britain by Henry Seymour and Charlotte Wilson, at that time the convenor of the Hampstead Historic Club, a private members-only debating club whose membership overlapped with that of the Zetetical Society.[10]

Finally, and of this there is no doubt, Howard was heavily influenced by the US writer and political activist Edward Bellamy, whose book *Looking Backwards 2000-1887* caused a sensation when it appeared in 1888. Written as a utopian science-fiction novel, it predicted a future where everything is publicly owned, everyone retires at 45, crime has all but vanished and a world of peace and plenty reigns throughout the globe, due to machinery taking over unpleasant work and the widespread use of credit. Howard was apparently so gripped by Bellamy's predictions that he read the book in a single sitting.[11]

If Howard was impressed by Bellamy's vision of the future, others were too, though some found much to criticise in the ways Bellamy thought it could be brought about. William Morris issued a firm corrective for the benefit of the UK's progressive readership with News from Nowhere (1890) in which the future is cooperative and democratic, but markedly less statist than the world envisaged by Bellamy. Morris did not want the government, however it was formed, dictating how everyone should live, and disliked industrialism and a factory-based economy based on the use of machines. He also imagined a world that was distinctly libertarian: in News from Nowhere there is no formal education for children who "often make up parties, and come to play in the woods for weeks together in the summer time", whilst their parents, though monogamous, are free to pursue romantic love with other, temporary, partners.[12]

Howard's own views were presented in his 1891 essay A City of Health and How to Build It. This proposed building at a far lower density than the typical suburban schemes then being developed by private builders. It also advocated abandoning the practice of adding additional residential "outgrowths" to existing towns and cities in a quasi-organic fashion, and recommended instead completely detached, newly created urban areas. The preponderance of such "outgrowths" that were appearing, particularly around London from the late 1880s, was marked and may have sharpened Howard's opinion that something needed to be done to counteract them. Many were promoted by Frederick Ramuz who hit on the idea of buying, whenever it came on the market, farmland that adjoined railway lines, breaking it up into "plots" (roughly 10 per acre) and selling these individually at mass auctions to whoever fancied building their own home. Active from 1888, when he promoted an ill-fated project at Hampton-on-Sea (adjoining Herne Bay), Ramuz had an enormous audience for his schemes, reflecting how many of the public continued to see cities as something to escape at the first opportunity. But other than a few unadopted roads he provided his developments with nothing, calculating instead that in time continued development from nearby towns would see them fall under the responsibility of the local authority in their area, which would then be obliged to provide appropriate facilities. Surely, something better, and more comprehensive than this rather desperate version of a DIY utopia could be provided? Howard thought so, and, like Morris, did not see the state as the body that would implement it: in his view of the future the ideal communities would have to be built with funding from trusts and sympathetic benefactors.[13]

Howard announced his scheme to the wider public in 1893. The venue chosen, the Congregational Memorial Hall in Farringdon Road, was a magnificent gothic structure, built in 1875 and dedicated to the two thousand puritan ministers who had refused to conform to the 1662 Act of Uniformity, and had thereby inaugurated "nonconformism".[14] The meeting was chaired by prominent Congregationalist James Branch, who also sat as Liberal representative for Bethnal Green South West on the London County Council, whilst others in attendance were Reverend Alderman Fleming Williams and Reverend J Bruce Wallace. The presence of Branch and Williams, an LCC Alderman, reflected Howard's latest role as "official reporter to the LCC", and underlined the extent to which progressive politics and nonconformity intertwined then. Williams was in fact Irish, having been born in Limerick. By 1881, he was living in Shoreditch and minister of Hoxton Academy Chapel, later serving as the minister of Rectory Road Chapel, Stoke Newington, where he earned the nickname "Flaming Williams" on account of his oratory. Chairman of the London Congregational Union he was known for his socialist views, and Shaw based the character of Morrell in his play Candida on him. Wallace had strong Irish connections too, and had been Pastor of the Congregationalist Church in Kingstown, Dublin. Later, in 1887, he founded a cooperative newspaper in Limavady, called The Brotherhood. Heavily influenced, like Howard, by both George and Bellamy, Wallace was also a keen advocate of the theories propounded by Leo Tolstoy, principally an opposition to the private ownership of land and a belief that living in self-governing anarchist communes was to be preferred to conventional society. An early member of the Fabian Society, alongside Shaw, HG Wells, J Ramsay MacDonald and Emmeline Pankhurst, by 1892 Wallace was Minister at the Southgate Road Chapel in Hackney, renaming it the Brotherhood Church, and was involved in the Kingsland branch of the Socialist Democratic Federation.

Howard now expanded his essay into a book, and did so, over several years, by working through the night at his kitchen table in the houses that his family occupied in a newly built, upmarket area of north Hackney.[15] A detailed text, complete with elaborate plans, drawn by Howard himself, illustrating the ideal towns and cities of the future, it was considered by the commercial publishers he approached to be too expensive to produce. None would agree to take it unless Howard provided some funds to offset this. The sum of £50 (equivalent then to approximately £25,000 today) was considered necessary, and Howard, who, despite working in the House of Commons and at the LCC, was of limited means, was eventually given this by George Dickman of the US Kodak company, who, like Howard, was a great admirer of spiritualist Cora Tappan.[16]

Howard's book *Tomorrow: The Peaceful Path to Real Reform* appeared in October 1898. It set out detailed proposals. Money would be raised via mortgages vested in "*...four gentlemen of undoubted probity...*" The newly built city would be managed by a Board of Management elected by its residents, who would be households that both rented and owned homes there. There would be 54 members and 27 non-elected officers each running a department. For anyone connected with nineteenth-century house-building it was clear that Howard was suggesting building at a density well below anything considered commercially viable. His scheme, as illustrated, recommended developing at only 5% of that practised then in contemporary urban areas, and, although influenced by Bellamy, George, Tolstoy and Kropotkin, there was no acknowledgement of the obvious practicalities such a radical strategy implied, namely that the US was 38 times, and Russia 100 times larger, than the UK.

Howard also claimed "*...If Labour leaders spent half the energy in co-operative organization that they now waste in co-operative* *disorganization, the end of the present unjust system would be at hand. In Garden City such leaders will have a fair field for the exercise of pro-municipal functions...*" This was politically naïve, even at the time. The idea that the urban masses and their leaders should self-fund and self-build their own garden cities and, after moving there, busy themselves in the administration of various democratic, municipal activities, was an astonishing assumption from someone who knew both Tom Mann and Ben Tillett, neither of whom showed much interest in such a project.[17] In addition, some of the details on how this would be implemented were vague. It wasn't clear, for instance, whether the electorate that voted for the 54 members of the garden city governing body would include women, or, indeed, if women could stand for office. Given that the campaign for female suffrage had been extant for three decades by the 1890s, this was a rather peculiar omission from an author who saw himself as being within the progressive caucus.

Nevertheless, Howard's connections amongst the political elite brought him a review in *The Times*, albeit his book was treated as a curiosity "*...Mr Howard is not content with half measures; like Sir Thomas More, he builds a Utopia – a charming 'Garden City' of 32,000 people in the midst of a little territory, all owned, planned, built and generally directed by the community itself. The details of administration, taxation etc., work out to perfection, and it is quite evident that if Mr Howard could be made town clerk, he would carry it on to everybody's satisfaction. The only difficulty is to create it; but that is a small matter to Utopians...*" Fellow Fabian, Edward Pease, adopted a similar tone on reading the work, commenting "*...We have got to make the best of our existing cities...*"

One must conclude that neither *The Times* nor the gradualist leadership of the Fabians were Howard's intended audience. Significantly his book sought to attract a kind of discerning middle-ground readership and was also reviewed in both *The Country Gentleman* and *The Lady's Pictorial*. When it came to assembling the like-minded souls who might take his project forward, Howard concentrated on progressive thinkers within the nonconformist community, and began giving lectures about the

garden cities of the future. The first of these took place at the
Stoke Newington Congregational Church on 3 December 1898,
with further talks following at Wallace's Brotherhood Church,
Southgate Road. Howard would speak in a darkened hall, with
illustrations from his book – marvellous, coloured, geometric
designs like gigantic snowflakes, transposed onto large glass
slides – projected onto a screen by a powerful lantern. These
showed perfectly interlocking roads (actually immensely broad
avenues), canals and railways serving six satellite towns (Garden
City, Gladstone, Justicia, Concord, Philadelphia, Rurisville) each
containing 32,000 people spread out over 14 square miles, with, in
the centre, a Central City of 18.75 square miles containing 58,000
people. In the gaps between these settlements were convalescent
homes, cemeteries, forests, farms, allotments, "homes for waifs",
"homes for inebriates", an insane asylum, industrial homes and
"epileptic farms". The entire apparatus, as shown, covered 103
square miles and accommodated 250,000 people. It must have
been the case that the beauty and perfection with which this
was proposed made an immense impression on audiences. One
can imagine them, exiting into the dank, smoky atmosphere of
late nineteenth century London, replete with trams, gin palaces,
factory chimneys and the stench from breweries, canals and
drains, thinking that they had glimpsed the future, and that it
was attainable. In acknowledgement of this, Howard joined the
Stoke Newington branch of the Brotherhood Association, which
promptly renamed itself the Garden City branch.[18]

It mattered not that Howard's illustrations came with
disclaimers: *"Plan cannot be drawn until site selected"* or *"Plan must
depend upon site selected"*. Nor did it matter that another Fabian,
HG Wells, had a markedly different view of the future. Almost
simultaneous with the appearance of *Tomorrow: The Peaceful Path
to Real Reform*, Wells published the immense dystopia *When the
Sleeper Wakes*. Echoing Bellamy this has a man going to sleep in
1897 and waking up in the London of 2100. It's quite a future:
aerial travel is common and no one lives in the country or small
towns any more. In fact, there are only four gigantic cities in

the entirety of the United Kingdom, agriculture is completely mechanised and all power is obtained from immense wind-farm arrays. Sadly, social arrangements have not moved apace with this. Instead, they have regressed with a small, wealthy, elite manipulating the population via a combination of oppression, impoverishment, technology and mindless pleasure. The book ends with a workers' uprising in full swing. Wells elaborated further on this topic in the subsequent novella *A Story of the Days to Come* (June 1899) in which the London of the 22nd century has a population of over 30 million, the most important of whom live in skyscrapers, and a whole range of technical innovations are common including moving walkways, air-travel and immense motorways between cities. In this instance, the countryside is largely abandoned. Wells clearly saw the dangers that technology – controlled by a capitalist elite – posed to the masses. Howard, in contrast, proposed a self-implemented salvation for the elect, and, by inference, a disengagement by them from the hurly-burly of day-to-day politics.

In early 1899, Howard travelled to Hindhead, Surrey – then, as now, a select residential area – to give one of his lectures. George Bernard Shaw attended[19], jocularly referring to it as an evening with *"Ebenezer the Garden City Geyser"* and apparently debunking some of Howard's assumptions at the subsequent discussion. It had little effect on the popularity of Howard's proposal. The same month that *A Story of the Days to Come* appeared, Howard returned to the Congregational Memorial Hall in Farringdon Road for a meeting, chaired by John Leng MP, that led to the formation of the Garden City Association, a collection of the great and the good that would seek to build the prototype garden city, and would in years to come become world famous as the Town and Country Planning Association.

Notes

(1) The building in question still stands at the junction of Tabernacle Street and Leonard Street, London EC2.
(2) Though some Native Americans, encouraged by Custer's defeat at Little Big

Horn, momentarily rose again in 1876, the year Howard returned to the UK.

(3) In 1871, the First Congregational Church of Chicago was located in a large, newly built, stone building and ideally placed to accommodate relief efforts. It had been founded 20 years earlier on another site by an anti-slavery group that split from the Presbyterian Church, and became nationally famous for offering sanctuary to escaping slaves.

(4) The main venue for free thought in London. Originally the John Street Institute, it was founded by Robert Owen in 1840 and used frequently as a meeting place by the Chartists. It moved to Cleveland Hall in Cleveland Street, which had been built with a legacy from William Saull in 1861. Tappan did not limit herself to serious audiences, and could also be found performing at the Weston Music Hall, aka the Holborn Empire, alongside a wide range of variety artistes.

(5) Before doing so Howard, who had invented a new version of the typewriter, attempted to sell this to the Remington Company at their New York works. He failed, but made several trips to and from the US in the years that followed, seeking to make money from his invention, which he claimed would "...*provide for narrower spaces between letters occupying little room, and for wider spaces between letters occupying much room, and for normal spaces between letters of normal width, so that, finally, when the printing is completed, the actual blank spaces between the letters printed will be substantially alike...*" In 1924 he invented a shorthand typewriter (the Phonotype) but neither this, nor his earlier efforts made him any money.

(6) Eventually increased to a height of 180 feet, by 1890, the status of the Home Insurance Building as the "first skyscraper" is disputed in favour of several other structures built in Chicago around this time.

(7) Hall, a doctor, was a prominent figure in economic thought from the 1780s. He was imprisoned in the Fleet Prison – for debt – in 1816, and died shortly after his release in 1825. His writings were later much admired by Karl Marx and Henry George.

(8) Both Chamberlain and Collings were adherents of the "Civic Gospel" a grouping that originally emerged in the late 1840s from attendees at the Unitarian Church of the Saviour, in Edward Street, Birmingham. From 1876 the movement was headed by Congregationalist divine Dr Robert Dale.

(9) Keir Hardie, a Methodist lay-preacher in addition to his trade union and political activities, failed in an attempt to enter Parliament at the Mid Lanarkshire bye-election (April 1888). He eventually served as MP for West Ham South 1892-1895, and Merthyr Tydfil 1900-1915.

(10) Kropotkin lived in Harrow, later moving to 6 Crescent Road, Burnt Ash, Bromley, a very typical, well-to-do, newly built suburban location for the time. His book *Fields, Factories and Workshops*, recommending decentralisation of the state, was published in 1899. While living in London he became friends with William Morris and George Bernard Shaw.

(11) *Looking Backward: 2000-1887* was the third biggest selling novel of its day, behind *Uncle Tom's Cabin* and *Ben Hur*. It has remained in print to this day. In 1897, Bellamy produced a sequel, *Equality*, set in 2000. In this the population has been dispersed out of overcrowded cities (Boston, Massachusetts, drops by 75%, from 300,000 to 75,000) to idyllic suburban and rural locations and most people are vegetarians.

(12) Morris had an unhappy experience in his membership of socialist organisations. He split (with others) from Hyndman's SDF in 1884 and set up the Socialist League, which he subsequently abandoned in 1890 after it had been taken over by anarchists. His views on romantic, consensual, relationships may have reflected his wife's lengthy affairs with Dante Gabriel Rossetti and Wilfrid Blunt.

(13) Ramuz was active in local politics in Southend-on-Sea where he was Mayor 1898-1900. Most of his schemes were in the Thames Estuary. Hampton-on-Sea failed completely due to coastal erosion, but others, at Rochford, Essex and Minster-in-Sheppey, Kent were quite successful. Typically, he would purchase up to 1,000 acres, divide it into plots (of around 3,000 sq ft each; roughly 10 per acre) and sell these for anything between £4 and £20 each. In 1900 values he would spend circa £3,000 acquiring a site and eventually recoup from plot sales up to £75,000. (In today's values, spending £1.2m and recouping £30m). He was able to do so due to the almost complete lack of planning regulations covering this type of development during his lifetime. His company, The Land Company, was by 1906 proclaiming in its brochures *"Land nationalisation is coming"* in the expectation that the newly elected Liberal government would preclude further schemes of his type. See https://www.rochford.gov.uk/sites/default/files/Issues%20and%20Options%20-%20Strutt%20and%20Parker%20Peggle%20Meadow%20-%20Attachment%203.pdf and also Patrick Wright *The Sea View Has Me Again: Uwe Johnson in Sheerness* (London: Repeater Books 2020) p138-142 for a discussion of Minster-in-Sheppey.

(14) The Fleet Prison originally occupied the site. This was demolished in 1842. Part of the land was bisected by the railway line connecting Herne Hill and Farringdon in 1866, after which the eastern portion was used (from 1871) as the location for Holborn Viaduct Station. What remained on the western part of the site was then sold to the Congregational Church. The Congregational Memorial Hall was frequently used as a venue for important events: in February 1900 the foundation meeting of the Labour Representation Committee (the precursor of the Labour Party) took place there.

(15) At Kyverdale Road and Durley Road, about half a mile north of the family's former address in Evering Road.

(16) By this point Tappan had remarried and was appearing as Cora Richmond, her new husband recording her lectures in shorthand for publication. For Howard, this funding would prove to be a stroke of luck, as Dickman's generous act would prove to be one of the last things he did. A few days later, whilst at the Kodak offices in London, he began to complain of severe abdominal pain. Taken home by ambulance he was operated on, but never recovered and died on 15 November 1898.

(17) Both were major figures in trade union organisation in the late nineteenth and early twentieth century. Mann would later be prominent in the moves that led to the foundation of the Communist Party. Tillett, who sat as a Labour MP 1917-1924 and 1929-1931, was much further to the right politically.

(18) Applying Howard's densities today, London (the GLA area) would have a population of no more than 1.5 million, a drop of 7.5 million (83%). Were the garden city model rolled out across the entire UK it would require the use of 28,000 square miles of land to accommodate the present UK population. Currently, according to the Ministry of Housing Communities and Local Government estimate, 8% of UK land is "developed". Howard's proposal, by spreading low-density housing amongst amenity space and other uses, would increase that to 30%.

(19) Why Hindhead? Possibly because both George Bernard Shaw and Edward Pease were resident in the area.

5

CHARITIES, PHILANTHROPISTS, LOCAL GOVERNMENT

During the time Howard was away in the US, and the time that he spent after his return at the House of Commons and LCC, others, engaged in the practicalities of providing housing in the UK, found much to do. The 1880s, in particular, were a period when the inadequacy of the housing that was available for the poor was much remarked upon. It was also a time when, despite emigration, particularly from Ireland, the population of the UK grew from 35 million in 1881 to 38 million by 1891, with most of the increase in English towns, particularly London which expanded from 4.7 million to 5.6 million during the same period. Typical of those expressing their concerns was George Sims, a journalist and playwright, who published *How the Poor Live* in *Pictorial World* and *The Daily News* in 1883. This was followed a few months later by *The Bitter Cry of Outcast London* by Andrew Mearns, who was prominent in the London Congregational Union. To exert direct political pressure, there was a Land Nationalisation Society (1881) with offices at 432 Strand and the pioneering zoologist Alfred Wallace as its first President, and an English League for the Taxation of Land Values (1883). Originally established as the Land Reform Union following a UK speaking tour by Henry George, this held regular meetings in Trafalgar Square, one of which, in 1887, ended in a riot. Several of its adherents would be successfully elected in the inaugural London County Council elections of 1889.

In 1884, Prime Minister William Gladstone, having won an outright majority in the 1880 general election, noted the way the political wind was blowing, and established a Royal Commission on the Housing of the Working Classes. With a membership that included Charles Dilke, (President of the Local Government Board and MP for Chelsea), the Prince of Wales, Lord Salisbury, (Leader of the Opposition), Lord Shaftesbury and Cardinal Manning, the leader of the Roman Catholic Church in England and Wales, and a keen advocate of social justice, this spent a year taking evidence, touring overcrowded urban areas and interviewing witnesses.[1] The outcome was the Housing of the Working Classes Act (1885), sponsored, in an openly bipartisan fashion, by Richard Cross in the House of Commons, and Salisbury in the House of Lords, after the formation of a minority Conservative administration. Importantly, the Act established the principle that local authorities could borrow money to address housing problems via the Treasury, using their local rates as security.[2]

For the while, though, the task of providing new homes remained something mainly carried out by privately funded, philanthropic, organisations. The Artizans, Labourers and General Dwellings Company commenced construction of their 2,200-unit Noel Park Estate in 1883. Designed, like their predecessor at Queens Park, by Rowland Plumbe, it was named after their Chairman, Ernest Noel MP, and built in an area made accessible by the opening of the Seven Sisters-Wood Green railway. The aftermath of Gladstone's Royal Commission and the raised public awareness about social justice and related issues that it generated also produced a wave of new providers of purpose-built social housing. These included the East End Dwellings Company, founded by Canon Samuel Barnett of Toynbee Hall, the Four Per Cent Industrial Dwellings Society (1885, founded by Lord Rothschild), the Guinness Trust (1890, founded by the Irish philanthropist Edward Guinness), the William Sutton Trust (1894) and the Samuel Lewis Housing Trust (1901, from the bequest of an English moneylender). All of these built high-density, model estates to serve the rapidly increasing urban population.

In tandem with this came an improvement in how such properties were managed, mainly due to the efforts of Octavia

Hill. A long-standing activist, she had originally worked with John Ruskin, who purchased 3 houses for housing the poor in Paradise Place, now Garbutt Place W1, in 1864. These were managed by Hill who, by using a team of women she specifically trained for this purpose, devised new methods of rent collection, tenancy and lettings procedures, resulting in her appointment to run the Ecclesiastical Commissioners' housing estates in south London.

Alongside this the 1880s saw a boom in private house-building, most of which was undertaken by builders who built an average of 4 houses per development. Building for rent, rather than sale, was the model most commonly pursued, assisted by low land values, low labour costs, the low cost of materials, and the restrictive terms imposed by many lenders on would-be mortgagees. In the 1880s, new houses in the Victoria Park area of Hackney could be rented for between £40 pa (small house) and £100 pa (large house), £21,000 pa and £52,500 pa respectively in 2021. New suburbs were being created too. Bush Hill Park, developed by the Bush Hill Park Land Company over 700 acres, was started in 1872 and finally completed 20 years later after a station serving the area had been opened in 1880. By 1901 houses there were being rented for 6s 9d per week. At a time when typical average earnings were £69 10s per year (£1 6s 8d per week) this was 18% of an average income. (In 2021 this would imply £106 per week for a 3-bed house... £462 per month).

At the other end of the spectrum was Bickley Park Estate, designed by Ernest Newton and consisting mainly of very large, detached houses for the upper middle classes, built in what might be considered the emerging "English vernacular" style, a melange of Elizabethan and Queen Anne period detailing reproduced in Victorian red brick. The Woodgrange Estate in Newham was less grand, though much prized by families seeking a respectable neighbourhood. Developed in the 1890s, by Archibald Cameron Corbett, MP for Glasgow Tradeston, it provided well-built, spacious accommodation at 307 habitable rooms per hectare, which, had it been rolled out uniformly across a square mile, would have housed a total of 99,391 people. Walking through Woodgrange Park today it remains a well-planned, desirable area, with street trees, front and back gardens and long avenues of 2-storey houses. Although barely a third the density of Kensington and Chelsea 50 years earlier, it was popular with the public and the rejection of this model by Howard and his disciples in favour of far lower levels of density is striking.

As too is the way they distanced themselves from the structures that were set up in the late nineteenth century to improve public housing. Whilst Howard was patiently devising his network of new towns, presided over by *"four gentlemen of undoubted probity"*, successive governments were implementing financial and democratic legislation that would fundamentally change people's lives. In 1888, Charles Ritchie, MP for Tower Hamlets and President of the Local Government Board in the 1886-1892 Salisbury government, presided over the passing of the Local Government Act. This established the London County Council and various County Boroughs elsewhere. Opposed by many in his own party, this was a very significant step forward, and, when combined with the powers introduced in the Housing of the Working Classes Act a few years earlier, led to the undertaking of very large-scale, new-build municipal projects. The same year that Sir William Harcourt proclaimed jocularly *"We are all socialists now"*, the inaugural LCC elections, in 1889, produced a majority for the Progressives, as the coalition of Liberal and Labour candidates was known.[3] An administration led by the Earl of Rosebery, later to be Prime Minister 1894-1895, took power in London, and quickly embarked on the construction of the Millbank Estate, on the site of the former Millbank prison, and the Boundary Estate, which swept away the *Jago* "rookery" in Shoreditch.[4] In social housing, then, as now, size mattered. The scale of the resources that the LCC could mobilise, and the amount of money it was allowed to borrow, meant that each of these was up to 7 or 8 times the size of the smaller schemes completed by the various companies set up by charitable benefactors. Tackling the *Jago* in particular was a much-praised objective. The area was notorious as a den of vice, and featured in fictionalised studies such as A *Child of the Jago* (Arthur Morrison, 1895) and, even after its demise, in *The People of the Abyss* (Jack London, 1903).[5]

Another practical alternative to Howard's immaculate plans for the cities of the future came in 1890 when William Booth published *In Darkest England and the Way Out*. An observation of contemporary urban conditions, this stated, about the most wretched *"...This submerged tenth – it is, then beyond the reach of the nine tenths in the midst of whom they live..."* A Methodist, who moved to Congregationalism in the 1850s when he associated with John Campbell at Whitefield's Tabernacle,[6] Booth had formed his own evangelical organisation, later known as the Salvation Army, by 1861. His book sold 10,000 copies on the day it was published and proposed solutions such as hostels for the homeless, waste recycling centres, skills workshops, job centres for the unemployed, access to banks and legal advice for the poor as well as women's refuges. It appeared midway through the multi-volume *Enquiry into Life and Labour in London 1886-1903*, by his namesake Charles Booth, a Unitarian. An early example of social cartography this had been devised from travels around the city, the end result of which was an enormous map of the metropolis, with each street coloured to reflect the income and social class of its inhabitants. The level of detail provided by Charles Booth's work makes for an interesting comparison with Howard's sketches.

The cumulative effect of the legislation, and of the initiatives followed by the house-builders, philanthropists and nascent local authorities was to accelerate the emergence of a new, orderly, late-Victorian streetscape. An urban environment characterised by high-density terraces, blocks of mansion flats, main roads lined by shops with residential areas above, stitched together by electric trams (introduced in Leytonstone in 1882) and prototype commuter train services running to and from city centre stations. The quality of what was built varied, of course. Contrary to what many maintain, the standard of Victorian housing construction was not uniformly high. A lot of properties were built without damp courses, many others were built on unstable ground (clay, in particular) or on land that had not been properly filled in after use as brick fields or quarries. But much of it was solid, and some, like John James Burnet's 1891 scheme at Charing Cross Mansions, in Glasgow, magnificent.

Further progress occurred in 1900 when Henry Chaplin MP, President of the Local Government Board in the 1895-1900 Salisbury government, established the London Metropolitan Boroughs, sweeping away the remnants of the vestries, only a few of which, such as St Leonard's Shoreditch, had attempted to provide social housing.[7] The 28 newly created local authorities set about devising their own housing and slum clearance programmes. For the moment, though, the initiative remained with philanthropists, some of whom opened privately funded "model" developments similar to those envisaged by Howard.

Among these could be found George Cadbury, a Quaker and the owner of the confectionery manufacturers of the same name who developed Bournville from 1893. Built slowly, it had evolved by 1900 into the Bournville Village Trust. Eventually covering 1,000 acres and home to 23,000 people, it was planned at roughly 20% of the density of inner urban areas in the 1890s and designed by its architect, William Alexander Harvey, in the then prevailing "Arts and Crafts" style, which tended in practical terms to mean mock-Tudor. In keeping with the Cadbury ethos, there were no public houses in the development, something that remains true to the present day. One hundred and five miles north-west of Bournville, William Lever, a Congregationalist, built Port Sunlight. A scheme of 800 houses, completed between 1899 and 1914 it was designed by William Owen, and had much the same appearance visually as Cadbury's scheme. Somehow, the ethos of a model settlement for workers at a cosmetics and toiletries factory seemed less serious than the endeavours of Cadbury, Peabody, Guinness and others. When added to Lever's foibles – he ran Port Sunlight as his own private town, where joining in community activities was compulsory and changing your job to work elsewhere meant losing your house – this was noted by the wider public and satirised in the stage musical *The Sunshine Girl*, which ran at the Gaiety Theatre, London, formerly the Strand Music Hall, in 1912 and 1913.[8] Both Cadbury and Lever launched their schemes within a few months of Howard's book, and, for practical reasons, both projects were much smaller than what Howard proposed.

Which is not to say that Howard was wrong to think on a grand scale. By the 1890s taxation on land was impacting on traditional landowners, to the point where Oscar Wilde in *The Importance of Being Earnest* (1895) had Lady Bracknell stating "*...What between the duties expected of one during one's lifetime, and the duties exacted from one after one's death, land has ceased to be either a profit or a pleasure. It gives one position, and prevents one from keeping it up. That's all that can be said about land...*" It followed that there was much agricultural land to be bought cheaply, and, in this context, it is of interest that Chaplin's successor as President of the Local Government Board, Walter Long MP, who held the position from 1900 to 1905, later became leader of the Country Landowners' Association in 1907, specifically to fight the devaluation of their main asset.[9]

Notes

(1) Manning moved from the Anglican to the Catholic Church in 1851. His views on social teaching, in which the state has a duty toward the poor, later found expression in the Papal Encyclical *Rerum Novarum* (1891) by Pope Leo XIII, subsequently one of the key foundation blocks of European Christian Democracy, and via that, the European Union.

(2) As a result of this, the Public Works Loans Board, which had expanded its remit to include lending money for the building of workhouses (from 1835), water supply and sewers (from 1848) and schools (from 1870) finally began to consider applications for housing schemes.

(3) Harcourt, MP for Derby, made the quote in *Fabian Essays*, a collection edited by George Bernard Shaw.

(4) Located in and around Old Nichol Street, the Jago was the only example of a historic London slum to be comprehensively redeveloped: the others changed over time as house-builders made inroads into their terrain. The London "rookeries" seem to have overlapped in area with preceding mediaeval "liberties": self-governing areas that were independently administered and separate from the structure of parishes that existed elsewhere. Thus, the Jago included some of the Liberty of Norton Folgate, and the St Giles rookery was within the extended Liberties of Saffron Hill, Hatton Garden, Ely Rents and Ely Place, which contained a population of around 10,000 in the mid-nineteenth century. Liberties were finally abolished by the Local Government Act (1888) with two exceptions – the Inner Temple and Middle Temple in London which continue to be self-administering local government areas.

(5) Among those elected to the LCC with Rosebery were John Burns, James Branch, John Benn (like Branch a Congregationalist, and grandfather of Anthony Wedgwood Benn) and Jane Cobden, daughter of Richard. The opposition Moderate Party included Thomas Corbett, brother of Archibald Cameron Corbett. The 1889 LCC had 2 current, 2 past and 23 future MPs.

(6) Prominent from the 1830s, John Campbell helped established Congregationalism as a separate dissenting tradition from Methodism. A keen supporter of the abolition of slavery, he spoke with escaped slave Frederick Douglass at the Congregational Chapel in Finsbury Circus in 1846.

(7) The Shoreditch Vestry built a total of 97 flats in 3 separate blocks in and around Provost Street in the final few years prior to their abolition. In comparison, the London County Council provided on the Boundary Estate 1069 flats, a laundry, 77 workshops and 188 retail premises in a scheme that completed in 1900.

(8) Lever held, and lost, a referendum on banning the sale of alcohol in Port Sunlight.

(9) Chaplin was a landowner too, owning extensive states in Lincolnshire.

6

HOWARD PERSISTS

By 1901, Howard's Garden City Association was being chaired by Ralph Neville KC, formerly MP for Liverpool Exchange. With the Cadbury family confirmed as significant supporters, a conference was held at Bournville.[1] George Bernard Shaw attended, and remained sceptical, particularly regarding the vague governance structures, but Howard now enjoyed immense influence. A second edition of his book appeared in 1902, by which point the Garden City Association had 1300 members, and no fewer than 101 Vice Presidents. In addition to Shaw and Neville, these included the Countess of Warwick, the Bishop of London, the various nonconformist house-builders (Cadbury, Rowntree and Lever), Cecil Harmsworth, HG Wells, Aneurin Williams, the book illustrator Walter Crane (a colleague of William Morris) and George Holyoake, one of the Rochdale pioneers from 50 years earlier.

Relatively few figures from the emerging Labour movement were to be found in the organisation, and the politics of the more notable members remained either erratic or decidedly centrist. The Countess of Warwick, for instance, had been the mistress of Edward VII in the 1890s, during which time her investments (in Tanganyika) were handled by Cecil Rhodes. She lived in Warwick Castle with her husband, the 5th Earl, a Conservative politician and one of the most senior freemasons in England, and yet she was also a member of Hyndman's Social Democratic Federation. Arthur Winnington-Ingram, Bishop of London, was noted both for his interest in social work in east London and his progressive views on housing. Regarding the latter, these were so advanced for the time that streets on the Hampstead Garden Suburb were named after him, including Bishops Avenue.[2] He adopted an extreme anti-German and jingoistic rhetoric after 1914. Both Harmsworth, from 1906, and Williams, from 1910 were Liberal MPs with Harmsworth also acting as Chairman of Associated Newspapers, the publishers of *The Daily Mail*.

The Garden City Association quickly registered as a company (the Garden City Pioneering Company Limited) and took premises at 77 Chancery Lane, London WC2. Negotiations began about buying a site at Chartley Castle, in Staffordshire, possibly selected because of a general proximity to Bournville. Here, 6.5 miles north-east of Stafford and adjoining a station on the Uttoxeter-Stafford railway, the land was level and theoretically could have been developed... except that it was difficult to see major employers locating there, and Howard's scheme depended on the new city being self-sustaining in employment terms. Whilst the practicalities of this were mulled over, Herbert Warren, the company's solicitor, heard that 3,822 acres of land between Baldock and Hitchin were becoming available for purchase. It was agreed that this was a better prospect, 34 miles from London, but not under metropolitan influence, and therefore a location where a new city could be built from scratch, where employers were more likely to relocate and where progressively minded people might move. The land was purchased, at a cost of £160,378, and a prospectus issued in September 1903 asking for a share issue of £300,000 (£125m today) to fund the project.

Looking at these figures, it is clear that Howard and his colleagues paid £41.96p per acre for the land they purchased in Letchworth. This is equal to a price today of £17,455 per acre at a time when average agricultural land per acre is reckoned to be worth £6,690[3]. Clearly, this was an expensive acquisition, and could only have been thought worthwhile on the basis that most of the housing built in the scheme would be for private sale, and, toward the upper end of that market. It was also the case that this expenditure was only for a fragment of Howard's plan – the land purchased was barely sufficient for Rurisville. Its surrounding settlements and their supporting array of facilities would clearly have to wait before they could be provided. Howard, who had never built anything, had grandiose ideas of what his garden cities should look like, and was given to comparing them to New York, remarking *"...we may have finer buildings in London, but there is nowhere anything like such a succession of fine buildings..."* In his mind Letchworth, as a prototype was intended to have both a "Fifth Avenue" (which Howard envisaged being 110 yards wide) and a "Central Park". According to Charles Purdom, employed as a junior clerk by the Garden City Pioneering Company from its foundation, and later a major figure in UK town planning *"...Howard was a good talker, but essentially simple-minded and fundamentally uneducated; his mind was that of an inventor... No invention is the work of a single mind, and that was true of Howard's. He was, however, extremely sensitive about what he had done, and though in his book he quotes the names of three writers who, he says, had influenced him, he picked up ideas from many sources. He would not, however, discuss the matter, and inevitably changed the subject when it was referred to. The much-criticized term garden city was got from A. T. Stewart's Long Island scheme of the same name, the beginnings of which Howard must have seen when in America, but he would not admit it..."*

This is an interesting comparison. Alexander T Stewart, an Irish-American who opened the first department stores in New York in the 1840s, lived to become one of the richest men in the world. In his retirement, from 1868, he began planning "Garden City", the building of which started in 1869 and continued slowly for many years. Whether or not Howard was actually aware of it is probably beside the point.[4] The key issue is that Stewart's Garden City, which was spread across 7,000 acres and has today a population of only 22,000, was an ultra-low-density residential district in a country that had an abundance of space. Whether such a project should ever have become the template for major developments in a much smaller country with an existing population density that was quite high, doesn't seem to have crossed Howard's mind, nor those of his colleagues. For Howard, matters were clear. Once one of the new garden cities had been announced, people would simply stream out of their overcrowded abodes in London and gratefully take residence in the new environment, leaving behind them depopulated areas that could be pulled down and replaced by parks and open spaces.

The reality, however, of planning and laying out a completely new town in isolation from any adjoining settlements, proved significantly more difficult than Howard and his colleagues had anticipated. By 1904, the share issue had not been taken up and, if Letchworth was going to emerge out of the fields any time soon, a more conventional approach to development would have to be pursued. The Rowntrees, the Cadburys and Lever, who had built model villages themselves, at this point carefully and diplomatically excluded Howard from any day-to-day management of the scheme. Recognising, though, his talent for political and social networking, he was retained and paid £350 a year (approximately £140,000 today) to promote and get publicity for the garden city project. About this move Charles Purdom would state *"...No one who knew him could regard Howard as a practical man, and it is a fact that he took an inconspicuous part in the task of building Letchworth and Welwyn; but it cannot be gainsaid that his garden city project was practicable in the highest degree. He had the vision, and presented it in explicit terms. He had no idea how the town he described was to be built, but he formulated its essential structure and economic basis, which was the creation of land values by converting rural into urban land..."* The final sentence here, possibly unwittingly, reveals the logic behind the garden city plan: buy land cheaply in rural areas (rural land is, and always has been, cheaper than urban land), build pleasant houses in a pleasant setting and sell them to private buyers. In theory, the sales values, though marginally lower than in traditional towns and cities, would, because of the lower land value, produce enhanced profits for the developer. In basing the economies of his project on this, Howard and his colleagues were doing no more and no less than a great many private housing developers had always done (and still do). Where they differed was in presenting the public with the notion of a completely new town, with many embellishments, reserved for an elect, discerning population who no longer wished to live in traditional urban settings. The problem was, in Letchworth in 1904, given how much the land cost the company, and whether there were sufficient people willing to migrate to such a setting, it was both unlikely that the anticipated profits would accrue and uncertain if selling the completed homes would be a quick process.

The company appointed Richard Parker and Raymond Unwin as architects. Howard had met them when he addressed the Manchester Ruskin Society in November 1901. Unwin, from Rotherham, had heard Ruskin lecture at Oxford in the early 1880s, and via his political connections, (at one time he was Secretary of the Socialist League in Manchester) had also met William Morris, whose "arts and crafts" philosophy he admired and emulated. Unwin's sister married Parker, who was from Chesterfield, making them brothers-in-law, and from 1902 they had been engaged in building New Earswick, a model village near York, for the Rowntrees.[5] A smaller scheme than Letchworth, this proceeded slowly with the properties being owned from very early on by the Joseph Rowntree Housing Trust. But, like Letchworth, it had ambitions, albeit on a reduced scale: two fruit trees were provided for every home, there were allotments and a "folk hall" for social activities.[6] It fell to Unwin to convert Howard's diagrams into a practical plan.

Doing this much was reasonably easy. Though Howard based his preferred densities and building dimensions on examples that had been extant since mediaeval times, his scheme proposed housing 30,000 people across 1,000 acres, which was low, but not unimaginable. The plan to build Letchworth as a gigantic cooperative failed early on – as would be the case today relatively few people wish to live in a self-managing cooperative. More to the point, it proved difficult to attract well-to-do house buyers to a new settlement that was in the earliest stages of construction, lacked many of the facilities of a traditional town, and required commuting to and from their place of work. This was despite the fact that a new station, Letchworth Garden City, was opened on the Hitchin-Cambridge line in 1903, to facilitate access to the area. Not surprisingly, the Garden City Pioneering Company soon adopted the approach that had worked at New Earswick: building traditional terraces of cottages for local workers, which, in this instance were placed, from 1911, under the management of the newly formed Howard Cottage Society.[7]

By then, Unwin had left to work, with Parker, on Hampstead Garden Suburb, taking over from Edwin Lutyens. Compared to Letchworth, this was – as a piece of architectural and master-planning work – a considerably easier project. Covering 243 acres, on what was then mainly countryside outside the London County Council boundaries in Golders Green, it consisted of Wylde's Farm and adjoining agricultural land near where the Charing Cross, Euston and Hampstead Railway (now the TfL Northern Line) opened a station in June 1907. The site had been purchased from Eton College by Dame Henrietta Barnett, wife of Canon Barnett of Toynbee Hall and the East End Dwellings Company, to provide 5,000 properties housing 13,000 people.[8] Barnett, who lived at Hampstead's North End, a mile to the south-east of the Hampstead Garden Suburb site, was highly motivated and socially conscious, and disliked what she had seen of how typical middle-class-type housing arrived in an area once a railway station, or, as was likely then, a tram route, had been opened. Admiring settlements like Bedford Park and New Earswick, she set out to ensure that what was built once electric trains were running to and from Golders Green was a cut above what would probably happen there if nothing were done to prevent it.

The back-story to Hampstead Garden Suburb is actually quite revealing. In a way that makes one think they were channelling John Galsworthy's *A Man of Property*, Eton College, the owners of the land, refused to deal with Barnett because she was a woman. This obstacle was duly surmounted by forming a committee to conduct the purchase, in which Barnett was joined by, among others, Lord Crewe, Earl Grey, Sir John Gorst, Sir Robert Hunter and the Bishop of London. The land itself was actually purchased by the London County Council – for £140,000, approximately ten times the price per acre paid in Letchworth – and vested in the ownership of the Hampstead Garden Suburb Trust Limited.[9] To approve this somewhat unusual and not particularly straightforward arrangement, and to circumvent the local authority (Hendon Urban District Council, established 1894), the Hampstead Garden Suburb Trust required, and got, its own Act of Parliament. This stated that its aims were to cater for all classes of people and all income groups, to provide housing built at a low density, to have wide, tree-lined roads, to replace boundary walls with hedges between houses, to give access to open space within the scheme (woods and public gardens) which would be free to all, and to have as little noise within the area as possible, with, in particular, the ringing of church bells prohibited.

The Trust, with Alfred Lyttelton MP as President and a membership that included Lever and the Cadburys, issued a share prospectus for £75,000 (considerably less than that required to get things moving in Letchworth) and commenced building in 1907. Due to its proximity to London and abundance of public transport links, this went well and, as set out in the Act of Parliament, some of the early properties were cottages available at a low rent. However, after 1919, rising construction costs meant that a limited company like the Trust could no longer afford to provide housing for "all classes of people and all income groups" and this part of their activities was quietly shelved. But it continued acquiring land and building and covered 800 acres by 1935. What emerged was a large, affluent, low-density suburb that had been set up with public funds, but, within which, the majority of the public who had funded it were unable to reside because of the expensive nature of the housing it provided.[10]

Barnett and her colleagues had persuaded the London County Council to acquire land outside its boundaries on the grounds that the opportunity arose to lay out and build a new garden city within easy reach of central London. They argued that they would develop something better than typical house-builder projects elsewhere. As an immediate precedent, they could point to the LCC cottage estate scheme in Lordship Lane, Tottenham (954 houses), construction of which started in 1904 and which, like Hampstead, was outside the LCC boundaries.

Looked at today, it is not clear how great a justification there was for their arguments. If one compares Hampstead Garden Suburb, with, say Eltham Park, some interesting points arise. The latter covered 334 acres (it was 37% larger than Hampstead Garden Suburb), was within the LCC area and required no public funds for land purchase. It was built from 1899 by Archibald Cameron Corbett, as his successor scheme to a similar development a few years earlier, where he built 3,200 houses, on agricultural land between Hither Green and Catford. Corbett paid £50,000 for his Eltham estate, far less than Howard or Barnett managed per acre, and it would appear on that basis alone that Eton College extracted a handsome profit from the sale of their holdings in Hampstead to the LCC. Corbett built rapidly, and completed his project far quicker than Letchworth or Hampstead Garden Suburb, and was assisted by the opening of Shooters Hill and Eltham Park stations, on the Lewisham-Dartford line, in 1908. Eltham Park contained a broad range of housing, from large stately properties for the well-to-do through to middle-class dwellings available at annual rentals of around £38 (14s per week then, approximately £284 per week now) with smaller terraced houses available for the working class at lower, weekly, rents in selected streets. With Howard, Barnett and the whole "Garden City" ideal, of course, the LCC were buying into a particular vision. And yet Corbett had a vision of his own too. His Hither Green-Catford scheme had been promoted as a "modern Hygeia", encouraging healthy living and healthy minds.[11] Plots of land were set aside for shopping parades (with residential accommodation above), schools, churches and local parks. There were also back-land sites where businesses and local small-scale manufacturing could be accommodated. Public houses were, however, banned. Corbett, a Presbyterian and supporter of the temperance movement, ensured that anyone buying or leasing a property on one of his developments was precluded from selling alcohol. Thus, from a moral point of view, he emulated Howard and, like Howard, he had his own celebrity supporters. Charles

Booth compared his development, which was popular with Methodists, to "...*a new Garden of Eden, with young married people and no public houses...*" in his *Life and Labour of the People in London*.[12]

The March 1907 LCC elections that followed the acquisition of the Hampstead site were a disappointment to many of those who had supported the Barnett proposal. The Municipal Reform (Conservative) candidates took control, defeating the Progressive (Liberal) group, in a neat local reversal of the sensational "Liberal landslide" result in the general election held a year earlier. If the intention had been to present the development of the LCC's first garden city as a coup for progressive minded people, this failed at the ballot box. But, at central government level (and many of the Progressive members of the LCC 1904-1907 were elected MPs in 1906), matters were different. The government headed by Henry Campbell-Bannerman (and from 1908 by Herbert Asquith) appointed John Burns President of the Local Government Board and began implementing a programme of legislation to improve housing, planning and urban conditions generally. There were Royal Commissions into Registration of Title (1906), Land Transfer (1908) and Housing of the Industrial Population of Scotland, Rural and Urban (1912) and a new Housing Act (1909). Most importantly of all, there was a Housing and Town Planning Act (1909). This banned the continued construction of back-to-back housing, obliged local authorities to draw up development plans for their area and strengthened legal standards for the construction of new homes[13].

Burns also took a major role in promoting the House and Cottage Exhibition held at Gidea Park in March 1910. In some ways the pre-1914 apogee of the garden suburb/garden city phenomenon, this took place because of the ambitions of Liberal MP, Herbert Raphael, to develop 650 acres of land that he purchased near Romford in 1897. Inspired by the example of Hampstead Garden Suburb, and claiming that he wished to give working-class families the chance to enjoy a new home, he set up the Gidea Hall Development Company, and set aside 450 acres of his land for the building of a garden suburb. (The bulk of the remainder was designated for use as a golf course). Building started in 1909, as soon as Raphael had secured the provision of a new railway station at Gidea Park, on the main line into Liverpool Street from Chelmsford. The foundation stone for the first dwelling on what was now called the Romford Garden Suburb was laid by Burns on 20 July 1910. He was fulsome in his praise, proclaiming *"...This is one of the most beautiful sites I have ever been associated with in twenty-five years' connection with Housing and Town Planning – surroundings formerly enjoyed in splendid isolation by the few... When this estate is completed, you will have one of the lowest death rates in England and Wales. You will be the envy of Bournemouth... The object is to bring the Town into the Country and the Garden into the Town, to secure something more beautiful and more human than the majority of houses and streets erected in and around London during the past hundred years..."*

Raphael, a man of artistic and literary interests (he was a trustee of the National Portrait Gallery) was keen to build something of lasting significance. Inspired by Henrik Ibsen's *The Master Builder*, he held a development competition with architects from across the UK, including Parker and Unwin, vying to build the most attractive home in the "arts and crafts" style. Advice was sought from Thomas Hardy, Millicent Fawcett, Arnold Bennett and Sir Edward Poynter (President of the Royal Academy) about what made the perfect house and how the most up-to-date and modern types of homes could be provided. The scheme, containing 140 houses and cottages, was ready by early 1911. Development costs by that stage totalled £80,000 (£26.3m in 2020), which implied an average pre-sales value of £571 then (£188,000 now).[14] The likelihood of working-class families buying into this was slight, and it was clear that, whichever way you looked at it, this was a fairly upmarket and expensive development, accessible at best for the middle classes. What the Romford Garden Suburb showed was the extent to which Howard's plans had been appropriated by housing developers and how much political support that had. The comments made by John Burns deserve some analysis. He would have known, for instance, that the density at Romford (and for that matter Hampstead and Letchworth) was very low, much lower, in fact, than the density on the first LCC cottage estate, built at Totterdown Fields, Tooting in 1901, when he was LCC representative for Battersea and Clapham. (Totterdown Fields had 1,244 houses on 38 acres).[15] Burns would also have been aware that – unlike Hampstead – no LCC funds were committed to the Romford Garden Suburb, and that the chances of a large amount of working-class housing being built there were low. Perhaps he was happy to support a political colleague, knew that in any event Romford Garden Suburb was more affordable than Hampstead Garden Suburb, and supported the ideals of quality design that Raphael embraced. But... even in 1910, schemes like this were never going to solve the UK's dreadful housing problems.

In the meantime, Letchworth had been slowly taking shape. Howard was sufficiently confident to set up the Garden City Pioneer Company Limited in 1902. By 1906 Ewart Culpin had been appointed secretary of the Garden City Association and a year later had founded the International Garden Cities and Town Planning Association, actively cataloguing similar projects around the world and campaigning within the UK to raise the profile of Howard's scheme. By August 1907, enough of Letchworth had been built for Howard to take a delegation from the World Esperanto Congress (held then in Cambridge) around the nascent city. Claims were made subsequently that Vladimir Lenin also visited that year, whilst he was in the UK for the Russian Social Democratic Labour Party Congress. Originally planned for Copenhagen, this had to be hurriedly reconvened in London after pressure from the local police caused it to leave Denmark. Held between 13 May and 1 June 1907 at the Brotherhood Church, Southgate Road, it was attended by all the leading figures of the movement: Lenin, Trotsky, Stalin, Maxim Gorky, Rosa Luxemburg and many others, all of whom dispersed after the daily sessions to addresses across the city where they stayed under pseudonyms. Lenin and many others at the Imperial Hotel, Russell Square, Bloomsbury, Trotsky in a kosher bakery in Brick Lane, Stalin at a working man's hostel in Fieldgate Street, Whitechapel and Rosa Luxemburg at The

Three Nuns Hotel, 11 Aldgate High Street.[16] The Brotherhood Church, with its Tolstoy associations, was an obvious choice as a meeting venue, and indeed, Lenin had even visited services there to experience the Christian-socialist teachings propounded from the pulpit. John Wallace, the minister, was an early resident at Letchworth and may even have met Lenin. But there is no proof that Lenin actually visited Letchworth. Russian archives contain copious material on every hour of every day in Lenin's life, and his whereabouts in 1907 (and on his other London visits in 1908 and 1911) are recorded in great detail. There is no mention of him visiting Wallace, or Howard, in Letchworth. Allowing for travelling to and from the town and spending about 2-3 hours there, he would have been away from his colleagues for a minimum of 5 hours. It seems more likely that this claim is either a garbled misrepresentation of the contact between Wallace and Lenin, or a fond basking in the reflected glories of the Russian revolution, presumably before knowledge of the purges and the Ukrainian famine were widespread, by a group of UK figures who saw themselves as similarly progressive, and part of the same political fraternity as the Russian exiles.[17]

Slowly but surely, Letchworth grew. Although attempts to acquire and/or use land in the vicinity for agricultural production, so it could be self-sustaining in food production, were abandoned, and only a few employers moved there (WH Smith was one), Howard remained optimistic, commenting in 1910 "...There is a most interesting society at Letchworth. Life is in many ways like Colonial life, bright, joyous and friendly; largely free from class distinctions, and without much regard for the narrower conventionalities..." The allusion here to "Colonial life", with its images of settlers occupying a conveniently empty land, is quite revealing, given Howard's time in the US, and the similarities of his scheme to the earlier New Zealand project. His remark about "narrower conventionalities" is also telling and reflects the number of free-thinkers, vegetarians and those interested in pushing the boundaries of sexual freedom who were choosing to live there. Among those visiting Letchworth to give lectures in the community hall there pre-1914 were ED

Morel, a prominent pacifist and anti-colonial campaigner, Bertrand Russell, Lloyd George and Ramsay MacDonald.

The truth was that Letchworth had more in common with US suburbs like Shaker Heights in Cleveland, Ohio and Pasadena, California, than it did with most contemporary UK housing schemes. The first of these was developed from 1911 by the Van Sweringen brothers who enforced a number of fussy standards and restrictions, including, for many years, barring African Americans as residents, to maintain what they saw as the integrity and desirability of their development. Built to an extremely low density, its population grew slowly, reaching 28,000 by 1950. The second, with which the architects Greene and Greene were involved from 1908, was a network of immense and hugely expensive bungalows (actually two storey buildings) built in American Arts and Crafts style on the outskirts of an existing US city. The residents of both would have been comfortable with the claims Howard made for Letchworth, and would have recognised his comments about colonial life. Culpin also visited the US at this time, where he spoke publicly about the desirability of building new low-density housing schemes as extensions of existing cities, rather than as isolated, stand-alone projects in their own right. This must have seemed, to Howard, a shift away from his vision toward something that Cameron Corbett and other "developers" would have more readily recognised. In this context it may be significant that Culpin had acquired, by studying in his spare time, qualifications in town planning and architecture, things that Howard conspicuously lacked. The fruits of Culpin's travels (and studies) were contained in his 1913 book *The Garden City Movement Up-To-Date*, which, privately, Howard resented.

None of these internal conflicts, though, affected the way Howard was seen by influential and well-connected people in the UK. There was a growing audience for his views and, in 1913, he was awarded a Civil List pension of £70 a year, roughly equivalent to £23,000 a year in 2020.[18] His embrace by the highest levels of the establishment was their way, perhaps, of acknowledging the progress that had been made since housing forced its way onto the

UK political agenda 70 years earlier. It also reflected who Howard tended to deal with when promoting his schemes, and who were the most natural supporters for them. Now in his early sixties, and uninvolved in the day-to-day management of Letchworth, he appointed Frederic Osborn as Secretary of the Howard Cottage Society in 1912. An autodidact, Osborn had left school at 15, and worked his way up from being an office boy to editing the Fabian Society magazine for its younger members. An admirer of HG Wells, and like Wells from south London, Osborn was active in the Independent Labour Party and first encountered Howard at a Fabian meeting. His appointment to the position in Letchworth would be the start of an involvement in housing and town planning, alongside Purdom, that would last until the 1960s.

That same year of 1912, Raymond Unwin published *Nothing Gained by Overcrowding*, which extrapolated a set of town planning and architectural theories from his work in Hampstead Garden Suburb. Proposing houses big enough to have gardens with vegetable plots where potatoes could be grown, he recommended a density of at most 12 per acre, almost a third of that deployed by the LCC on its cottage estate in Tooting. Chiming neatly with Howard's views, it had even greater resonance, given Unwin's standing as a qualified professional architect. Around the same time, Ruislip Manor Garden Village, covering 133 acres, showed yet again what Howard's ideas meant in practice. Built from 1911, on land that became available when King's College Cambridge decided to emulate Eton College and sell up, it eventually covered 5992 acres. A careful geometric plan of streets, arterial roads, houses and shops, it had its own railway station (Ruislip Manor, on the Metropolitan Railway) and working-class housing provided by the Ruislip Manor Cottage Society, with, in more select areas, large detached properties at only 3 per acre. This is how the house-building industry applied Howard's ideas in practice and, like Hampstead Garden Suburb, Ruislip Manor took until the 1930s to complete.

With the bricks and mortar came a crop of late Victorian and Edwardian urban and suburban writers who explored the social hinterland that was being created. Some, such as Arthur Morrison and HG Wells, had been popular in the 1890s. Morrison was noted for realistic crime thrillers, including a series of stories about an amoral working-class detective Horace Dorrington set in the continuing squalor of east London. Wells for his part enjoyed enormous success with *Love and Mr Lewisham* (1900), *Kipps* (1905) and *The History of Mr Polly* (1910) all of which celebrated the ascent and subsequent social mobility of lower middle-class figures. London also produced Edwin Pugh, who enjoyed immense popularity pre-1914 with works like *A Street in Suburbia* (1895) and a series of appreciations of Charles Dickens, whose cockney, lower-class, characters he echoed. At the other end of the social spectrum, John Galsworthy explored the immense wealth and privilege of the upper classes in *The Forsyte Saga* (from 1906), about a family who owed their social position to having been successful house-builders since the mid-nineteenth century. Outside London, C Allen Clarke, who was active in both the Independent Labour Party and the Social Democratic Federation, wrote novels set in Lancashire and Yorkshire, whilst Arnold Bennett in *Anna of the Five Towns* (1902) and *Clayhanger* (1910) portrayed the Potteries towns around Staffordshire and Stoke. Possibly the most interesting work from this time would be *The Ragged Trousered Philanthropists*, written in 1910 by Irishman Robert Noonan (under the pseudonym Robert Tressell) which is about the antics of private house-builders and decorators, and the miserable conditions, poverty and job insecurity they inflict on their workforce in order to guarantee their profits. Noonan died in 1911 and his novel only appeared in April 1914, with much of its political material removed. For many years a difficult work to obtain, it became an immensely influential text in left-wing and trade unionist circles, virtually a *samizdat* publication, and was eventually credited with helping to win the 1945 election for Labour.

Long before that, though, a Bosnian Serb, Gavrilo Princip,

fired two shots at point blank range at a car carrying the Archduke Franz Ferdinand and the Archduchess Sophie, after it had taken a wrong turning in its official drive through Sarajevo on the morning of 28 June 1914. Both died. Five weeks later Austria-Hungary and Imperial Germany were formally engaged, after a series of declarations of war, in a massive and bloody conflict with Serbia, Imperial Russia, Belgium, France and the UK. Within each of these countries a huge disruption of the normal peacetime economy took place as production was redirected toward military requirements. In the UK, the substantial workforce that house-building required was either absorbed by the armed forces or built factories and barracks instead. As a result, very little new housing was completed for the next five years. Exceptions were made, though, for the wartime Ministry of Munitions who commissioned Raymond Unwin to design neat garden-city-type schemes at Gretna and Eastriggs in 1916-1917 to house the influx of employees needed for their factories in both locations. A larger version of these, the Progress Estate, was provided to accommodate the extra workers required by the Woolwich Arsenal. Containing 1,086 houses and 212 flats it took only 12 months to build and closely followed the specifications laid out by Unwin and Parker in their work at Letchworth and elsewhere.[19]

In Letchworth, John Buchan arrived, taking up residence there whilst working for Lord Beaverbrook as Director of Information, and using the town as the setting for his Richard Hannay novel *Mr Standfast*. Another arrival was Herbert Morrison, at that point Secretary of the London Labour Party, who was sent there to do civilian work, having declared himself a conscientious objector. Frederic Osborn, though, disappeared. Like Morrison a conscientious objector, he left to live quietly in London when conscription was introduced in early 1916. Here, supported by his wife he went to and from the British Museum Library, "studying the history of community projects" and succeeded in avoiding military service, or any other kind of service, for the remainder of the war. The fruits of his research appeared in 1918 when J M Dent published his book *New Towns After the War*. One suspects this was a "done deal" given that Dent's printing and binding works was located in Letchworth, one of the few notable businesses to have done so. They published the enormously popular and influential Everyman Library, meaning that the appearance of Osborn's book automatically placed him amongst the likes of Rousseau, Adam Smith, Conrad, GK Chesterton, Wordsworth, Sir Arthur Eddington, Tolstoy and many others. It isn't clear what the sales figures were for *New Towns After the War*, but it proved an influential work. In it, Osborn very gently distanced himself from Howard, stating *"... He used to see me off on my missionary tours with comforting words like these: 'My dear boy, I hope you have a pleasant trip; but you are wasting your time. If you wait for the authorities to build new towns you will be older than Methuselah before they start. The only way to get anything done is to do it yourself.' To the rest of us this was unacceptable advice. We had all taken minor parts in building the First Garden City founded by Howard at Letchworth. We considered that the practicability of building new towns had been shown – as indeed it had, beyond all cavil. We did not think another mere demonstration, another trial model, was necessary. We wanted the idea applied in all the regions of Britain as a national policy..."*[20] Howard and Osborn remained close, though, despite this difference in approach and emphasis. The same was not true of Howard and Culpin, whom Howard outmanoeuvred at this time, replacing him as Secretary of the Garden City Association with Charles Purdom.[21]

For Osborn, it was simple. Instead of getting the great and good (and the very wealthy) to join together, profess lofty aims and build whatever they could whenever they could, he argued instead that the State should provide £500m (£92.5 bn in 2021, far more than is now spent on housing and equal to 10% of current government expenditure), which would be disbursed by loans covering up to 90% of the development cost of the 100 new towns he proposed, all of which would be developed on garden city principles, with the plans approved by "government experts". When complete these would be transferred to local authorities. This approach was immediately supported by Herbert Morrison and a National Garden Cities Committee was set up in London with GDH Cole, Professor Patrick Abercrombie and Charles Purdom. Whilst it began the long, serious business of getting political support for such a radical departure from traditional government policy, Ebenezer Howard, and a group of his friends and supporters went for a long walk one Sunday in October 1918 and selected the site for their second garden city: Welwyn.

Notes

(1) The event at Bourneville was actually co-chaired by Neville with Earl Grey, who would later be involved in the creation of Hampstead Garden Suburb. The programme for the Bournville event can be viewed at https://media. stridetreglown.com/wp-content/uploads/2018/10/17145250/Bournville-GCA-Conference-1901.pdf

(2) Now the most select street of all, and much favoured by oligarchs.

(3) See https://www.savills.co.uk/research_articles/229130/302436-0

(4) Stewart emigrated to the US from Lisburn, Antrim in 1818. He opened the largest retail premises in the world on Broadway in 1846, and later owned the Grand Union Hotel, the Metropolitan Hotel, the Globe Theater, and Niblo's Garden, all well-known New York landmarks of the time. He sent aid to the people of Chicago in 1871 after the disastrous city fire, so Howard may have known of him for that reason.

(5) New Earswick was built as a suburb of York and is just over 2 miles north of the city. At the time it was served by a station on the York-Market Weighton-Hull railway. However, this route closed in 1964.

(6) Development was slow – only 175 houses had been built by 1915. Today the Joseph Rowntree Housing Trust own and manage over 1,000 homes on the site.

(7) Unwin was also involved with the Brentham Garden Suburb – known as the Pioneer Co-Partnership Suburb – which consisted of 680 houses built mainly between 1901 and 1915 though infill development continued through to the 1950s. The Howard Cottage Society still exists today as First Garden City Homes, having merged with Welwyn Garden City Housing Association in 2020.

(8) Henrietta Barnett started her involvement in housing and philanthropic work as one of the women trained by Octavia Hill. On Wylde's Farm, see: https://www. hgstrust.org/documents/hampstead-trust.pdf

(9) See https://discovery.nationalarchives.gov.uk/details/r/2e073f30-263b-488a-92 a1-66a7f5cf23d4 Only 243 acres were built on, 80 set aside to form an extension to Hampstead Heath. The land value therefore was £576 per acre (then) or £224,000 per acre (now) an astronomical sum for agricultural land.

(10) In later years Unwin and Parker did the initial planning for Wythenshawe. Five miles south-west of Manchester, this was identified by Patrick Abercrombie in 1920 as an area where a garden city covering 2,500 acres could be laid out. Little of this was done, however, and, following boundary charges in 1931, most of the housing there took the form of traditional council estates built by Manchester Corporation.

(11) Named after a proposed scheme in Ohio that was much remarked upon but never built.

(12) Mention should also be made of the Sutton Garden Suburb, proposed from 1912

by Thomas Wall, of sausages and ice cream fame. Originally intended to provide 1,000 homes only 134 had been completed by 1915 when building stopped. Post-war the undeveloped land was sold off to local builders who abandoned attempts to develop it as a coherent whole. Wall's company was acquired by Lever brothers in 1922.

(13) Back-to-back housing meant sharing a communal wash-house and lavatories. As such it was similar to the early 1844 scheme built by the Society for Improving the Condition of the Working Classes in Lower Road, Pentonville. Despite the restrictions imposed by the 1909 Act, Leeds City Council continued building variations of the back-to-back house until 1937.

(14) The increase in average income per person has been used to calculate these figures: what has become clear in recent years is that inflation in house prices has lifted property values far beyond where they ought to be had they remained linked to wage inflation, leading to real issues regarding the definition of "affordability".

(15) Totterdown had 32 houses per acre, and works well as a scheme. Raphael stipulated no more than 6 per acre. Port Sunlight was 8.

(16) The Three Nuns Hotel was a large imposing tavern, restaurant and hotel directly adjoining Aldgate Station. Luxemburg's account of her journey to find it indicates how little London had changed since the time of Dickens and underscores, despite 50 years of relative progress, why Ruskin, Morris and others wanted to escape Victorian/Edwardian cities: "*I travelled through the endless stations of the Dark Underground and emerged both depressed and lost in a strange and wild part of the city. It's dark and dirty here. A dim streetlight is flickering and is reflected in puddles and pools. (It's been raining the whole day.) To the left and right in the darkness the brightly coloured restaurants and bars give off an eerie glow. Groups of drunken people stagger with wild noise and shouting down the middle of the street, newspaper boys are also shouting, flower girls on the street corners, looking frightfully ugly and even depraved.*" Quoted at https://rosaluxemburgblog.wordpress.com/2012/05/13/on-this-day-13-may-1907/

(17) On the claims made by Purdom and Osborn about Lenin see https://www.bbc.co.uk/sounds/play/b01r9r3x The 1907 congress at the Brotherhood Church was a great triumph for the Bolsheviks, who emerged as the largest group within the Russian political movement in exile. Stalin kept a set of minutes of the event, in which he diligently recorded the names of those speaking and voting against Bolshevik candidates and resolutions. This can be viewed at https://www.marxists.org/reference/archive/stalin/works/1907/06/20_2.htm

(18) By way of contrast, WB Yeats was awarded £150 the same year.

(19) The War Office sold the estate in 1925 to a subsidiary of the Royal Arsenal Co-Operative Society. Tenants were able to purchase their homes from 1967, and many did so. In 1980, the remainder of the tenanted properties passed into the ownership of Hyde Housing Association.

(20) Recorded in the 1942 reprint of the same. See http://cashewnut.me.uk/WGCbooks/web-WGC-books-1942-1.php

(21) A search of the Howard archive records almost nothing about Culpin at all. The only file available (D/EHo F24), and promisingly titled "Howard-Culpin correspondence" turns out to be about the organising of a banquet on 19 March 1912 to celebrate the publishing of Cecil Harmsworth's *A Man and his Book: The Triumph of the Garden City Idea*. Held at the Holborn Restaurant, 129 Kingsway, this brought together Earl Grey, Lord Robert Cecil, Sir William Lever, Sir Ralph Neville and many other luminaries to celebrate Howard's career. Culpin's role appears to have been to arrange the seating plan.

7

1919-1939:
THE LONG BUILDING BOOM

Despite widespread popular belief to the contrary, no one in British politics actually said *"homes fit for heroes to live in"*. The phrase has stuck, though, as evidence of a different time, back in our grandparents' (or great-grandparents') days when priorities were different and, after the making of immense sacrifices, a grateful state gave something back to the people. However, as with many misremembered memories, urban myths and so on, there is truth in the recollection. The words may be wrong, but something of that type did happen at the end of the First World War.

Having secured an armistice with Germany on 11 November 1918, Prime Minister David Lloyd George immediately requested a dissolution of Parliament, so that a general election could be held on 14 December. During the ensuing campaign, he stated on 24 November *"What is our task? To make Britain a fit country for heroes to live in"*. No mention of homes there, but, in fairness, how the UK's domestic arrangements could be improved had exercised him for some while. In July 1917, he had established a Ministry of Reconstruction to take forward proposals for reform of the civil service, Irish devolution, women's suffrage, additional employment rights and significant housing improvements. The latter were based on a paper put forward by a committee led by garden city advocate Seebohm Rowntree. This recommended that 300,000 new houses should be built by local authorities who would either be reimbursed after three years for the cost they incurred in doing so, or given a grant beforehand by the government to pay for the construction. The incoming Minister of

Reconstruction, Christopher Addison, modified this further, by increasing the target to 500,000 new homes and confirming that the government would provide a grant equal to 75% of the cost incurred by the local authority. The remainder was expected to be covered by the local authority increasing their annual rates by 1d (0.42p then, £82.32p today). If, however, the gap between central government and local government funding could not be closed by doing this, then the government would cover the shortfall. It was a revolutionary proposal.

After Lloyd George's overwhelming election victory, the task of implementing this fell to Addison. Appointed President of the Local Government Board by Lloyd George, he stayed in post a few months later when this department was expanded and renamed the Ministry of Health. By 1919, it had been calculated there was a shortage of 610,000 homes, because house-building ceased during the war. To address this, Addison sponsored the Housing Act 1919, which put into law the subsidy arrangements approved by the Ministry of Reconstruction and fixed rents for the new homes local authorities would build at the level tenants would have paid in 1914. As to what the new homes should look like, and whether houses were preferred to flats, he relied heavily on the input of Raymond Unwin, who had been appointed Chief Town Planning Inspector at the Local Government Board in December 1914. Unwin produced a Housing Manual, illustrated with model house types, including three that he (and Parker) had built at New Earswick for Rowntree. Thus, when local authorities began building, much of what they provided on their new estates closely resembled Howard's pre-1914 garden cities.

In the early stages of implementing the legislation it was popular and bipartisan. The Labour Party, now the official opposition,[1] supported the measures, and produced, via Averil Furniss and Marion Phillips, *The Working Woman's House*, a book suggesting specific design improvements so that housework, child care and the business of running one of the new homes would be as convenient as possible for women.[2] Among the many developments that appeared because of Addison were Northfield,

Edinburgh, designed by Reginald Fairlie, schemes in Portsmouth and Weybridge by Henry Lanchester[3] and a significant estate in Whiston, Lancashire by Herbert Rowse[4]. A total of 213,000 new homes were directly provided by the legislation, and a large number of these were completed in 1922. By then, though, their anticipated cost had risen from £385 per unit to £910 (approximately £72,000 to £171,000 in 2021 prices).[5] In a coalition government where 73% of the MPs were Conservatives, questions were quickly raised about Addison's competence and whether he and his department were getting value for money. He was replaced as Minister of Health by Alfred Mond in April 1921, and, after hanging around for a few months as Minister without Portfolio, resigned completely from the government in July.[6] But though trimmed and much criticised, his system of subsidies survived.

In the first flush of optimism about building a country fit for heroes to live in, Welwyn was presented by Howard, Purdom and Osborn as part of the solution, ideally as one of 20 "satellite" towns surrounding London. A shrewd Herbert Morrison, by that point serving as Mayor of Hackney, pointed out that "satellite town" was a US term, describing places like Cambridge, Massachusetts or Oakland, California. Whether this observation was intended as a reproach wasn't clear, but doubts of whether or not low-density garden cities ought to be the primary objective would grow steadily from this point onward. Howard's trump card remained his rejection of government funding, and his reliance on well-connected board members. For Welwyn that meant a company with a membership that included Lord Lytton, whose family seat was at Knebworth House, and who would later be appointed Governor of Bengal. The land for Howard's second scheme, some 2,400 acres, included 700 acres purchased from Lord Salisbury, with the total acquisition cost before any building had started coming to £100,000 (£16.5m in 2021 money). To try and recoup some of this Howard went fundraising among wealthy UK expatriates on the French Riviera, without much success. As a result, work at Welwyn proceeded slowly, and at a markedly slower pace than that on most of Addison's estates. This was despite the terms offered to those who wanted to live there being quite advantageous: a house at Welwyn could be purchased for £765 (£144,000 today), and modest homes were available to rent at 3s per week (15p then £28.20p today). Attracting private sector employers to Welwyn proved difficult, though, and in its early years most of the employment within Welwyn was in the administration and statutory services that the town relied on and provided to itself. A cyclical relationship developed: people moved there to rent or buy a home, worked for the company that ran the town, the company paid them their wages, and they then paid back most of that to the company via rent, mortgage payments or domestic utility bills. It was not unlike Pullman, Chicago: a "company town", and one with which Howard would have been familiar.[7] Welwyn, however, by virtue of the UK's tangled system of local government, could at least claim to be democratic, with its electors participating in elections to Welwyn Rural District Council and Hertfordshire County Council.

As had been the case with Letchworth, and almost every other similar development, the town only really took off after Welwyn Garden City got its own railway station in 1926. The year before this Howard had visited the US, where he tried to persuade Henry Ford to fund garden cities, having heard that Ford had built homes for his workforce on the outskirts of Dearborn. It transpired that Ford wasn't interested in any wider investment in housing, particularly overseas.[8] During his visit Howard spoke in New York about how the US had provided him the inspiration for his garden city plan, confirming "...*I have lived long enough in America to know that the people of this great country... have, among other qualities, the somewhat extraordinary power of conceiving and following out new ideas... I feel that civilisation is on a new threshold, and that possibilities lie before us which the Americans will do more to point out to the other nations of the world than has ever entered into the minds of any of us...*"[9] He was knighted in 1927, at the age of 77, whilst planning a visit to Radburn, New Jersey where a new model of low-density housing was being created, and died a year later. It fell to Frederic Osborn to take his ideas forward, initially as manager of Welwyn Garden City, and later, through to the 1960s, via his involvement with the Town and Country Planning Association.

Howard accomplished much in what can only be considered an extraordinary life. He was living at a time when a consensus had already been formed in some circles that cities and towns were best avoided, and living instead in the country, with all its perceived health attributes, was to be preferred. As well as this, he was living when migration from the UK was running at a very high level, and played a key role in shaping public views about the ideal type of property one ought to aspire to own. In the century between Napoleon's defeat at Waterloo, and the German invasion of Belgium, it has been estimated that 22.6 million people left the UK and Ireland to live abroad. The overwhelming majority of these (62%, or an average of 140,000 per year, every year) headed toward the US, with the remainder dispersed between Canada, Australia and New Zealand. A small minority (3.5%) opted for South Africa, possibly because it had already been settled by the Dutch. Apart from civil servants, soldiers, sailors, administrators and a handful of significant commercial figures almost nobody chose to migrate to the remainder of Africa, India and the extensive imperial realms further east.

This migration was driven by several factors, including unemployment, under-employment and poor pay caused by cyclical depressions, together with brutal land clearance programmes in Scotland and Ireland. Virtually every family in the UK and Ireland was affected. Although some migrants, like Howard, did return (and it is calculated that about 35%-40% were doing so, especially in the latter part of this period), most left for good, and most did better in their new countries than they would have done had they stayed at home. Having relatives who lived in the US, or what became known as the white settler Dominions, was quite normal. And they might well have their own house in a new suburb or a completely new town, be in somewhat better paid employment and – relatively speaking – free of the class assumptions (and restrictions) that were typical back home. What

Howard devised, in the eyes of many, was a way to avail oneself of these opportunities without having to leave the UK.[(10)]

Politically, Howard was regarded as being progressive, and even possibly an early type of socialist. Certainly, he came out of a cooperative, internationalist tradition that was common within non-conformism. However, he never really identified with the growing labour movement and, as has been shown, he thought that many trade unionists were expending their energies on fruitless class struggle, rather than trying to build a new, hermetically sealed, Jerusalem of their own at home. What seems to have been the case is that he recognised from very early on, probably from his many years minuting the deliberations of Parliament and the London County Council, the importance of obtaining the support of powerful establishment figures. Once he had achieved this in the 1890s, though he was happy to continue an association with the likes of the Cadburys, Rowntrees and Lever, he moved on quite quickly from having any direct connections with the political left.

As to why he was so successful, raising the funds to commence two garden cities and spawning many imitators, one needs to consider how much the public identified with his idyll, as part of a wider trend that normalised the culture of America, and the rather similar white settler regions of the British Empire. It wasn't just the fact that, throughout the nineteenth century, most middle-class and working-class families had members who had migrated away from the UK. Many of the upper classes and aristocracy had married into US money during this period too. On top of this, came the increase in US culture helped by the rise of the cinema, and the increasing availability of a number of gadgets (the telephone, radio, the motor car and so on) that became common after they had first been made available to the wider public in the US. The notion that building US-style suburban developments in the UK was incongruous, and best avoided, probably wouldn't have occurred to most people.

Howard insisted on avoiding government funding for his projects. Initially he was probably wise to do so: in the 1890s there was no tradition of the state funding house-building in the UK, and not too much activity from local authorities either in terms of providing it. But after 1919 it was wrong to maintain this stance. In fact, all the examples of suburban and garden city schemes in the UK from the mid-nineteenth century onwards were bedevilled by their reliance on private funding. Most took quite some time to complete as the developers and house-builders reined in work whenever an economic downturn occurred. Letchworth and Welwyn were no different in this respect. Nor did they provide, in sufficient volume, the numbers of new properties required either to ensure that all households had a reasonable home of their own, or to replenish and increase the number of homes fit for human habitation as earlier, older dwellings continued their decline. They were a niche product, for a niche group of consumers.

The arguments that Howard made for well designed, pleasant streets of spacious housing, would, as noted, have puzzled the likes of Archibald Cameron Corbett who from the 1890s onward built many of the eastern suburbs of London with far less fanfare than attended Howard. Comparing and contrasting the two it is not clear how significant the advantages of Howard's garden city actually were. However, one thing is certain: they came with two significant flaws. The first of these concerned the governance of the development. The company overseeing the garden city raised money via rents, ground rents and selling leases. After it had deducted administrative expenses and the cost of maintaining the communal facilities that "sold" the scheme to the public in the first place, whatever profit was left remained with the company who could use it to build more homes, or to provide a wider range of non-housing benefits. This was fine, and in the early years both Letchworth and Welwyn did that as far as they were able. The problem was, although the company directors were no doubt publicly spirited in the early years of the development, there was no guarantee they (or their successors) would be 50 or 60 years later. They might be inclined to sell-up, or they might seek to alter the complex articles of association of the company to make them more advantageous to themselves. It was never clear how democratic or accountable they really were.[11] The second problem came with the extent of the maintenance required by the design itself. Garden cities were noted for an abundance of open space, verges, grassed areas, flower beds, trees, ornamental shrubs and other features. Keeping all of this in pleasant condition became an increasingly expensive process. The later replication of these design features in new towns post-1945 eventually created significant environmental problems. It should be noted that, although we might cut Howard some slack by pointing out that the problems of the consumer society and its throwaway culture were probably not foreseen in the 1890s, other types of urban and suburban development being built then, and subsequently, avoided this future problem by restricting the amount of public space to the highway, pavement and traditional open spaces, such as parks. It can be argued that this was, ultimately, more sustainable.

*   *   *   *   *   *

Addison's departure from the government was part of a gradual rightward shift. By the autumn of 1922, the Conservatives, who had a majority within Parliament as well as within the government, ended Lloyd George's coalition. In the ensuing general election, they won an overall majority of 75 and their leader, Andrew Bonar Law became Prime Minister. Found to be dangerously ill with cancer only seven months later, Bonar Law gave way to Stanley Baldwin. In December 1923, Baldwin called a general election on whether to introduce trade tariffs across the British Empire that restricted foreign imports or continue with free trade. The result was a hung Parliament, in which the Labour Party, with 191 MPs were now the official opposition. Baldwin resigned on 22 January 1924 and Ramsay MacDonald became Prime Minister of a minority Labour government.

In the early 1920s, UK politics were fairly chaotic in comparison with the monolithic two-party system that had prevailed prior to that, and the changes that ensued – such as Ramsay MacDonald entering Downing Street – reflected the

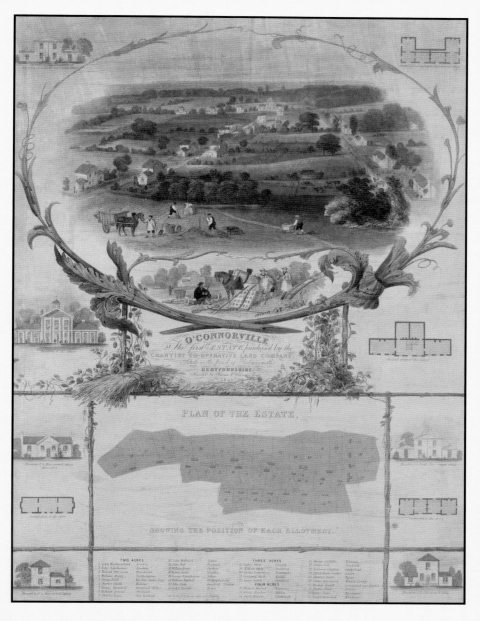

A plan of O'Connorville, the settlement proposed by the Chartists in Rickmansworth, Hertfordshire in 1845-1846. An early attempt to encourage a large-scale migration out of the UK's burgeoning towns and cities, most of the Chartist developments failed.

One Chartist scheme that succeeded was at Great Dodford, Worcestershire where some of the original homes, on their plots of land, remain.

Not everyone thought urban conditions couldn't be improved. The Metropolitan Association for Improving the Dwellings of the Industrious Classes built Metropolitan Buildings, St Pancras Square in 1848, the first five-floor block of completely self-contained flats. Destroyed by enemy bombing in April 1941 it was opposite St Pancras Church.

Harking back to a Gothic-mediaeval past, Philip Webb designed and built the Red House for William Morris in 1859-1860. Lesser versions of this type of design proliferated in the years that followed, down to the mock Tudor suburbs of the inter-war period. Ironically Morris only lived five years in the property, moving back to a flat in Bloomsbury in 1865.

Fore Street, Moorgate, on a relatively clear day. Birthplace of Ebenezer Howard, this is the type of environment he sought to escape from.

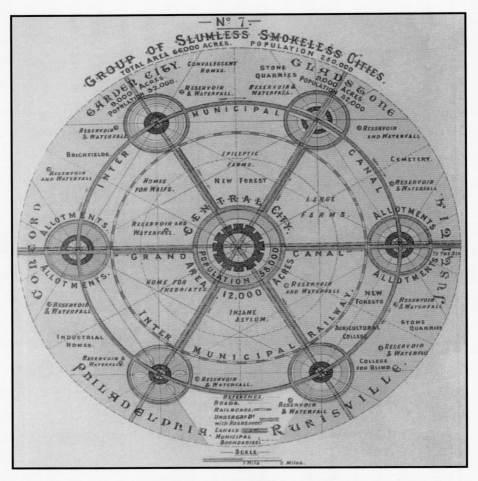

Ebenezer Howard's elaborate 1898 plan for an interlocking set of Garden Cities.

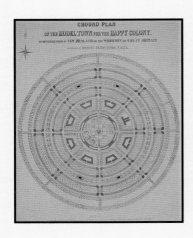

Howard's scheme is uncannily similar to Robert Pemberton's 1854 proposal for a new colonial settlement in New Zealand.

Whilst Howard drew up his plans, new urban homes were being built. The London County Council Millbank Estate (1895) was typical of these and much emulated.

St German's Estate, Hither Green – one of several built around London by Archibald Cameron Corbett. Remaining popular today, these were built to a significantly higher density than Howard's proposed Garden Cities.

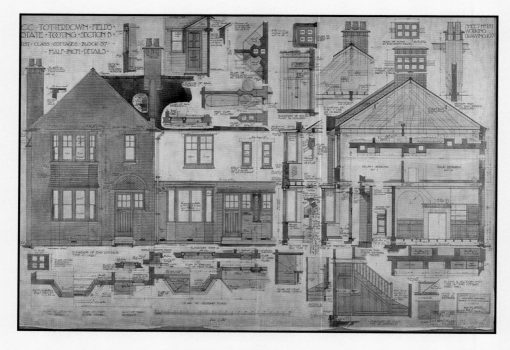

The London County Council also built town house (or cottage) estates, the first of which was at Totterdown Fields, Tooting in 1901. As with Archibald Cameron Corbett their density was much higher than anything recommended by Howard.

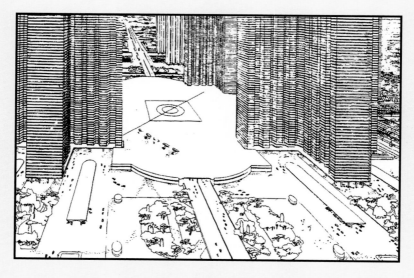

After the destruction caused by the First World War completely new visions of urban architecture emerged. This is Le Corbusier's 1922 Ville Contemporaine.

Reduced versions of
Howard's Garden Cities were
built by the Metropolitan
Railway, becoming known as
Metroland as a result.

Founded in 1929,
Radburn, New Jersey
with its cul-de-sacs and
footpath-only access
to houses, was much
influenced by Howard.
Many schemes of this
type were built in the
UK after 1945.

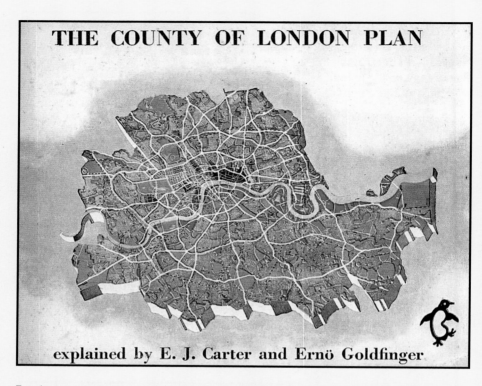

THE COUNTY OF LONDON PLAN

explained by E. J. Carter and Ernö Goldfinger

Forshaw and Abercrombie's County of London Plan, as explained for the popular reader by E J Carter and rising star Erno Goldfinger.

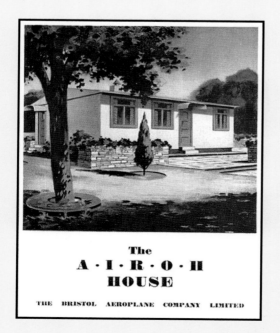

The
A · I · R · O · H
HOUSE

THE BRISTOL AEROPLANE COMPANY LIMITED

Churchill knew that huge amounts of new housing were needed after 1945 – but wanted to provide this via simple, factory-produced 'pre-fabs'.

extension of the franchise that had been introduced by Lloyd George in late 1918. Commonly this is regarded as the point at which women were allowed to vote in parliamentary elections. But this is only partially true. From 1918 women over the age of 28 could vote (age equality with men, 21, was only introduced in 1928), but the more important factor introduced then was the abolition of the property qualification for all electors. The historic requirement to be a freeholder and/or ratepayer before you were entitled to vote disappeared. Thus, in 1918, all adult men over 21 were enfranchised. Before that date, with most men either renting or living as lodgers, virtually all working-class males had been disenfranchised. Lloyd George's 1918 Representation of the People Act actually tripled the electorate and gave as many working-class men votes as it did women of all classes. In electoral terms this produced huge gains for the Labour Party, and led within a few years to the first Labour government.

John Wheatley, MP for Glasgow Shettleston, was appointed Minister of Health in Ramsay MacDonald's first administration. A fiercely intellectual Irish Catholic, Wheatley was the author of *Eight Pound Cottages for Glasgow Citizens* (1913) which advocated using the profits generated by the Glasgow municipal tramways to subsidise council house-building, with the completed dwellings available at a rent of £8 per year, 3s 9d per week. (£50.41p per week today). An elected member of Lanarkshire County Council from 1909, he had studied local government finance in some detail and quickly introduced a Housing (Financial Provisions) Act. This reinstated Addison's system of subsidies, and increased them to a level of £9m a year (£1.168bn today). It also set up training schemes to produce qualified building workers in collaboration with the appropriate trade unions. Under Wheatley's Act, local authorities were given subsidies over a period of 40 years, to build council housing, and guaranteed against any losses. It aimed to increase council house-building from 135,000 per year (Addison's Act had built a maximum of 110,000 in 1921-1922) to 450,000 per year over a ten-year period, thus solving the UK's housing shortage. The properties were to be built to a high standard, suitable for skilled workers and were aimed primarily at the prosperous working class, rather than the destitute or homeless.

Although Wheatley's Act was tinkered with and scaled back by successive Conservative governments, around 500,000 new homes were built because of it. The London County Council used it to build the bulk of the Becontree Estate and to commence Downham Estate, both "cottage estates" that owed a lot to Howard's approach.[12] The effect of the legislation sponsored by Addison and Wheatley, combined with the political enfranchisement of working-class men and women was to make the provision of housing an issue that remained at the forefront of politics, and of importance to all governments, in a way that had not been so marked pre-1914. In practice a bipartisan attitude prevailed and, significantly, a particularly large number of new council homes were built in 1927-1928, when Neville Chamberlain was Minister of Health in the Baldwin government.[13]

Although the provision of council housing was now an accepted part of the political agenda, in terms of overall numbers, the private sector continued to lead the way. In fact, it would be during the inter-war period that it built more homes than at any other time, before or since. By 1924, construction numbers were running at 120,000 a year and they rose steadily, peaking at 294,000 in 1935-1936. Between 1930 and 1940 private builders completed 2.9m homes, with local authorities adding a further 0.78m during the same period. In effect, there was a house-building boom driven by the continued low cost of land, low wages, the low cost of living, the low cost of materials, low interest rates and a large pool of labour. To maintain costs at an acceptable level, developers built out from town and city centres, spreading networks of new streets to either side of existing main roads, many of which acted as "arterial roads", ie, the local authority provided mains services beneath them which the developer could access to facilitate rapid, efficient development. One consequence of this trend was that the population of all the old northern towns declined throughout the inter-war period as suburban development on their outskirts accelerated.

Howard would have recommended much of this and traditional examples of his oeuvre duly appeared at Townhill Garden City, Swansea and Swanpool Garden Suburb, Lincoln.[14] These were limited in size, however, and grander examples, now regarded as synonymous with this era, came in what would be called "Metroland": the parts of Middlesex and Buckinghamshire that adjoined the commuter route into Baker Street. Developed by the Metropolitan Railway, prior to their absorption into London Transport, these were "garden suburb" schemes built along its route by its subsidiary company Metropolitan Railway Country Estates Limited. Operating in partnership with builders they launched the Harrow Garden Village (213 acres, 1928) and Rayners Lane (250 acres, 1931)[15]. Nor did the demise of the Metropolitan Railway end this. In 1934 De Havilland sold the Stag Lane airfield (in Edgware) to Laing Homes, and a scheme of 1,000 houses and 150 shops was quickly erected. Queensbury Station was built to service this.

What the Metropolitan Railway did throughout the 1920s was an embellished version of what Cameron Corbett had been doing in the 1890s, greatly assisted by private landowners on the fringes of London and other cities selling tracts of agricultural land to housebuilders. In 1927, for instance, the Rector of West Wickham (Kent) sold the glebe lands before he retired to a builder. A decade later several square miles of these had been built over with houses available at up to £2,500, five times the price of a smaller inter-war house at that time. Less expensive, but much larger in scale, was the immense sprawl of property completed by the builders New Ideal, Wimpey and Wates around Bexleyheath in the 1930s. In fact, between 1925 and 1940, a huge phalanx of new housing was completed, connecting Woolwich with Dartford and stretching around, through Kent and Surrey, to Croydon.

In terms of what this looked like, it was definitely Howard-lite. A type of "English vernacular" housing, often mock-Tudor, that bowdlerised the earlier careful designs that had characterised Letchworth and other pre-1914 schemes. Density remained fairly low and some of the accoutrements of garden suburbs were retained (streets lined with fruit trees remained popular) but this was definitely house-builder territory, a product that could be built rapidly. Not that these aesthetic distinctions mattered overmuch, as typical inter-war housing was popular both politically and with the public. A new 3-bedroom house in the south-east of England cost £500 in 1935 (£350-£400 elsewhere), the equivalent of £77,000 today. Land values were typically only £200 per plot, equivalent to £30,000 in 2020, by which point, due to house price inflation, they were usually 3-4 times higher in real terms. In the 1930s you could buy a property if you had a satisfactory reference from your bank and a 5% deposit, (£25 then, £3,850 now). In practice, though, with mortgages much more difficult to arrange at this time, many of the homes were built for rent and were a good investment for their owners, because of cheap money and low interest rates.

The impact of this was spotted by JB Priestley in *English Journey* (1934) *"This is the England of arterial and by-pass roads, of filling stations and factories that look like exhibition buildings, of giant cinemas and dance-halls and cafes, bungalows with tiny garages, cocktail bars, Woolworths, motor-coaches, wireless, hiking, factory girls looking like actresses, greyhound racing and dirt tracks, swimming pools and everything given away for cigarette coupons... You need money in this England, but you do not need much money. It is a large-scale, mass-production job with cut prices"*. The way such development advanced along main roads was also caught by George Orwell in his *Road to Wigan Pier Diary*, where he noted on 2 February 1936 *"Walk from Wolverhampton to Penkridge (10 miles) very dull and raining all the way. Villa-civilization stretches almost unbroken between the two towns"*. The prospect of say, London and Birmingham becoming connected via continuous "ribbon-development" along the A41 seemed very real, and a desire to prevent the rapid spread of suburbia was one of the factors in the foundation of the Campaign to Protect Rural England by town planner Patrick Abercrombie in 1926. Which is not to suggest that Abercrombie was against garden cities. Rather, he supported properly planned developments of this type, and wanted ersatz-Howard variants curtailed. A similar view was taken by architect Clough Williams-Ellis, who wrote about the dangers of unregulated house-building in his books *England and the Octopus* (1928) and *Britain and the Beast* (1937), the latter a collection of essays that he edited. A firm advocate of the arts and crafts ethos, Williams-Ellis provided suggested designs for many of the garden suburbs that emerged just before and after the 1914-1918 war. Mainly, though he specialised in small terraces of cottages in rural locations. From 1925 he gradually designed and built his own village, Portmeirion, in mock-Italian village style. It took 50 years to complete, but was sufficiently advanced by the 1930s to be visited by George Bernard Shaw, HG Wells and Noel Coward. This is the philosophy of Howard, Osborn and Purdom taken to extremes: a fantasy place, well executed but essentially an exercise in "retro-architecture" and leading inexorably to Disneyland, which is Portmeirion on a massive, highly commercial scale.[16]

The reservations expressed by Abercrombie, Williams-Ellis and others eventually bore fruit in the findings of the Barlow Commission. Established by Prime Minister Neville Chamberlain in July 1937, this was an official endorsement of much of Howard's philosophy and owed much to lobbying by Osborn and the Town and Country Planning Association. Reporting in 1940, it recommended that manufacturing be dispersed around the UK rather than concentrated in old industrial areas, and that properly planned new towns and cities should be built to accommodate its required workforce.[117]

Similar views were also coming to the fore in the US. Here Lewis Mumford, an intellectual within several disciplines and a friend of both Frederic Osborn and Frank Lloyd Wright, argued that urban sprawl was bad and that existing suburbs were unsatisfactory. His ideal was a city built to a recognisably human form and scale, in a way that respected existing social structures and values. Mumford was heavily influenced by Patrick Geddes, a major figure in UK zoology, botany, sociology and town planning from the 1890s, whose views, had in turn, guided Raymond Unwin.[18] By the 1920s, then, a US-UK consensus seemed to have emerged about the most beneficial and desirable type of development. An example of this transatlantic approach had been built at Radburn, New Jersey, in 1929. Covering 149 acres, this eventually housed just over 3,000 people, making it low-density, but by no means at the bottom of that scale. Its key features were its geometrically laid out terraces of housing that were separated from each other by abundant grass verges and planted areas, and only accessible via footpaths. A limited number of broad public highways were provided within the scheme, but otherwise a lot of walking within its interior was required. The object was somehow to contain the prevalence of motor vehicles whilst accommodating them and leaving safe areas for pedestrians, especially children. Known as "the Radburn layout" it quickly became the classic US suburban design. Architect Clarence Stein produced additional examples in Chatham Village, Pittsburgh (from 1932) and in two locations within Los Angeles (by the 1940s), but its greatest success under his auspices came via the New Deal-funded schemes at Greenbelt, Maryland, Greendale, Wisconsin, and Greenhills, Ohio from 1935. The plan for Greenbelt, which was built on government-owned land, was approved in person by President Roosevelt, a level of official endorsement most architects and planners (outside of the Soviet Union) would have died for, and much of the town was designed to operate as a cooperative. Prospective residents were carefully selected: it was located in a part of Maryland that was racially segregated and early plans to allow part of the town to be occupied by African American families were quickly jettisoned as too controversial. Applicants had to be married couples, earn between $800 and $2,200 per year (roughly between £26,000 and £88,500 now) with the husband, specifically, employed. Female-led households were not entertained.

Greenbelt was the subject of considerable publicity efforts, and features in the latter half of the 1939 documentary, *The City*. Devised by Lewis Mumford, and with a score from Aaron Copland, this provides an extremely polished view of how the problems experienced in densely populated cities (particularly with traffic congestion) could be overcome by rigorous planning and high-quality design. Greenbelt is shown as new, in bucolic settings and with a healthy, fit, all-white population clearly enjoying life. In its early years the community hosted many visitors, anxious to see for themselves how a planned environment of this type worked in practice. Raymond Unwin came in March 1938 and was extremely impressed, noting that many of the houses with pitch roofs resembled designs found in Letchworth and Welwyn Garden Cities. In time, the Greenbelt concept was widely exported, and was adopted for public housing in Canada, Australia and the UK, despite the fact that, when coupled with other political and planning decisions, its low density and extensive maintenance requirements led to issues with antisocial behaviour and environmental decline. Today, Greenbelt, Maryland covers 6.3 square miles and houses 23,000 people, a density only 10% that of a typical inner London/inner city area.

* * * * * *

Not all utopias took the form of garden suburbs, however. In fact, it was possible to be inspired by William Morris and his use of high-quality art and design and end up in a very different place to Howard, Osborn and Mumford. One figure who emerged in the 1920s with a markedly different take on geometric layouts, traffic issues and how best to enhance green space was Charles-Édouard Jeanneret. Born in Switzerland, and originally apprenticed to a watchmaker, he had built his first house by the time he was 18. By 1910, he was living and working in Germany alongside Mies van der Rohe and Walter Gropius as an assistant at the practice of Peter Behrens during a period when Behrens undertook many commissions for immense industrial buildings. Arriving in Paris in 1917, he worked initially as an artist, adopting the name Le Corbusier ("the crow-like one"), and finally arrived at town planning with his 1922 design for a city of 3 million people: *Ville Contemporaine de trois millions d'habitants*. At this stage there were still parallels with Howard. Neither had any formal architectural qualifications and both were proposing large, geometrical designs. Unlike Howard, however, Le Corbusier had a background in the practicalities of building and development and had spent 17 years working his way through various drawing positions in architects' offices. More importantly, unlike Howard (and Morris), Le Corbusier sought his solutions by looking to the future, rather than replicating an idealised past. And he was aware of the need to use space effectively when trying to accommodate rapidly increasing populations within countries that were not particularly large.

Unashamedly high-density, the *Ville Contemporaine* aimed to prevent congestion in city centres via a network of broad new roads, and like Mumford's ideas (but on a much larger scale) provided landscaped green space in any area not required by blocks of flats, offices, roads, public facilities (schools, churches, administrative buildings) and transport infrastructure. Visually, some of this looks rather like the accounts of the cities of the future that featured in HG Wells's works a decade or two earlier. Le Corbusier's city has 24 immense tower blocks (each with 70 floors and housing 5,000 to 8,000 people each) surrounded by a great many 17-floor "medium-rise" blocks housing around 2,500 people. The ground-floor space in all of these residential buildings would be occupied by shops, cafes and launderettes, with swimming pools and nurseries on the roof. Rapid construction was favoured, almost exclusively in concrete and glass, with prefabricated sections being slotted into place wherever possible.

Ville Contemporaine was theoretical, the work of a dreamer planning a new world. In 1925, sponsored by his friend Gabriel Voisin, a car and aircraft designer, Le Corbusier went a step further with *Plan Voisin*, a specific design for completely rebuilding part of Paris. The objective here was the debourgeoisification of the city by bringing the working classes back to the centre (where the affluent had always lived) from the unsatisfactory accommodation they inhabited on the fringe. Phalanxes of high-rise flats dominated Le Corbusier's vision, for which immense amounts of demolition and clearance would have been required. In normal peace-time situations few countries would wish to undertake such a radical project. One that did, and where the democratic difficulties encountered by widespread demolition were no obstacle, was the Soviet Union. Here, where his promise had been noted some years earlier, Le Corbusier built the Tsentrosoyuz building, the HQ of the Central Union of Consumer Co-operatives. A hugely ambitious structure that used substantial amounts of reinforced concrete, it was completed in 1933, following shortages encountered during the first Five Year Plan. By then Le Corbusier had added a couple of urban housing projects to his portfolio: the Cité de Refuge, in Paris and Immeuble Clarté, in Geneva, both 1932-1933. The former was a Salvation Army hostel, one of several such schemes that he undertook on behalf of the philanthropist and socialite Winnaretta Singer, the Princesse de Polignac.[19] The latter, a scheme of 45 apartments, was his first large residential scheme to be built to completion. An earlier commission, the Cité Frugès, on the outskirts of Bordeaux (ironically in a suburb), had been aborted in 1926 when only 25% complete.

In the midst of this gradually burgeoning reputation, he published his manifesto, *The City of Tomorrow and its Planning* (1929), a widely praised work that brought him to the attention of the English-speaking world. Reviews were particularly favourable in the US where *The Nation* stated *"...Le Corbusier ranks with Freud, Picasso, and Einstein as a leading genius of our time. The only great architect alive, he has turned his attention from the individual house to town-planning. And the result is 'The City of Tomorrow', a book not for the aesthetes but for statesmen..."* Writing in *The New York Evening Post*, Edgar Johnson was equally fulsome *"...M. Le Corbusier's extremely important book is an analysis of the problem of the city and a solution. It sidesteps none of the issues, admits the inevitable growth in population, the need for speed and centralization, and provides a reasoned and thorough overcoming of the difficulties. This book is, both practically and artistically, a work of vision..."*

It made less impact in the UK, where, with the exception of Maxwell Fry, unashamedly modernist architects were a rarity. But, examples of modern residential developments did, nevertheless, begin to appear: Cropthorne Court, Maida Vale, by Giles Scott, (who later did Battersea Power Station) in 1928; the Isokon

Building, Lawn Road, Hampstead and Embassy Court, Brighton, both 1934-1935, by Wells Coates; and Appleby Lodge, Manchester, which had 100 flats, by Peter Cummings in 1939. Le Corbusier never built anything in the UK, and his influence, initially, was quite restricted. A more obvious determining factor, for those interested in resolving the problems of high-density urban living, came from the study of how European cities provided housing in medium-rise blocks of flats.

Council housing pre-1939 was typically built to a density of 615 people per hectare. This is equivalent to 249 people per acre, against Howard's preference for 3-4 in his original garden city plan, and 23 in Bournville. On paper this looked as if horribly dense and antisocial schemes were being developed by local authorities. In practice, they worked perfectly well. Under Herbert Morrison, from 1934 the LCC built many estates made up of high-density, 5-floor blocks, these being complimented in *Housing and Slum Clearance in London* (Quigley and Goldie, 1934) thus "... *The new estates built by the LCC in Kennington and Stamford Hill... come as close to perfection in their type as anything in Germany, Holland or Austria, and they definitely surpass the most expensive block of flats built in the West End of London...*"[20] Like Patrick Abercrombie, the LCC also recognised the problems posed by ribbon development and, in August 1935, introduced its own "green belt" to try and curb this.

The LCC, and other major urban local authorities, were also much exercised by slum clearance. They were able to act effectively in this area because of Arthur Greenwood MP, Minister for Health in the second Labour government, who passed the Housing Act 1930. This provided extensive subsidies for slum clearance, and related them to how many people were rehoused, rather than how many properties were demolished. Thus, it became popular, and financially viable, to knock down much of the housing in multiple occupation within which a significant proportion of the working classes lived, and replace it with purpose-built, self-contained new homes. Between 1934 and 1939, using these powers, 250,000 properties were demolished, more than had been achieved in the previous half-century. It was a tribute to the politicians of this period that, even after Greenwood had left office in 1931, his legislation remained intact and was retained by Neville Chamberlain and Sir Edward Hilton Young, the latter being particularly vigorous in its execution.[21]

The descent of much nineteenth-century (and earlier) housing into poorly maintained multiple occupancy had long been noted. It was particularly obvious in London where decline affected many streets and squares in what are today fashionable areas. To address this, a Royal Commission into London Squares was established in 1927, to protect them and to prevent further deterioration. Some parts of London, like Somers Town, were in notably poor condition, and as a result benefitted from concerted improvement efforts, in this case the Ossulton Estate (310 flats) built by the LCC between 1927 and 1931 and the Sidney Street Estate (250 flats) built from 1935 by the St Pancras House Improvement Society.[22] Elsewhere in London, concern about slum conditions in Ladbroke Grove and Notting Hill Gate – where many once grand buildings and squares had declined dramatically – led to the founding of the Kensington Housing Trust in 1926. Chaired by Lord Balfour of Burleigh, it acquired early on a swathe of property from the Great Western Railway, and even promoted its work on film. *Kensington Calling*, an 8-minute-long silent with captions appeared in 1930, with footage of a grossly overcrowded 5-floor house in the area that was lived in by 48 people.[23]

The use of cinema as a medium led to *Housing Problems* (1935), made by John Grierson and Edgar Anstey. Shot in black and white on 35 mm sound stock, it was widely shown in cinemas as part of a full evening's entertainment, as well as separately at film clubs, universities etc. Over 13 minutes it firmly sets out the case for slum clearance, with replacement housing coming via modern methods of construction, including the use of concrete and steel framing in blocks of flats. A model of Quarry Hill Estate in Leeds is shown. This was subsequently built in 1938 and consisted of 938 flats in blocks between 6 and 8 floors high: so high, for the time, that lifts were fitted, an almost unique occurrence in a social housing estate. Inspired by the Karl Marx Hof in Vienna, Quarry Hill came with its own bus station.[24] On garden cities *Housing Problems* restricts itself to a mere 12 seconds of coverage, cautiously admitting "*...where there is enough room, and where the price of land is not too high, it's possible to build cottage estates and give each house its own garden...*" The message in both films was almost the opposite of what Howard would have wanted: houses should be retained and refurbished, new flats should be built in high-density developments, and demolition and landscaping (on the scale Howard envisaged) avoided. It is interesting to compare how Howard's efforts in publicising the housing solutions of the future – via elaborate slide shows in church halls, targeted at a specially invited, rather well-to-do audience – contrast with the films used to promote good housing in the 1930s. These were seen and appreciated by millions of ordinary people via cinema, the mass medium of its time.

The UK's sustained private sector house-building boom lasted through to 1940. Thanks to Greenwood and his subsidies, 1939 was also a good year for council housing. Adding together both council and private house-building, the years from 1935 to 1939 saw 350,000 completions annually, a remarkable figure, and it was in this period that London reached a population of 8.1 million. There was also additional legislation. In 1936, the minimum size of a "habitable room" was defined (at 50 square feet) meaning that landlords could not legally class anything smaller than this as a bedroom. The rise of new social landlords was also facilitated with legislation passed allowing seven or more residents of a block or street to form a "Housing Society". By the end of the decade spending on official housing in the UK was calculated as being £37.3m per annum (£12.645bn in 2020 money) with the parliamentary grant for housing being £4m (£1.356 bn in 2020 money).[25] In terms of overall numbers there was no shortage of dwellings in the UK in 1939, though many, as noted by Grierson, Anstey and others, were in deplorable condition.

This was the state of play in 1936, the year that Frederic Osborn took over the Town and Country Planning Association, when – according to him – garden cities were in danger of going out of fashion. It was clear that the future could well involve a clash between two competing approaches to meeting the UK's need for more and better homes.

Notes

(1) The 1918 general election produced a Parliament in which – on paper – 18 different parties were represented. In practical terms, though, 11 different groupings emerged. Lloyd George remained Prime Minister, supported by 526 MPs: 380 Conservative, 127 Liberal, 13 Labour, 3 Labour Unionists, 2 National Party and 1 Independent. The opposition consisted of 181 MPs: 73 Sinn Fein, 61 Labour, 37 Liberal, 7 Irish Nationalist and 3 Independents. Sinn Fein refused to participate, and set up their own legislature in Ireland, meaning that Labour became the official opposition to a Lloyd George government that had a majority of 418. However, Lloyd George was entirely reliant on the large bloc of Conservative MPs, who could have formed a majority government without him.

(2) It can be viewed on line at http://digital.slv.vic.gov.au/view/action/singleViewer.do?dvs=1614277601751~982&locale=en_US&metadata_object_ratio=10&show_metadata=true&VIEWER_URL=/view/action/singleViewer.do?&preferred_usage_type=VIEW_MAIN&DELIVERY_RULE_ID=10&frameId=1&usePid1=true&usePid2=true

(3) Lanchester, whose first major commission was the Bovril Factory at 148 Old Street EC1, was noted for producing a major town planning scheme for Delhi as well as extensive bungalow suburbs in Rangoon and Zanzibar.

(4) Rowse's finest residential architecture is considered to be an estate at Woodchurch, Birkenhead, work on which started in 1945. The land had been purchased as far back as 1926, when it was intended to accommodate a local authority-owned garden city, an idea that the council abandoned in the 1930s.

(5) Note that in 1921-22 the Public Works Loans Board lent nearly £49 million for housing, equivalent to roughly £12bn today. Actual UK spend today is £2bn. See: https://www.bbc.co.uk/news/business-59032791 25th October 2021.

(6) The financing for the house-building programme was made available by Chancellor of the Exchequer, Austen Chamberlain. Addison had begun his career as a doctor at Barts Hospital, and was originally a key political ally of Lloyd George. He lost his seat in Parliament in 1922 (he was MP for Shoreditch) and subsequently joined the Labour Party, serving as a senior minister in Attlee's 1945-1951 government.

(7) George Pullman, the US railway and engineering tycoon purchased 4,000 acres south of Chicago in 1880 where he built his main factory and a town for its workers. The latter – housing 8,000 people at a density Howard would have approved of – was completely controlled by Pullman, with no democratic structures to gainsay his arrangements. In 1893, after an economic downturn, he laid off staff without reducing the rent due on their housing. When rioting began following evictions, he secured the use of the US Army to maintain order. After 34 people were shot dead, Pullman was later annexed by the city of Chicago. See https://www.nps.gov/pull/learn/historyculture/a-brief-overview-of-the-pullman-story.htm

(8) In 1919-1920, Henry Ford built 250 homes near his main automobile plant at Dearborn, Michigan.

(9) Quote from Robert Beevers *The Garden City Utopia: A Critical Biography of Ebenezer Howard* p177.

(10) The cost of migrating was £3-£4 in 1850, about 2 years' pay. In 1910 a steerage class ticket on Cunard from the UK to New York was priced at $37.75c, or at the exchange rate then £7 16s (£2,550 now).

(11) In early 1956 the directors of First Garden City Limited – the body that owned and administered Letchworth – voted to abolish the limits on the dividend they could award themselves. A specific act of Parliament, the Letchworth Garden City Corporation Act, passed in 1962, was required to amend this and ensure that the city continued to function in the manner prescribed by Howard.

(12) Becontree, which was outside the LCC area, was built between 1921 and 1937, eventually containing 26,000 homes housing 115,000 people. Addison presided over an opening ceremony in 1935. Downham, built between 1924 and 1930, was smaller with 6067 properties. Covering 522 acres, this was equal to 11-12 homes per acre, a level slightly higher than that preferred by Howard.

(13) As with the earlier involvement of Austen, his half-brother, Neville Chamberlain was always aware that he was following in the footsteps of his father Joseph Chamberlain, and like him had been Mayor of Birmingham.

(14) Townhill was designed by Raymond Unwin pre-1914, but was only completed after Addison's subsidies became available in 1919. Swanpool Garden Suburb was an attempt, in 1919 and 1920, to build privately funded accommodation for the employees of Ruston and Hornby, a local engineering works. It was abandoned after 113 of the projected 3,000 homes had been completed.

(15) On Metroland see: https://discovery.ucl.ac.uk/id/eprint/57/1/Ian_Dunsford_MPhil_TP_Dissertation.pdf

(16) Lewis Mumford was an early visitor to Portmeirion, commenting *"...In a sense, Portmeirion is a gay, deliberately irresponsible reaction against the dull sterilities of so much that passes as modern architecture today... It is prompted by the impulse... to reclaim for architecture the freedom of invention – and the possibility of pleasurable fantasy – it had too abjectly surrendered to the cult of the machine..."* Whatever one's views of them, both Disneyland (as a leisure destination) and facsimile-style housing of the Portmeirion type, are popular. Portmeirion itself was later the setting for the 1967-1968 fantasy sci-fi TV series *The Prisoner* as well as one of the locations used for *Brideshead Revisited*, the 1981 Evelyn Waugh adaptation.

(17) Chaired by Sir Clement Anderson Barlow, formerly Conservative MP for Salford 1910-1923. It proposed a planned industrial strategy, in which the dispersal of industry was partly regarded as a civil defence measure to minimise bombing damage in the event of war, with new towns being built to facilitate this. Published in 1940, most of its findings were implemented after 1945.

(18) Geddes, who had no formal qualifications in either town planning or architecture, corresponded with Unwin extensively over a period of 40 years. In 1914, they were appointed by Dublin Corporation to comment on proposed new housing schemes. Geddes's approach was informed by his sociological theories derived from his study of zoology (under Huxley) and an interest in eastern religion. He produced plans for the redevelopment of Bombay and Tel Aviv, the latter of which was built.

(19) Winnaretta Singer, an heiress to the Singer sewing machine fortune, emerged as a patron of the arts in France in the 1890s. She funded the construction of many Salvation Army hostels in Paris from 1910, hiring Le Corbusier to work on several of these.

(20) Co-author Hugh Quigley was a prominent economist in the 1930s, during which period he ran the XYZ Club, introducing Keynesian economic theories to the Labour Party.

(21) Young served as Minister of Health from 1931 to 1935, having, like Addison, originally entered politics as a Liberal supporter of Lloyd George. He was also associated with the Bloomsbury group and a friend of John Maynard Keynes.

(22) St Pancras House Improvement Society later became St Pancras Housing Association and still exists today as part of Origin Housing. It was founded by Basil Jellicoe, a prominent figure in the UK's small Anglo-Catholic branch of Anglicanism, who persuaded Edward, Prince of Wales to become an early supporter of his efforts. Somers Town also contains Oakshott Court, designed in 1976 for the GLC by Peter Tabori, on the site of Polygon Buildings, 288 Midland Railway tenement dwellings dating from 1894, which in turn replaced The Polygon, a 1784 development that once housed Mary Wollstonecraft, Charles Dickens and others: much of the history of housing development in London compressed here onto one single site.

(23) See: https://www.youtube.com/watch?v=ciw8Ww6Gx4c For background on the early Kensington Housing Trust block Crossfield House, see: https://www.rbkc.gov.uk/pdf/Delegated%20Decision%20Report%20Sept%202012%20Appendix%203.pdf

(24) Quarry Hill Estate was built using some steel-framing and pre-cast concrete elements, an early example of this type of construction, and, as used here in prototype, one not without problems. Leeds City Council took a decision to demolish it in 1973, at a time when refurbishment of such schemes remained unfashionable. Karl Marx Hof still exists in Vienna. A flat within it was used as the apartment of Max (Dirk Bogarde) in the 1974 film *The Night Porter*.

(25) Quoted in David Edgerton *The Rise and Fall of the British Nation: A Twentieth Century History* p232-233.

8

HOWARD'S IDEAS PREVAIL

When the Second World War started only 25% of UK households lived in homes that they owned (compared with 10% in 1914) and 75% rented. Of the latter, only 10% were local authority tenants. An enormous part of the population – 65% in total – rented "privately", this definition covering housing associations, industrial dwellings companies and landlords managing everything from properly self-contained accommodation through to houses in multiple occupation with shared cooking and washing facilities. House-building itself had slowed virtually to a halt by the spring of 1940 as the diversion of manpower and materials to wartime uses took precedence. Thereafter only a tiny number of new homes were completed: between 1940 and 1945 just 113,000 of all types would be built.[1]

It had been expected that the outbreak of a war would be immediately accompanied by mass bombing raids, something featured decades earlier in the writings of HG Wells, and then seemingly confirmed by the destruction in April 1937 of the Basque city of Guernica during the Spanish Civil War.[2] Official policy on this in the UK had been made clear as early as November 1932 when Prime Minister Stanley Baldwin declared, when stating that the UK would not pursue unilateral disarmament, *"...I think it is well also for the man in the street to realise that there is no power on earth that can protect him from being bombed. Whatever people may tell him, the bomber will always get through..."* This was not to mean, though, that the government regarded itself as helpless. In the years that followed elaborate precautions were put in place to minimise civilian casualties, including plans to evacuate women and children out of large urban areas. The Home Office set up an Air Raid Precautions department in 1935 and began recruiting Air Raid Wardens from 1937.

Many of these plans were put into operation in August and September 1939, only for very little – by way of aerial destruction – to occur. The bulk of those evacuated in the autumn of 1939, for instance, had moved back home voluntarily by the spring of 1940. When Churchill became Prime Minister in May 1940, with the war escalating, he welcomed Neville Chamberlain's decision to remain in the government, expecting that Chamberlain would *"look after the Home Front for me"* whilst he concentrated on military and naval strategy.[3] In fact, although Churchill brought Labour and Liberal figures into his administration, apart from Ernest Bevin (whose role was to mobilise the national workforce and provide an effective war economy), they had mainly secondary positions. The key post of Minister of Health, with responsibility for housing as well as medical services, was held by Malcolm MacDonald (1940-1941), Ernest Brown (1941-1943) and Henry Willink (1943-1945) none of whom was a Labour MP. Similarly, the position of First Commissioner of Works was occupied by Lord Tryon, Lord Reith, Lord Portal and Duncan Sandys respectively, none of whom was a Labour (or even Liberal) representative. It is hard not to draw the conclusion that Churchill wanted the support of the Labour Party mainly because it enabled him to wage war, not for any broader set of objectives. In so far as he thought about post-war arrangements at all in the early months of his premiership, he assumed that these could be devolved to Chamberlain, the architect of much of the pre-1939 house-building boom.

If that were his assumption it disappeared in September 1940 when Chamberlain resigned on grounds of ill-health. Coincidentally, the mass bombing of UK cities commenced the same month. It had a severe impact, killing over 43,000 people and injuring another 52,000 over the next eight months. Approximately half the casualties inflicted by the Luftwaffe occurred in London. Estimates of how many buildings were destroyed and damaged vary, but figures suggesting 70,000 completely destroyed and 1,700,000 damaged (many of which were then abandoned) are quoted. By November 1940, 25% of the population of London had left the city, most making their own arrangements to live elsewhere.[4] It was true, of course, that these figures were much less than those suffered subsequently in Russia, Germany or Japan. It was also true that a great many of the damaged houses were duly patched up and brought back into use, and that most of those made homeless found accommodation with friends or family. But the overall impact, which saw fairly extensive areas of London and other key UK cities remain derelict with many abandoned properties and a substantial number of households voluntarily rehousing themselves away from likely target areas, did not change.

The scale of the damage in London - clearly visible to government ministers as they went about their business - meant that from early on in the conflict, with victory far from assured, bullish proposals were made for post-war reconstruction. In early 1941, Lord Reith, First Commissioner of Works, asked the LCC to draw up proposals to completely rebuild London. Reith set out the parameters the government were setting in how this should be carried out in a speech on 17 July 1941: *"...There are four main points in both the Interim Report and the Government statement. The first is a standard of maximum values; the second, a definition and appropriate special treatment of reconstruction areas; the third, a general strengthening of planning control to safeguard the future while plans and the full post-war planning system are being worked out; the fourth, a central planning authority. On the first, a standard of maximum values, the Government have made the 'announcement of intentions' which the Committee recommended as sufficient for present purposes. The announcement of the principle—that is, that values for public acquisition or control of land should not exceed those of March, 1939—should not and does not prevent legitimate dealings in land meantime, but it should and does give us sufficient warning to prevent undesirable speculation and speculative dealings of any sort. Caveat emptor! If there be any of the vampire breed who expect to profit in this particular direction from the war, they will have cause to regret their action and they will find themselves in error...*[5] In other words: the government would set land values, with these not exceeding March 1939 prices, there would be centralised planning, and planning rules themselves would be strengthened. By the time Reith and the government committed to this, the LCC had appointed Patrick Abercrombie to draft a County of London Plan, work that he would carry out with John Forshaw, Chief Architect of the LCC.

Abercrombie had been associated with Osborn, Purdom and Howard from 1918, via his membership of the National Garden Cities Committee. It might have been thought that his appointment by the LCC signified a preference for low-density solutions to housing and planning issues. In fact, his outlook was more nuanced than this, and his approach to issues generally was heavily influenced by Baron Haussmann and the École des Beaux Arts.[6] Between 1853 and 1869, Haussmann had accomplished an immense reconstruction of Paris at enormous expense. Much of the old, cluttered city was torn down and replaced by mile after mile of multi-storied apartment blocks built above ground-floor commercial space. Density was high (as it was too, in the early Victorian London equivalent of this) and a huge proportion of the population was moved to facilitate the plan. Haussmann himself enjoyed autocratic powers, and whilst his plan delivered a new, ideal city, it also had a military purpose. The wide, broad boulevards made it easier to clear demonstrators (or even revolutionaries) out of the way by the use of artillery fire, and the green belt of recreational land that surrounded Paris contained 38 forts, built between 1840 and 1890 for the defence of the city.

As early as 1914 Abercrombie had shown an interest in re-planning a large UK city. In that year he entered, and won, a competition to provide a plan for Dublin.[7] By 1922, he was acting as adviser to Cork, after which he returned to Dublin in 1925 to complete the Dublin Civic Survey. This was intended to rebuild areas that had been devastated between 1916 and 1923 during the Irish War of Independence and the Civil War that followed. Much of the Civic Survey (and of Abercrombie's earlier plan) was never implemented: to this day Dublin lacks the underground rail network that was envisaged over a century ago. What did happen, after a fashion, was the expansion of various low-density suburban areas like Crumlin and Drumcondra.[8]

As far as most people in the UK were concerned, though, Abercrombie's reputation rested on his work with the Council for the Preservation of Rural England and in particular his 1929 report *The Thames Valley from Cricklade to Staines: A survey of its existing state and some suggestions for its future preservation*. This certainly tapped into the feeling of the time: that largely unregulated ribbon development spreading out of existing cities was in danger of "joining up" much of the country in one extended suburban sprawl.[9] Appointed chair of town planning at University College, London in 1935, Abercrombie was back in Dublin a year later to work on further plans for remodelling the city. These emphasised open-space provision within the centre and recommended a green belt up to six miles wide around the city within which some low-density development would be permitted. When finally appointed by the LCC, Abercrombie was 62 years old, impeccably well-connected and regarded as the leading UK expert in strategic town planning. Always immaculately dressed, his bearing was patrician veering to haughty, an impression confirmed by his wearing a monocle at all times. Forshaw, his colleague, had been chief architect of the Miners' Welfare Committee in the 1930s prior to joining the London County Council, where, by 1941, he had responsibility across the metropolis for clearing land that had been damaged in air raids and disposing of the debris that resulted from this.

The knowledge that a major report was being written about the future planning of London produced, as was to be expected, a lively correspondence from those with a specific professional interest in whatever recommendations it might produce. As early as 16 January 1942 a pessimistic Frederic Osborn was commenting *"Most planners are too much cowed by the City-in-Being"*[10]. Throughout that year he found himself increasingly crossing swords with Erno Goldfinger, a Hungarian émigré architect who favoured an unashamedly modernist approach. In a series of articles for *The Architectural Review* Goldfinger, who had built little at that point, put forward his own definition of how space should be used to maximum advantage and attacked Osborn, observing that his writings *"state as axiomatic truths the one-sided arguments of the Garden City Movement"*.[11] At its simplest, Osborn wanted an abundance of low-density garden cities outside London, to which a high proportion of the city's population (and its employment) would be moved, whereas Goldfinger wanted most of the city demolished and rebuilt in situ, to a much higher density, Le Corbusier style. At the extreme end of the spectrum were the members of the Modern Architectural Research Group (MARS), founded in 1933, who produced their own Plan for London in June 1942. Led by Morton Shand, a kind of upper-class connoisseur and friend of Le Corbusier, MARS brought together Wells Coates, Maxwell Fry and John Betjeman as well as a host of other figures.[12] Their plan – heavily influenced by Nikolay Alexandrovich Milyutin's 1930 design for a linear city – would have involved demolishing most of London and starting again from scratch.

Not surprisingly, gigantic proposals of this type were avoided by Abercrombie and Forshaw. Even so, when published in 1943, *The County of London Plan* was judged to be *"a profound disappointment"* by Osborn. Despite such mutterings it was the subject of an exhibition at County Hall, London, which ran from July to August 1943 and drew 75,000 people, including the King and Queen.[13] Further afield, news of the debate at home about planning for the post-war world was even studied in some POW Camps, including Stalag Luft III, noted in later years as the site of *The Great Escape*. In fact, with the UK now part of an international coalition that was clearly prevailing against Germany and Japan, at this point public interest in the post-war world was running at a very high level. Penguin books, who had already published *Living in Cities* by Ralph Tubbs, a colleague of Goldfinger's, now asked Goldfinger and EJ Carter to explicate what the report meant in practice in a Penguin special.[14]

Despite the immense acclaim for *The County of London Plan*,

Osborn remained in despair, commenting on 7 September 1943 *"90 to 95 per cent want houses and gardens and don't want this... The LCC is led by middle-class Labour Councillors right out of touch with popular opinion."* This was a cutting remark, albeit one made in private correspondence. To whom might it have applied in Osborn's eyes? The 1937 LCC elections produced 69 Labour and 49 Conservative councillors, with the Labour contingent including 3 former MPs and 9 current MPs, including Herbert Morrison, Lewis Silkin, George Strauss and John Wilmot, all of whom would hold senior positions in the Attlee government. There was also the Earl of Listowel, who sat as an LCC councillor, and, like the quartet just mentioned, would later serve under Attlee. A further 12 LCC members would be elected Labour MPs in 1945. That the LCC was operating as a kind of incubator, providing personnel for a future Labour government, reflected Morrison's efficient management of the Labour Party across London in the 1920s and 1930s, something very much designed to produce Labour supremacy in the capital. Was Osborn referring, perhaps, to Peggy Jay, one of the *"Hampstead middle-class Labour grande-dames"* whom Morrison had groomed to facilitate his takeover of the LCC? Or if not her, suspicion falls on Ewart Culpin, ousted by Howard from the Garden City Association in 1918. Culpin had served on the LCC since 1925, and had qualified as both a town planner and architect, designing council housing in Bermondsey, an area he would later represent.[15]

In the event Osborn's fears were groundless. Abercrombie kept a foot in both the modernist and garden city camps. In 1944, he produced a sequel, *The Greater London Plan*, known subsequently as the "The Abercrombie Plan". This introduced the idea of satellite towns, and recommended that much of the population of London and other cities should be moved out to them. His proposals were extremely detailed, and took as their starting point his view, which Howard would have shared, that there was inadequate open space in existing cities and towns. He recommended a future allocation of 4 acres of public amenity space for every thousand people living in an urban setting, the equivalent of 174 square feet or

16 square metres per person. Whilst many inner-urban areas in the 1930s and 1940s had resident groups, or local politicians, who were vocal in their demand for additional open space, it isn't clear how Abercrombie reached his figures, or why he made the assumptions that he did.[16] It is worth considering that, if the same formula were used today, it would require the conversion of 395 square miles of UK *urban* land into public open space. Abercrombie also called for most major roads within London to be expanded to dual carriageways and either elevated above or placed in tunnels below the new urban fabric. Additional arterial roads would be built and treated as "parkways", with substantial planting on either side (including wooded areas) to muffle their noise from the surrounding residential and commercial buildings. He also suggested that all the railway bridges across the Thames ought to be abolished (instead the lines would tunnel beneath central London, to and from colossal subterranean termini) and be converted into road crossings with a couple of substantial extra bridges added for good measure. It was almost, but not quite, as ambitious as the MARS Plan.

The view that something exceptional had to be done about housing, and the built environment generally, extended beyond Abercrombie, Osborn and the LCC. Churchill too had thoughts about this, creating the posts of Minister of Town and Country Planning, from December 1942, and Minister of Reconstruction, from November 1943. Both were held by Conservatives, and the Labour Party was kept securely away from any such responsibilities. With so much destruction across the UK's cities these initiatives were understandable, and the government's intention was to make an immediate impact on the problem via a programme of Emergency Factory Made (EFM) housing. This would erect hundreds of thousands of temporary bungalows, quickly named "prefabs" by the public, wherever there was some empty land. Prefabs had the advantage – at a time when traditional building materials were in short supply and the construction industry still lacked manpower – of being assembled from mainly non-traditional materials. A prototype, "the Portal" (named after Lord

Portal, Minister of Works and Planning) was exhibited at the Tate Gallery in May 1944. Sponsored by the UK automobile industry, and built of steel – which turned out to be in equally short supply – it was quickly abandoned in favour of other prefabricated designs that used concrete panels, aluminium and even asbestos. Some could be assembled in 41 minutes, and there was also a complementary range of slightly more elaborate prefabricated houses that could be built in 2-3 days. The intention with all of these was that none would remain in use for more than 10 years. By then, normal market conditions would have resumed, something which in Churchill's eyes would mean a continuation of the inter-war private housing boom with a few substantial council house and flat building projects thrown in for good measure.[17]

The final stages of the conflict brought further destruction to the UK, notably via the use by Germany of the V1 (from June 1944) and V2 (from September 1944) which between them damaged or destroyed over a million buildings, mainly in London and the south east, before attacks finally ceased in March 1945. By then, Goldfinger and Carter's *The London County Plan* had appeared. It sold 100,000 copies and a precis of it was distributed to the armed forces. Illustrated with attractive hand-drawn maps and diagrams, it pointed out in particular the advantages of building properly spaced 7- to 10-floor residential blocks. Goldfinger and Carter also discussed issues of density and overcrowding, and clearly illustrated, as had Abercrombie and Forshaw, the need to decant 2 million people out of London. New planning powers would be used, with all urban areas in future carefully divided into residential, leisure, industrial or employment areas. To demonstrate how this would work in practice, they selected Shoreditch as an example, providing "before" and "after" illustrations showing the impact of these theories.

Churchill was not in favour and personally rejected the garden city/dispersal thesis in a cabinet meeting in April 1945, commenting *"Ah yes… all this stuff about planning and compensation and betterment. Broad vistas and all that. But give to me the eighteenth-century alleyway, where footpads lurk and the harlot plies her trade, and none of this new-*

fangled planning doctrine...[18] By then the war against Germany was in its last stages and he had already committed, in October 1944, that the end of the war in Europe should determine the date of the next general election. At a meeting with Clement Attlee on 18 May 1945 both agreed that the government should continue until the defeat of Japan, which, at that point, might not have been until 1946, or possibly even 1947. Attlee was immediately advised afterwards by Bevin and Morrison that in their view an election should be held that October, when the current Parliament rose. With this in mind, and after taking soundings at a party conference, Attlee went back to Churchill and told him Labour would be leaving the government. Bevin and Morrison had good reason for insisting that Labour take this course of action. Although in their infancy, polls by the British Institute of Public Opinion showed in February 1945 that Labour were leading the Conservatives by 47% to 27%, with this commanding lead narrowing to 45%-32% by June. In their view, they had a chance of winning a general election.[19]

Churchill's response to Labour leaving his government on 23 May 1945 was to disregard the polling data – if he took much notice of it at all – dissolve Parliament and call a general election. The highly personalised Conservative Party manifesto that appeared shortly afterwards (*Winston Churchill's Declaration of Policy to the Electors*) opened with an attack on his former coalition partners "...*I had hoped to preserve the Coalition Government, comprising all Parties in the State, until the end of the Japanese war, but owing to the unwillingness of the Socialist and Sinclair Liberal Parties to agree to my proposal, a General Election became inevitable, and I have formed a new National Government, consisting of the best men in all Parties who were willing to serve and some who are members of no Party at all...*" Despite approaching the campaign as a yes/no endorsement of Churchill as leader, on housing the Conservative campaign produced a surprisingly detailed set of proposals. They were explicit in stating that because of rising costs both local authorities and private builders would be subsidised by the state, the first two years post-war would see 300,000 new permanent homes built (albeit many of these would be "factory-made permanent houses") as well as between 150,000 and 200,000 additional "well-equipped temporary houses". In addition to this rents would be controlled via a new system of Rent Tribunals.

Churchill also committed to assist the reconstruction of urban areas by fixing land values at 1939 levels and *to secure for the future the best use of land in the public interest, including proper reservation of open spaces and the best location of industry and housing*.

In contrast to this, Labour went into the election with a manifesto overseen by Herbert Morrison and Ellen Wilkinson, the text of which was written by either Patrick Gordon Walker or Michael Young.[20] It had little specific to say about housing, preferring instead a set of generalisations, that were in many ways quite close to the Conservative position: modern methods and materials *"will have to be the order of the day"*, price controls on the cost of building materials would be enforced by the state and a programme begun that would continue until *"every family in this island has a good standard of accommodation"*. To facilitate this Labour committed to setting up a Ministry of Housing and Planning, exercising the housing powers of the Ministry of Health with the planning powers of the Ministry of Town and Country Planning. Finally, Labour repeated Attlee's statement of 1937 that it would nationalise land, caveating this by stating it was something it *"would work towards"*. It would ensure fair compensation to landowners affected by this, against which a new source of revenue would be set up, derived from the better use of the land in question. There was no mention anywhere in the Labour manifesto of how many properties it might actually build.

Similarly, the Liberal party avoided specifics. Proclaiming *"... There is a house famine in the land..."*, they planned like Labour to create a Minister of Housing, and like both the main parties they would control the cost of building materials. From here they went on to concentrate on the rural aspects of housing (most of their remaining seats were rural), making, inter alia, the assertions *"... Great Britain is a small country with a vast population..."* and *"...The fullest use must be made of agricultural land for food production..."* [21]

The absence of any costings, by any of the main parties, was curious, given the scale of the undertakings to which they were committing. One explanation for this may be that with the standard rate of income tax running at 50% in 1945 (10s in the £), the public were used to (and understood) the idea of large-scale, dramatic spending programmes.[22] Polling day was held on 5 July 1945. After votes had been cast by, and collected from, UK servicemen overseas, the result was declared on 26 July: Labour had an absolute majority of 147 over all other parties. Churchill departed and Attlee formed a government.[23] Aneurin Bevan became Minister of Health. Lewis Silkin went to the Ministry of Town and Country Planning with George Tomlinson installed as First Commissioner of Works. Contrary to the manifesto commitment there was no Ministry of Housing and Planning.[24]

But, in the late summer of 1945, there was much to celebrate. To universal surprise, and after atomic weapons had been used against two of its largest cities by the US, Japan surrendered only 20 days after Attlee became Prime Minister. The opportunity thus opened up, long before it had been expected to become possible, for widespread social change. The vision the new government would follow in housing was spelt out in the documentary film The *Proud City: A Plan for London*. Produced by Edgar Anstey and directed by Ralph Keene, this recycled footage from *Housing Problems* and war time newsreels, and features Forshaw and Abercrombie spelling out their proposals for the reconstruction of the city post-1945. Like *Housing Problems*, it focusses on Stepney as an illustration of how best to proceed. The benefits of clear, detailed, bureaucratic planning – involving all government agencies as well as the private sector – are spelt out with great emphasis, with Abercrombie stating, very firmly, that London has *"...mean hideous slums of which any city ought to be ashamed..."* and *"...all these bad things must go and the sooner the better..."* whilst lamenting that *"...we have allowed uncontrolled ribbon development..."*[25]

The film doesn't actually articulate what will happen, but viewers would surely have concluded that there would soon be a new world, where a lot of demolition and reconstruction would take place in a very short space of time, ribbon development would be prevented and traffic would be accommodated via a massive array of new multi-lane arterial roads. (This is illustrated with footage of US urban motorways). The film ends with Lord Latham, Leader of the LCC, and an advocate at the time of a new regional authority that would stretch far into the Home Counties, batting away criticism that any of this was unachievable. In particular he deals sharply with the traditional canard that there would be difficulties with the finances: *"...It will certainly cost a great deal of money. But not more than unplanned building and certainly less than war..."* Screened in cinemas through 1946, much of this had been in Howard's vision half a century earlier. Now, modified by Abercrombie, and backed by substantial state funding, it would be implemented.

Notes

(1) Both the figures for housing tenure and the numbers of dwellings built 1939-1945 are included in Butler and Butler, *British Political Facts 1900-1994* and were drawn from data held, at that point by the Department of Environment.

(2) Wells was much taken, from very early on, with the impact aerial bombing might have on civilisation. *The War in the Air* (1908) and *The Shape of Things to Come* (1933) both depict massive destruction caused by fleets of bombers.

(3) Quoted in Robert Self *Neville Chamberlain: A Biography* (2006).

(4) Estimates of Blitz casualties vary. Dear and Foot in *The Oxford Companion to World War II* (2001) give figures of around 43,000 killed and up to 139,000 injured. The estimates given to Parliament were lower.

(5) See https://api.parliament.uk/historic-hansard/lords/1941/jul/17/post-war-rec onstruction#S5LV0119P0_19410717_HOL_22

(6) On Abercrombie, Haussmann's influence on him, and his proposals for Dublin, see *The Irish Times* 5 February 2003 at https://www.irishtimes.com/ opinion/an-irishman-s-diary-1.347850. As early as 1913, in *Town Planning Review*, Abercrombie had commented *"Haussmann's modernisation of Paris is the most brilliant piece of Town Planning in the world"*.

(7) Abercrombie was awarded a £500 prize for his 1914 Dublin plan. (Equal to around £150,000 today). For details of his plan, and its subsequent modification see https://www.irishtimes.com/opinion/an-irishman-s-diary-1.347850 and https://comeheretome.com/2013/02/22/patrick-abercrombies-vision-of-dublin-1922/ and Abercrombie, Sydney Kelly and Arthur Kelly, *Dublin of the future: the new town plan, being the scheme awarded first prize in the international competition* University Press of Liverpool, Liverpool (1922). (The report is online at https://www.rte.ie/centuryireland//images/uploads/further-reading/Ed92-DublinOfTheFuture1.pdf). Raymond Unwin designed a garden suburb of 428 houses at Marino, near Drumcondra, which was built 1922-1926. The Crumlin scheme, built 1926-1936, consisted of 136 houses built for the workers at the Guinness brewery on land donated by the Earl of Iveagh.

(8) Abercrombie's recommendation for a substantial underground railway system in Dublin – which he replicated in his later London plan – was not formally taken up until 1972. Granted permission to proceed via a Railway Order in 2011, work has yet to commence.

(9) See Patrick Abercrombie *The Preservation of Rural England*, London (1926). Abercrombie co-authored his 1929 book with the Earl of Mayo and Stanley Adshead. Literary representations of the opposition to ribbon development during this period ranged from George Orwell's *Coming Up for Air* (1939), which is set in a Thames Valley market town that has been swallowed up by suburban housing, to Betjeman's missive *Slough* in his 1937 poetry collection *Continual Dew*.

(10) See Page 21, *The Letters of Lewis Mumford and Frederic J Osborn: A Transatlantic Dialogue 1938-1970* Ed Michael Hughes London (1971).

(11) Quoted in Kynaston *Austerity Britain 1945-1951*. Born in Hungary, Goldfinger had Polish nationality, and initially worked in Paris where he employed the young John Cage, later a major figure in avant-garde art and music, as his assistant. Resident in London from 1934 he married Ursula Blackwell, a relative of Blanche Blackwell, mistress of Ian Fleming.

(12) On the MARS Plan for London see https://drawingmatter.org/the-mars-groups-plan-for-london-1933-1944/. Betjeman's involvement with this is curious, given his later reputation as a founder member of the Victorian Society.

(13) Details of the exhibition can be found at https://municipaldreams.wordpress.com/2014/07/08/the-county-of-london-plan-1943-if-only-we-will/

(14) Carter combined his work as librarian of the RIBA with being Secretary of the RIBA Refugee Committee. In the latter capacity he was responsible for bringing key Bauhaus figures like Walter Gropius and Laszlo Moholy-Nagy to the UK in 1934. Both found themselves with little to do in the UK – where modernism had shallow roots at that time it would seem – and left for the US in 1937. The departure of Gropius was commemorated by a dinner at the Trocadero Restaurant on 9 March 1937, attended by Abercrombie, HG Wells, Henry Moore and many others. The menu card for this event, designed by Moholy-Nagy can be seen at https://www.architecture.com/image-library/ribapix/image-information/poster/menu-card-for-dinner-in-honour-of-professor-walter-gropius-on-march-9th-1937-at-the-trocadero-restaurant-piccadilly-london-on-the-occasion-of-his-leaving-england-for-havard-university-the-toasts-menu-and-front-cover/posterid/RIBA94505.html During his stay in the UK Moholy-Nagy was also commissioned by John Betjeman to provide photographs to illustrate his book *An Oxford University Chest* and worked on the documentary films *Lobsters* (1935) and *New Architecture and the London Zoo* (1936), the former of which can be watched at https://player.bfi.org.uk/free/film/watch-lobsters-1936-online

(15) After being outmanoeuvred by Howard, Culpin's political career saw him stand unsuccessfully as the Labour candidate in Islington North in the 1924 general election, after which he sat on the LCC 1925-1946.

(16) Abercrombie's assumptions ignored existing open space, such as traditional parks, squares, churchyards, cemeteries, playing fields, allotments, grazing land and so on. In some cases, boroughs already met his stringent requirements by virtue of existing land use. What he concentrated on was areas where there was deficiency, irrespective of whether the local authority as a whole might already have "sufficient" open space, and to meet this, he advocated demolition and clearance to create new parkland. Some of these projects, such as Burgess Park in Southwark, took more than 50 years to complete. Many of Abercrombie's

proposals and much of his approach can also be found in later reports like *Traffic in Towns* (1960).

(17) Details of what the temporary housing looked like can be seen at https://www.youtube.com/watch?v=B7kfL0-QhpM

(18) Quoted in Kynaston *Austerity Britain 1945-1951* P 31. The target of Churchill's comments appears to have been William Morrison, his own Minister of Town and Country Planning.

(19) As well as the opinion poll data pointing against a Conservative win, Labour had gained 18 seats at parliamentary by-elections between 1935 and 1939. After the wartime "truce" was introduced (in which the three main parties agreed not to contest by-elections against each other) additional left of centre gains continued to be made by Commonwealth (3 seats), Eire Labour and even the SNP (at Motherwell, in April 1945). Support for the Liberal Party also rose from 12% (February 1945) to 15% (June 1945). See Butler and Butler, *British Political Facts 1900-1994*.

(20) Gordon Walker worked for the BBC at the time, and would later sit as a Labour MP 1945-1964 and 1966-1974. Young was employed at Political and Economic Planning, a prototype UK "think-tank".

(21) Each manifesto can be read in detail at http://www.conservativemanifesto.com/1945/1945-conservative-manifesto.shtml, http://www.labour-party.org.uk/manifestos/1945/1945-labour-manifesto.shtml and http://www.libdemmanifesto.com/1945/1945-liberal-manifesto.shtml

(22) The standard rate of income tax in the UK stood at 5s 6d in the £ in 1939 (27.5%) and rose to 10s in the £ (50%) in 1942, remaining at that level until 1947. It had been 1s 2d in the £ in 1914 (5.8%). In 2021 it sits at 20%, the same level it was at in 1923.

(23) The full result in 1945 was: 393 Labour; 200 Conservative, 13 National Liberal, 12 Liberal, 10 Ulster Unionist, 3 Independent Labour Party, 2 Communist, 2 Irish Nationalist, 2 Independent, 1 Commonwealth, 1 Eire Labour.

(24) Silkin had entered politics as a Liberal member of the LCC in 1925, switching to Labour a year later. He preceded Herbert Morrison as Leader of the Labour Group on the LCC, and was elected Labour MP for Peckham in 1936.

(25) The film can be viewed at https://www.youtube.com/watch?v=lZyUJ2CCQF8

9

Implementing Howard

The reputation of Aneurin Bevan rests on his time as Minister of Health, during which he worked tirelessly to establish the National Health Service. The enduring appeal of the NHS, and the regard with which it continues to be held, ensures that, even today, he enjoys an almost legendary status as a totemic, all-wise, left-wing giant. MP for Ebbw Vale from 1929, his radicalism initially led him to align himself with Mosley's economic proposals, though he quickly refused to follow Mosley out of the Labour Party in 1931. Later, his support, alongside many communists, for a Popular Front against Germany, Italy and Spain led to his expulsion, and that of Sir Stafford Cripps and George Strauss, from the Labour Party in March 1939. Prior to this he had also inveighed against rearmament and conscription, enjoying an immense reputation for doing so with much of the party membership. The first of the trio to be readmitted (in December 1939), Bevan went into the 1945 general election proclaiming: *"We enter this campaign at this general election, not merely to get rid of the Tory majority. We want the complete political extinction of the Tory Party, and twenty-five years of Labour Government."*

With no new Ministry of Housing and Planning set up, Bevan retained housing within his brief as Minister of Health. His view was that a National Housing Service should be formed, broadly comparable to the National Health Service... a kind of gigantic council housing department assembled from all the local authority housing in the UK, with hundreds of thousands of properties, millions of tenants and vast numbers of staff, working out of

central, regional and local headquarters. The government would
direct, and fund, a huge house-building programme that would
completely transform the UK. As well as this there would also
be, for those who still chose to buy or rent privately, government
grants to ensure that every home was brought up to a good level
of repair. In particular, Bevan wanted significantly better space
standards for council housing than those used in the 1930s, even
by Morrison's LCC, and took his cue in this from the deliberations
of the Dudley Committee.[1]

Produced by a committee established in 1944 by the Ministry
of Health's Central Housing Committee, the Dudley Report had
concluded that local authorities were too much in hock to the
space and design standards adopted in 1919, and largely drawn
at that point from the ideas of Raymond Unwin. Dudley and his
colleagues noted how adept 1930s house-builders had been at
judging the type of home the average renter and buyer wanted, ie,
how successful they had been at meeting the needs of the lower
middle classes and upper working classes, and recommended that
future council housing should reflect this, rather than what had
been considered adequate around the time of the First World War.

Accordingly, Bevan wanted the idea that council housing was
solely for the "working class" removed from official guidance
and terminology, and in pursuit of higher standards lowered the
guidelines for desirable municipal housing densities to 350 people
per hectare, a reduction of 43% on typical densities within LCC
estates pre-1939. As to what new housing developments should
look like, he was unashamedly conventional, stating in 1949 "...
*We should try to introduce in our modern villages and towns what was
always the lovely feature of English and Welsh villages, where the doctor,
the grocer, the butcher and the farm labourer all lived in the same street. I
believe that is essential for the full life of citizen ... to see the living tapestry
of a mixed community...*"[2]

Not much modernism here, and an end point not at all
dissimilar to that long advocated by Howard and Osborn. Bevan
was also clear, as Howard had been before him, that quality was
essential, stating in a speech in Margate in 1947 "...*while we shall*

be judged for a year or two by the number of houses we build ... we shall
be judged in ten years' time by the type of houses we build..." What this
meant in practice were homes with unprecedented refinements,
such as two indoor lavatories. The average new 3-bedroom council
house grew in size from 860 square feet (pre-1939) to 1,055 square
feet (1951) as Bevan both increased the amount of space families
had, and reduced the number of properties per hectare/acre to
provide more open space.

As indicated in their election manifesto, Labour was not
intending to build new homes solely within urban areas, or even via
existing local authorities. Lewis Silkin, and his Ministry of Town
and Country Planning, had been established in 1945, to provide
the legislative and bureaucratic framework needed to ensure that
"*up to 20 new towns*" would be built by the government. That these
might fall short of the existing examples of Howard's vision at
Letchworth and Welwyn was noted as early as October 1945 by
Osborn who asserted "*...Among both the upper and middle classes
the word 'garden city' stands for a working-class housing estate, with just
a touch of philanthropy. It has therefore been something to approve but
on no account to live in...*"[3] His fears were allayed somewhat by an
invitation to join the New Towns Commission chaired by Lord
Reith, and set up by Silkin"*...to consider the general questions of the
establishment, development, organisation and administration that will
arise in the promotion of New Towns in furtherance of a policy of planned
decentralisation from congested urban areas; and in accordance therewith
to suggest guiding principles on which such Towns should be established
and developed as self-contained and balanced communities for work and
living...*"

Reith, Osborn and their colleagues duly concluded that there
was a clear need to build new towns, with their construction being
undertaken by development corporations funded and supported
by central government. They also made recommendations
setting out the basic design parameters that would be followed:
developments should have a population of up to 60,000, should
be built as far as possible on greenfield sites, should consist mainly
of single-family homes built to a low density and be organised in

neighbourhoods around a primary school and nursery schools, a pub and shops selling staple foods. They were also keen to endorse Howard's original guidance about ensuring the population was actively employed locally, rather than just to create something that became a dormitory suburb of a larger urban area.

Officially, this became policy. But there were interesting variations on this theme appearing, now that it was clear that something radical would be done to sort out the UK's housing issues. In *Farewell Squalor: A Design for a New Town and Proposals for the Redevelopment of the Easington Rural District* CW Clarke, surveyor to Easington Rural District Council (which despite its name, was actually quite an industrialised area) set out the case for building Peterlee, starting with an explanation that rather cut across the views later espoused by Bevan *"...It is now generally accepted that a full social, cultural and educational life cannot be achieved with the village as a unit... Let us, therefore, close our eyes on the nineteenth century degradation and squalor, and let us only look with unseeing eyes on the sordid excrescence of the first decade of this century, let us blind ourselves to the septic and ugly building wens and ribbons perpetrated and planted on us between the wars, but let us open our eyes and look brightly forward and onward to the new town, the new living... Peterlee..."*

To achieve this, the original intention in Peterlee was to house many of its incoming population in modern flats within multi-floor blocks designed by Berthold Lubetkin. The idea that new towns might provide a high proportion of their homes in blocks of flats, distributed at a low density, seems to have distressed Osborn, who began claiming, from 1946, that it was cheaper to build houses than flats, and invoking Raymond Unwin's 1912 book *Nothing Gained by Overcrowding* by way of evidence.[4] The truth of this isn't clear, even today. He needn't have worried so much. In Peterlee, the National Coal Board objected to the depth of the foundations required by Lubetkin's blocks. What was eventually built was much more conventional, which would have pleased Osborn who was eventually won around to the government's proposals for how the new towns should be developed by the scale of the programme.

But it must be doubtful if his opposition, and that of the

Town and Country Planning Association would have altered events anyway. By the mid-1940s the belief in planning was so strong, and the determination to rebuild post-war Britain so marked, that politicians – and via them the electorate – were being offered many variations of Howard's original garden city design. If Peterlee was one such, another was Sir Charles Reilly's *Outline Plan of Birkenhead* (1947) which built on Reilly's own belief, expressed in language that chimed with that of Bevan, in *"...a semi-new planning principle ... that of houses round greens, as in pre-Industrial Revolution England, and the greens themselves arranged like the petals of a flower round a community building, the modern equivalent of the village inn..."*[5] A book advocating this, Lawrence Wolfe's *The Reilly Plan* was reviewed in *Tribune* by George Orwell, who remained somewhat sceptical, noting of some of the more radical proposals *"If you prefer to live in a kitchen-less house, you can have all your meals delivered from the meals centre in thermos containers which are left on the doorstep like the milk, the dirty dishes being removed afterwards by the same agency. A town can be built up of as many Reilly 'units' as there is need and space for... the main idea of the plan is to split the town up into self-contained communities, practically villages, of about 1,000 people each".*[6] Reilly's reversion to the mid-nineteenth century ideal of a substantial community building at the centre of a development, with a central eatery (an idea that was rarely, if ever, implemented) and a centralised heating system, for the entire development, required substantial amounts of land to make it work, resulting in low-density, sprawling schemes. The central, or "district" heating system would though become common to most of the larger post-war municipal estates.

The first new town to be designated was Stevenage, announced in 1946. It was followed by Crawley, Harlow, Hemel Hempstead, Newton Aycliffe and East Kilbride (all 1947), Hatfield, Welwyn, Peterlee and Glenrothes (all 1948), Basildon, Bracknell and Cwmbran (all 1949) and Corby (1950). Some of these self-selected: Howard's (and Osborn's) unfinished garden city at Welwyn was included, Newton Aycliffe and Cwmbran both had trading estates established in the 1930s, and Corby was the site of a pre-war steelworks that had expanded rapidly. In other words, this was not quite the beginning of a fresh initiative, rather it was a new government taking over and expanding existing projects, and utilising ideas that had been in the public domain by that point for over 50 years, as to how they should be carried out.

It is also commonly supposed that a degree of political consensus existed about this. If it did, it was absent from very early on, when a substantial legal battle had to be waged to get Stevenage started. Silkin addressed a public meeting there in May 1946 which quickly developed into a shouting match, with him saying "...*It is no good your jeering: it is going to be done...*" whilst the audience denounced him for using Gestapo tactics, let his car tyres down and erected signs at the local railway station telling travellers they were arriving at 'Silkingrad'. Hostility proceeded from this via a Judicial Review (led by a distinctly right-wing Residents Association) stating that the public in the area hadn't been properly consulted. Silkin fought and reversed a High Court decision to grant the review at the Court of Appeal and, eventually, the House of Lords. It was a messy process throughout, and even Ewart Culpin was an objector (he thought too many new towns were being grouped too close together in Hertfordshire, thus compromising Howard's original vision). Silkin's first choice to chair the Stevenage New Town Development Corporation, Clough Williams-Ellis, resigned in 1947 due to his inability to achieve anything.[7] Pressure was also brought to bear on Silkin in Parliament where he was challenged on the qualifications of those appointed to the Development Corporation.[8]

Some important arguments lurked beneath all the political and emotional point-scoring being made here. Stevenage was a small, established market town (early closing: Wednesday, market day: Saturday according to *The AA Road Book of England and Wales*, 1950) with a population of around 6,500. This was larger than either Letchworth or Welwyn when both were selected by Howard as garden city sites. The idea that an existing town would be greatly expanded (with the original inhabitants being subject to compulsory purchase) raised hackles, and, in truth, was not something that had ever been stressed in all the talk, over the decades, about building "new towns" of whatever type. Culpin's objection was interesting. Was it necessary to have four of the new towns in one not very large county? Could not some of them have been in Kent? The problem that would arise by having them grouped thus would be not dissimilar to the issues new towns were supposed to address, namely ribbon-development. Whilst there would be a better regulated landscape, travelling through Hertfordshire might in time become like travelling through the sprawl of towns and suburbs between New York and Washington DC: passing rapidly from one low-density development to another via strips of wooded and farmed land. The Stevenage objectors made some reasonable points.

Politically, though, things were much simpler. Historically, Stevenage was part of Hitchin constituency, which had never previously been Labour. Its wartime Conservative MP, Seymour Berry, (Deputy Chairman of *The Daily Telegraph*) lost by only 346 votes in 1945 to the Labour candidate, Philip Jones. The Conservatives were well aware of the impact made by Herbert Morrison's building programme on the political control of the LCC.[9] Was the Labour government now employing these same methods to ensure political control nationally? Some at least of them thought so, and, in terms of public perception, they were helped by the appointment of Monica Felton as Clough Williams-Ellis's successor. Felton, reputed to be Silkin's mistress, was extremely left-wing, and went as far as to visit North Korea after the outbreak of the Korean War, urging the UK government to withdraw from the conflict and send UK troops home. This won her the Stalin Prize for Peace, and dismissal from her position in Stevenage on her return.[10] By then Labour had lost the seat. Jones was beaten, in 1950, by Nigel Fisher, a centrist Conservative, who remained in situ until 1964, when Shirley Williams was elected. And even though Stevenage New Town hadn't progressed very much by the time Attlee gave way to Churchill in 1951, sufficient land had been acquired, and contracts entered into, to ensure that it progressed unhindered. The Conservatives were well aware of the need to build more homes, and the popularity this would bring them, even if they were prepared to engage in specific local campaigns against selected projects, and individuals.[11]

* * * * * *

Building new towns was only one part of the new government's housing agenda. It also concentrated resources in inner urban areas, where an immense amount needed to be done to address war damage, slum housing and overcrowding. If Lubetkin, who had arrived in the UK in 1931, found himself unwanted in Peterlee, there was much demand for his services in London. Heavily influenced by Le Corbusier he opened his account with the Finsbury Health Centre in 1938, after which his practice won the competition to provide a new housing estate at Spa Green.[12] Work on this finally began in July 1946, with Bevan laying the foundation stone. Originally limited (pre-war) to 5 floors, demand for housing after 1945 led to the main blocks being increased to 8 floors. Small, but symbolic, it provided 129 flats. Lubetkin's ability to fit a lot of good quality housing onto difficult sites brought him and his colleagues commissions in Bethnal Green where, from 1953 to 1954, they built the Dorset Estate and the Lakeview Estate, both of which relied on height and reinforced concrete. They followed this with the Cranbrook Estate, which had 15-floor blocks and finally Sivill House (19 floors) in the mid-1960s. The Dorset Estate, and Sivill House, which provided between them 342 homes, were built on virtually the same site as Columbia Square and Columbia Market, Baroness Burdett-Coutts's philanthropic venture of almost a century earlier.

Elsewhere, the London County Council produced high-density, medium-rise blocks, much influenced by pre-war housing schemes in Vienna, on the Woodberry Down Estate, Stoke Newington from a design by Sir Leslie Martin and Abercrombie's colleague JH Forshaw. As with Spa Green, this had been around as a project since the 1930s (the LCC had purchased the land in 1934) but building work didn't begin until 1949 and would stretch through until the early 1970s by which time 2,013 new homes in 57 blocks had been provided. Another development that lasted over several decades took place in a heavily bombed area between Brixton and Camberwell where Martin and his team built the Loughborough Estate. Here, from 1950, over 1,000 new homes were built, the most attractive of which were 11-floor blocks of flats and maisonettes. So attractively were these turned out that they drew praise from John Betjeman in *The Spectator* "...*When one compares their open-ness, lightness, grass and trees, and carefully related changes of scale from tall blocks to small blocks, with the prison-like courts of artisans' dwellings of earlier ages, one realises some things are better than they were... Maybe it has no place for someone like me, but it gives one hope for modern architecture...*"

These were not views shared by Frederic Osborn, who complained "...*the wholesale building of multi-storey flats at 40 an acre today in Stepney and Bermondsey is less enlightened than the building there of terrace houses at much the same density 100 years ago...*" He also observed privately to Lewis Mumford that "...*in London just now the local authorities are building eight and ten storey flats intended for families, though with an average floor area of only 650 square feet, compared to the 1,000 or 1,050 square feet for the current two storey house*".[13] Given the date of Osborn's comments this may have been a swipe at Lubetkin. Certainly, by 1949 he was railing against the LCC's proposal to increase density on the next stage of its Roehampton scheme, from 12 to 28 dwellings per acre. His friend Lewis Mumford noted that same year that planning in the UK appeared to have divided into two separate, and usually hostile camps, one (within which Osborn was counted) favouring "*the suburban type of open plain*" and the other, led by modernist architects producing "*a barbarous Le Corbusier/London County Council type of overcrowding*". There was some truth in this observation. Osborn's comments, though, failed to address how the LCC and the various Metropolitan Boroughs that made up London then, should have met housing need on small, irregularly shaped sites without abandoning development altogether. They also failed to consider, given costs and other competing priorities, whether any government ought, in effect, to restrict its housing programme so as to only provide properties built to very generous space standards. This argument, as voiced by Osborn, would be taken up and deployed by the Conservatives post-1951. The truth of the matter was that Lubetkin, Martin, Forshaw and many other architects were providing hundreds of thousands of urgently needed new homes on modern inner-city housing schemes across the UK during this period, very few of which would have happened had Churchill been returned as Prime Minister in 1945, relying as he did on temporarily housing people in "prefabs" until the private sector could re-commence its large-scale, 1930s-style building programmes.

There was action in the suburbs too. Taking its cue from Abercrombie's London Plan, and Attlee's electoral landslide, the London County Council embarked on its own programme of building mini-new towns. All of these, like its earlier Becontree Estate, were on sites outside its own boundaries and were often on land that had been purchased in the 1930s by Morrison or during the war by Charles Latham. By 1947, extensive new schemes had been started in Harold Hill, Aveley, Debden, Hainault, St Paul's Cray, Borehamwood and South Oxhey, the latter two in Hertfordshire, thus adding to the impression that that county was rapidly becoming an adjunct of London. Each of these was a fully integrated community in its own right, with shops, offices, industrial estates, schools, leisure facilities, bus, train, and, in some cases, underground services.[14] Between 3,000 and 7,500 homes were built in each location. The fact that all of them were within the newly designated Metropolitan Green Belt did not cause significant problems: waivers to allow development were sought and granted. In appearance these were all Howard-style garden cities, albeit on a smaller scale, and with many modernist flourishes. Most of the homes were houses, everything was mainly low-rise, and density was not high. Nor was the idea of building beyond city boundaries confined to London. In 1949, Abercrombie produced a Clyde Valley Regional Plan which advocated moving 50% of the population of Glasgow outside the city, insisting this was the only way by which local housing shortages could be speedily addressed. In the event, a compromise was struck: by the 1960s Glasgow had opted for high-rise, Le Corbusier-style blocks to meet its housing targets, and these were built within the city boundaries, albeit on sites designated as green belt.[15]

The initial impact of all these new policies in the immediate post-war years was actually quite limited: London, for instance, remained a growing city and its population would peak at 8.2 million in 1951. The public knew, though, that something had shifted and a better future was coming. Despite all the arguing about space standards, or whether development should be in traditional cities or on new garden suburb sites miles away, the February 1949 *Homes for London* exhibition, sponsored by the LCC and warmly endorsed by Bevan, was exceptionally popular.[16] A couple of years later the Festival of Britain staged, in Poplar, a Live Architecture Exhibition showcasing the best of modern design and pointing out that the alternative was inadequately regulated private housing built to a lower standard. Those venturing to the Poplar site – and nearly 87,000 did – could visit a Town Planning Pavilion and tour newly completed properties on the Lansbury Estate, a massive project specifically highlighted in Abercrombie and Forshaw's *County of London Plan*. Here new 3-bedroom flats cost £1 9s a week (£1.45p then, roughly £97.50p in 2021 prices). By the time it closed in September 1951, the Live Architecture Exhibition counted amongst its visitors 90 delegates from the International Federation of Town and Country Planning and the Duke of Edinburgh. It remained a popular example of post-war UK architecture for many years afterwards, Lewis Mumford claiming in 1953 *"...I have not looked at all that Europe has to offer since the war, but I shall be surprised if Lansbury is not one of the best bits of housing and urban planning anywhere ... the aesthetic results are remarkably good..."*[17]

* * * * * *

The final part of the Attlee government's housing triptych was the 1947 Town and Country Planning Act. This codified and regulated

UK town planning to a much greater degree than had previously been the case. It required virtually every type of development to be formally consented to via a system based on council planning committees. Most statutory bodies, and most governmental agencies retained powers to override local decisions (subject to judicial review), but in practice almost everything had to be done at local level. In time this developed into a system where there were frequent examples of schemes that were clearly desirable but were refused in some areas due to pressure on committee members from public lobbying and locally prominent campaigners. The degree of involvement by UK local politicians in planning applications after 1947 (and via that level of involvement, the degree of lobbying that they were subject to) was unprecedented compared to many other advanced economies, where, after determining priorities and setting them out in a local, borough, regional or even national plan, adjudicating on the applications was usually left to the paid employees of the state (local or national), subject to occasional legal overview. Whatever the benefits of such an intensely bureaucratic and highly politicised system, one outcome of the planning regulation operated by the UK after 1947 was that the country became noted for its protracted public enquiries into major infrastructure projects.

The 1947 Act also established a mandatory Green Belt around London and other major urban areas. Much talked about, its implementation prevented the continuation of the "ribbon development" that had been such a feature of the inter-war period and also curtailed the growth of Ramuz-style "plot lands" with their DIY bungalows and unadopted roads.[18] Both were welcome features. Less certain – over time – was why some of the land protected as "green belt" had been selected for that designation in the first place. The degree of inflexibility built into the Act was a subject of constant criticism, not all of it ill-founded.

The codifying of the planning system and the designation of a statutory green belt were both policies of which Howard would have approved, representing as they did a pushing back by the state against the *laissez-faire* liberties of the market. This was, however, as far as the Attlee government went. Absent from any legislative proposals, despite a lineage that stretched back at least 150 years, was land nationalisation. Mentioned as an objective in Labour's 1945 manifesto, it vanished from UK politics at this point, never to be revived. A proposal for a 100% levy on the profits accrued by private owners from appreciating land values was equally short-lived. One item that did survive for a while – having been invoked as a wartime measure to regulate the use of materials and manpower – was the requirement placed on private sector builders to acquire a building licence prior to developing properties for sale. This had the effect of limiting how many homes for sale were built. But, with most large-scale private construction companies carrying out contracts to build the UK's burgeoning council and new town estates it had little actual impact on their fortunes.

* * * * * *

With most of his time taken up by the establishment of the National Health Service, it is remarkable how much Bevan achieved in the housing field, and in particular how many new homes were built during his period in office. Despite restrictions on the availability of buildings materials (particularly bricks) and skilled labour, 1,192,000 new homes had been provided by 1951. This included 156,000 "prefabs". Properties built for sale amounted to 189,000, 16% of the total, with private sector completions typically varying between 25,000 and 40,000 per annum. At 148,000, council house completions in 1947 were the highest ever recorded, and were even higher between 1948 and 1951, comfortably exceeding anything achieved in the 1930s. This was despite Bevan's imposition of higher standards. Throughout this period, though, he remained under constant scrutiny and attack by the Conservatives who adopted the line that even more might have been done had space standards remained at previous levels. This was true, and had resonance with many of the electorate, particularly those who remained stuck in unsatisfactory private rented property waiting for a new council home of their own.

Bevan bridled at such criticism, and it may have led to his famous utterance in July 1948 that the Conservatives were *"lower than vermin"*.

What was significant was the shift made by the Conservatives to embrace house-building as an electorally popular policy. Their manifesto for the October 1951 general election, which reflected decisions taken at their 1950 conference at Blackpool, contained the statement *"...Housing is the first of the social services. It is also one of the keys to increased productivity. Work, family life, health and education are all undermined by overcrowded homes. Therefore, a Conservative and Unionist Government will give housing a priority second only to national defence. Our target remains 300,000 houses a year. There should be no reduction in the number of houses and flats built to let but more freedom must be given to the private builder. In a property-owning democracy, the more people who own their homes the better..."* To achieve this, they kept the structures put in place by the Attlee government, adding to them a Ministry of Housing and Local Government, something Labour had planned but failed to implement. There was a consensus at the highest levels in UK politics that housing production and improvement was something that only the state could tackle effectively. Most of Howard's vision had reached the statute books, and, remarkably, was being implemented via the generous availability of state funding. Because of this, the UK, even under a Conservative government, built more "new towns" in the 1940s and 1950s than anywhere except the Soviet Union.

Notes

(1) This can be read online at https://books.google.co.uk/books?id=rGJNAAAAMAAJ&printsec=frontcover&source=gbs_ge_summary_r&cad=0#v=onepage&q&f=false The report is notable for its reliance on experts: out of a membership of 19, there was only one politician, Megan Lloyd George, Liberal MP for Anglesey. The committee was established by Bevan's predecessor, Ernest Brown, Leader of the National Liberal Party.

(2) The comment was made in an extensive speech by Bevan in the House of Commons on 16 March 1949, which can be read in full at https://api.parliament.uk/historic-hansard/commons/1949/mar/16/housing-bill The number of interruptions is of note, and typical of how Bevan was treated by the Conservative opposition.

(3) Comments made in a letter from Osborn to Mumford, 21 October 1945. See *The Letters of Lewis Mumford and Frederic J Osborn: A Transatlantic Dialogue 1938-1970* Hughes p106-110, and also quoted in *Austerity Britain 1945-1951* Kynaston p174

(4) Around this time (April 1946) Mumford attempted, without success, to interest Osborn in the work of the Polish architects and town planners Szymon and Helena Syrkus. Fully signed up supporters of a Le Corbusier-style approach, they presided over much of the reconstruction of Warsaw after 1945.

(5) A copy of Reilly's plan can be read at https://archive.org/details/outlineplanforthecountyboroughofbirkenhead Reilly was principally an architectural theoretician and teacher. He built little of his own work, but helped design part of Lever's Port Sunlight scheme. In 1909 Lever sent him to the US to study methods of town planning there, and on his return he undertook St Barnabas Church, Shacklewell, London E8, the building for which he remains best known.

(6) In *The Collected Essays, Journalism and Letters of George Orwell Volume 4: In Front of Your Nose 1945-1950* p113-117.

(7) Given his pedigree and involvement throughout his life with Portmeirion, Williams-Ellis might have seemed an odd choice: but in the 1930s he had supported modern architecture in his book *Architecture Here and Now* (1934, with John Summerson), and given Bevan's views about modern villages may have seemed a perfect match.

(8) For a full discussion of Silkin's difficulties at Stevenage see https://core.ac.uk/download/pdf/220156737.pdf and also *Austerity Britain 1945-1951* Kynaston p161-162.

(9) In 1931 the LCC elected 83 Conservative, 35 Labour and 6 Liberal councillors. This changed in 1934 to 69 Labour and 55 Conservative. By 1937, it was 75 Labour and 49 Conservative and in 1946 it was 90 Labour, 30 Conservative, 2 Liberal and 2 Communist. It was commonly believed that Morrison pursued the construction of large municipal housing estates in areas with Conservative representation to tilt these locations electorally toward the Labour Party. There is no proof of this and the statement ascribed to Morrison (that he would *"build the Tories out of London"*) appears to be an urban myth. No evidence of it can be found prior to the 1960s: it appeared at the time the Conservative Party were replacing the LCC with the GLC. An example of this quote being attributed to Morrison is Leo McKinstry, *"Labour is stealing your country"*, *The Spectator*, 24 July 2004, p. 20. In fact, although Morrison's LCC built substantial numbers of homes, a large number were outside the County of London entirely.

(10) Felton represented St Pancras SW on the LCC, 1937-1946. After this she was chair of Peterlee New Town Corporation, where she was the subject of scurrilous rumours about her relationships with male staff. Her visit to North Korea, which was followed by her broadcasting to the UK from Moscow, was debated in the House of Commons on 14 June 1951, with calls from the Conservative ranks that she be charged with high treason (which carried the death penalty). See: https://api.parliament.uk/historic-hansard/commons/1951/jun/14/mrs-felton-visit-to-korea The tone of the debate, with much innuendo and doubt about her qualifications (she had a PhD from the London School of Economics), was deeply sexist.

(11) Although prepared to let most of the new town proposals proceed when they returned to power in 1951, the Conservatives did abandon one of the schemes, at Mobberley, Cheshire after opposition from local MP Lt Col Walter Bromley-Davenport MP. For some of the exchanges on this see: https://api.parliament.uk/historic-hansard/commons/1949/jun/28/new-town-mobberley

(12) Lubetkin's background is the subject of some debate. From Georgia, it appears that he fought in the Red Army during the Russian Civil War, after which he studied and worked in Berlin and Paris. The birth certificate that he produced to gain entry to the UK appears to have been a forgery, designed to obscure his Red Army service. For more on his design for Spa Green Estate see: https://www.locallocalhistory.co.uk/municipal-housing/spa-green/index.htm

(13) See *Austerity Britain 1945-1951* Kynaston p332 for more in this vein, from Osborn, and others. Osborn was involved in increasingly bitter disputes with both the RIBA and the LCC and by 1950 had fallen out with Mumford over density levels.

(14) Latham favoured expanding the LCC boundaries a considerable distance into the surrounding Home Counties. An entirely logical step, this reflected transport and commuting links as well as being in keeping with Abercrombie's *Greater London Plan*. Taking an independent, long-term view of this type, however, was frowned on by many of his colleagues who assumed such an expansion would cost Labour its political control. Latham resigned on 15 July 1947 "for personal reasons", being succeeded by Isaac Hayward, who had led the campaign against extending the LCC boundaries. Hayward was close to Herbert Morrison. It is interesting to speculate what might have happened had a Greater London Authority of Latham's type been established by the Attlee government.

(15) Abercrombie's report was written to counter Glasgow Corporation's *First Planning Report* (1945, written by Robert Bruce, City Engineer) which advocated a massive, Soviet-style reconstruction of Glasgow within its existing boundaries. This would have seen virtually the entire city demolished. For more on this see: https://www.glasgowlive.co.uk/news/history/soviet-bloc-glasgow-plan-17033205

(16) A film of the exhibition showing Bevan can be viewed at https://www.britishpathe.com/video/VLVA3CTFE3PIDQ8U5AIWDOM6NJ4YM-LV237/query/Bevan

(17) For a full account of the housing component of the Festival of Britain see https://www.british-history.ac.uk/survey-london/vols43-4/pp212-223

(18) The Ramuz plot-lands (and much of the inter-war ribbon development) were often built without planning consents of the type needed post-1947. All that was required to facilitate them was an agreement with the local parish vestry (or local council) on the arrangements for sewage, road access and lighting. In some areas not even this was required, particularly if what was being proposed was not deemed a permanent building: people just bought their own land and built a property, usually a chalet-style bungalow.

10

THE CONSENSUS YEARS

Harold Macmillan was 57 years old in 1951, and his appointment as Minister of Housing and Local Government was his first significant peace-time political role. After a conventional upper-class education – Eton and the Grenadier Guards – he declined to complete his degree course at Oxford, embarking instead on a political career. An admirer of Lloyd George, he was elected Conservative MP for Stockton-on-Tees in 1924, lost the seat in 1929, won it back in 1931 and remained in situ until 1945, declining the opportunity of a safer constituency and going down, inevitably by that point, to defeat in the Labour landslide. [1] Re-elected elsewhere within a few months at a convenient by-election, Macmillan's inter-war record, particularly his hostility to appeasement, commended him to Churchill, who stressed the great importance on meeting the house-building target in the Conservative manifesto, stating *"It is a gamble–it will make or mar your political career, but every humble home will bless your name if you succeed"*. This was true, in the sense that attaining any objective in politics might be a bit of a gamble, but Macmillan had many things working in his favour.

Firstly, he was able to rely during his time in office on a largely bipartisan commitment to high quality public services together with levels of personal taxation that provided more than sufficient funds for his objectives. The strain of operating a wartime command economy had increased the standard rate of income tax in the UK to 10s in the £ (50%). Attlee's government cut it to 9s (45%) in 1947, only for the Churchill administration to put it back up to 9s 6d (47.5%) five years later, a year after they took office. It remained at what today would be regarded as an extraordinarily high level until the end of the decade when it was still at 8s 6d (42.5%).[2] Secondly, the new government rowed back on the space standards Bevan had set. The size of an average 3-bedroom council house dropped from 1055 square feet in 1951, to 947 square feet in 1952 and finally to 897 square feet by the end of the decade, an overall fall of 15%.[3] Thirdly, the Churchill government increased both the speed of construction, and the number of properties built, by increasingly adopting prefabricated designs, and building proportionally more flats than houses. Fourthly, and finally, the Conservative pledge was to complete 300,000 new homes a year not, as some thought, 300,000 new council homes per year. To reach this target the private house-builders were allowed a much freer rein than they had enjoyed under Attlee and Bevan. By the decade's end they were virtually deregulated, and producing, more or less, the same volume of homes they had achieved in the 1920s and 1930s. Thus, Macmillan, with his own ministry at his disposal, met his targets because, whilst there was plenty of money available for housing, he built smaller, cheaper units and increasingly diversified into private sale.[4]

But it would be wrong to regard this as merely sleight of hand. Churchill and Macmillan presided over years of very high housing completion, and established another new town, Cumbernauld, the third in Scotland, in 1955. From 1954, additional government subsidies were provided for slum clearance, as the backlog of historic neglect in urban areas was finally tackled. Carefully compiled official statistics showed that 60% of houses in York had an outside WC, this figure rising to 90% in Sunderland. Macmillan sought to eliminate this as rapidly as possible. It would be fair to state that the period from 1945 to 1955 represented a time when both political parties were travelling in the same direction, albeit with a slightly different emphasis. What was also true was that both Bevan and Macmillan regarded the improvement of housing conditions as a priority.

It was also a period when architects' reputations were made on

the basis of their public housing work; a time when working in a
local authority architects' department had the same kind of artistic
glamour found in later years by those who designed opulent hotels,
corporate headquarters and bespoke residences for oligarchs. The
roll call of those who built the new Britain was impressive: within
the new towns were George Grenfell-Baines (Newton Aycliffe and
Peterlee), Sir Frederick Gibberd (Harlow) and Geoffrey Jellicoe
(Hemel Hempstead) whilst among those making their mark in
local councils were Philip Powell and Hidalgo Moya (Churchill
Gardens, Pimlico – a major example of inner-city clearance and
reconstruction that produced 1,600 new homes), Sir Colin Wilson
(Wyke Estate, Hackney, for the LCC and heavily influenced by Le
Corbusier) and Sir Denys Lasdun, a former colleague of Lubetkin
(Keeling House, Bethnal Green and much else).

Not everyone regarded this as progress. In particular, Frederic
Osborn, the UK's best-connected advocate of Howard's theories,
and still active throughout the 1950s and 1960s via his role with
the Town and Country Planning Association, railed against the
influence of Le Corbusier on young architects, claiming they had
gone *"...indecently, inhumanly wrong..."* He visited France to look at
Unité d'Habitation, Le Corbusier's great scheme at Marseilles,
soon after its completion, noting (in his view) its *"economic and social
absurdity, and with less amplitude... technical absurdity"*. Osborn also
found Macmillan hard to deal with, complaining in March 1953
that he had been *"stampeded by the agricultural lobby"* into building
flats rather than houses and had also stopped the development of
Congleton as a new town.[5] As evidence of this, Osborn referred
to the Ministry of Housing manual *The Density of Residential Areas*
in which Macmillan had written *"it is important to save every acre
that can be saved"*. But surely anyone aware of the physical size of
the UK in relation to its population would realise that, wouldn't
they?[6] For Osborn it was simple, people should just be given what
they want, a point he made throughout his correspondence, citing
various surveys about what the public liked and preferred. By
1954, he was campaigning to prevent development of housing at
30 units per acre (roughly the density found in urban areas today)

and pointing out how unfair it was that the housing subsidy local authorities received was £2,301 per flat, but only £845 per house. After Macmillan's exit (in October 1954, he became Minister of Defence) Osborn found his successor, Duncan Sandys, *"far more respectful... to me personally, than Macmillan was"*.

This may have been so, but it didn't stop a continued stream of Le Corbusier-inspired projects coming to fruition, including the Alton Estate in Roehampton, built by the LCC and their most ambitious project since Boundary Estate[7]; Park Hill, Sheffield opened by Macmillan, by this point Prime Minister, who proclaimed it would *"draw the admiration of the world"*[8]; and Golden Lane Estate in the City of London, notable for Great Arthur House, in appearance almost a vertical Mondrian, and, when complete, briefly the highest residential building in the UK.[9] All of these were either being designed or built by the mid-1950s, a time when being Minister of Housing was a recognised path to a successful political career, and one trodden then by Macmillan, Duncan Sandys, Keith Joseph and later by Richard Crossman and Anthony Crosland.

Nor was this just about building boxes for people to live in. The construction of new towns, new estates and new blocks was undertaken at a time when local government, and in particular the LCC, acted as a major sponsor of the arts. Many of the new developments were decorated with cutting edge pieces of sculpture or murals, the latter relatively commonplace. Artists like Victor Pasmore, for instance, worked on Peterlee New Town. The summation of this publicly funded cross-fertilisation between architecture and the wider arts came in August 1956, at the *This Is Tomorrow* exhibition at the Whitechapel Gallery. This matched architects, including Erno Goldfinger, Sir Colin Wilson, James Stirling and Alison and Peter Smithson, with sculptors, graphic designers, abstract artists, sociologists, photographers, printmakers, structural engineers and cultural critics.[10]

Most people associate *This Is Tomorrow* with Richard Hamilton's magnificent pop-art collage *Just what is it that makes today's homes so different, so appealing?* What the show was really seeking to do, though, was to integrate the provision of housing with design in general, stressing the external environment and the impact of how the public accessed information in an era of mass production. Nor was this just kite-flying by leftist intellectuals. The mainstream too embraced change. The Daily Mail Ideal Home Exhibition of 1956 included a House of the Future, as envisaged by Alison and Peter Smithson.[11] Footage of this shows something akin to a capsule, or series of interconnected pods, within which everything is operated by a remote control. A man and woman (presumably an actor and actress) are shown, both wearing the type of streamlined, figure-hugging clothing seen in 1950s science fiction films. At one point the woman shows the man what appears to be either a transparent ball gown or a négligée, presumably manufactured from a man-made fabric, in keeping with the light, carefully designed interior where everything is clean, simple and easy to maintain. No bulky wardrobes here. Context is important: a significant amount of what was shown at the exhibition emphasised space travel, rockets, and astronauts. Just 53 years after the Wright brothers took to the air for a couple of hundred yards in North Carolina, London had been bombarded by inter-continental missiles and long-distance jet travel was commonplace. Many wondered what might happen in the next 50 years: expectations were of manned space flight and cities on the moon at the very least.[12] Today, the Smithsons' House of the Future looks utopian and mildly foolish. But in 1956 it was seen as what might be typical within 5 to 10 years, given the exponential rate of technological progress in the twentieth century.

*   *   *   *   *   *

How much the wider public noticed the intellectual battles fought about housing throughout the 1940s and 1950s is a moot point. When peace came in 1945 most UK households rented privately, and many of these shared kitchens and bathrooms with other families. Much of the UK's housing stock was in poor condition and owner-occupation remained the privilege of a minority. Most of the country's larger cities exhibited war damage, London to a considerable degree, where vacant, cleared sites remained common for another 20 years. What people experienced, and surely noticed, were the practical effects of a significant housing shortage.

As early as 1945 there was an organised squatting campaign, involving 300 families who moved into empty mansion flats in Bloomsbury and Kensington.[13] Government action followed swiftly – targeting those who advocated such activity – and the official view remained that the public should await the arrival of new homes at whatever speed was possible. Thankfully, and due to the efforts of Bevan and Macmillan, in the years that followed completions accelerated. Indeed, in the two decades after 1945 4.473m new homes were built (nearly three-quarters by local authorities and new towns) a rate of building that was, on average, approximately four times that achieved from the mid-nineteenth century through to 1914.[14] Many of these were provided in suburbs or garden cities/new towns. Trying slowly to fill in the bomb-damaged gaps in inner cities was very unfashionable, and in truth more expensive.[15] Thus, many of the households rehoused after 1945 were offered brand new properties in an area that was often some distance from where they lived. But, contrary to many prevailing urban myths, people *were* offered a choice. And the choice might be either to remain in their existing home, and if that home was one requisitioned and managed by the local authority under wartime powers possibly buy it from the council[16], or to stay wherever they were until a new home became available for them in their current location, or to move to a new home provided much more quickly in a different area. Nor did moving to a new area have the same dislocating factors that came later: the two decades after 1945 were a period of almost continuous full employment, with the lowest ever unemployment figures (185,000) being announced in July 1955.

In terms of what the public saw, an important factor in their experience, they would have noticed that, as local authorities implemented the new legislation and drove forward their own building programmes, they emulated the design and layout of the new towns, creating many other miniature garden suburb and garden city schemes across the UK.[17] As with the "official" new towns a great many of these addressed the increase in car ownership by adopting the "Radburn" design for positioning blocks and terraces that had so interested Howard at the time of his death. Along with the typical Howardesque design features of playing fields, allotments, grass verges, large cultivated flower beds and properties often "set-back" a considerable distance from the nearest pavement, this meant living in an environment with a very considerable amount of open space. Whether people ever really wanted this, or not, isn't clear. Certainly, they wanted new homes, and in an area where there was employment. They may, though, have been just as happy living in an early LCC-style cottage estate, or something akin to a Cameron Corbett development, rather than somewhere with a density level derived from nineteenth-century US suburban housing. The public, however, weren't consulted and the long-term maintenance issues of so much open space remained an undiscussed issue for decades.[18]

One effect of the policies that had been advocated by William Morris and endorsed/embellished via Howard, Abercrombie and Osborn was that the UK's traditional cities and urban areas suffered a sharp (and deliberate) depopulation for decades after 1945, as millions of people were energetically relocated out of them by central and local government. The population of London, for instance, fell by 25% between 1945 and 1985. The horror expressed by Morris, Howard and others at the urban conditions they saw in the nineteenth century suggests that they would have deemed this a good thing. Certainly, the award of a knighthood to Osborn in 1956 reflected a strong "establishment" endorsement for this approach. But, by the end of the 1950s, Osborn was fighting off an attempt by property developers to take over the trust that ran Letchworth: reliable governance, it will be recalled, had always been a weak point in Howard's plan. Nor was that all. Lewis Mumford, a long-standing friend of Osborn, visited the UK in 1953 and 1957 and considered that the new towns were too open, wasteful of space and lacking in variety. In 1957 he commented "...

the New Towns had not gone beyond the planning principles of Letchworth or Welwyn and had, indeed, been bound down by an arbitrary set of space standards to be nothing other than a more extensive and voluminous reproduction of these earlier efforts..." If Mumford, who was far from being the type of revolutionary modernist who usually derided garden cities, felt that about Stevenage, Harlow and their ilk, it was hardly surprising that the intellectual climate within which debate on housing and planning took place remained ambivalent, at best, toward Osborn and his views.

In 1963, at the age of 78, Osborn produced a riposte of sorts to this criticism, publishing, with Arnold Whittick, *The New Towns: The Answer to Megalopolis*.[19] This suggested that, however poorly executed some of the new town/garden suburb ideas had been, they were still preferable to "Megalopolis": the conjoined urban/suburban sprawl that linked many adjoining US cities and was particularly observable along the Boston-New York-Washington corridor. This remained true (the UK then remained nothing like the US) but a cynic might have pointed out that the Letchworth-Hitchin-Stevenage-Welwyn route was not dissimilar, albeit on a smaller scale, and was, on that basis, a conjoined mini-megalopolis within Hertfordshire. The same year found Osborn admitting "*... there are powerful pressures... for further increases of density. They come from (a) the shortage of land in old cities (b) from the architectural obsession with the phony concept of 'urbanity' coupled with the artists boredom of love of gimmicks and (c) from the agricultural and country preservationist obsession with 'saving land'*" Mumford, in correspondence with him, said that the layout of Letchworth and Welwyn "*required a change in the pattern of density if the essential virtues of a small city were still to be preserved and furthered*" and pointed out that he hadn't noticed this when visiting both in 1932.[20] It was a powerful argument. Could a low-density environment of that type contain enough people to pay for the provision of the services that the population of the area required? What would happen if circumstances changed, and the funding were no longer available?

Notes

(1) Whilst considering whether to recontest Stockton-on-Tees in 1930, Macmillan narrowly failed to get selected as the Conservative candidate in Hitchin, the seat that encompassed Stevenage. Had he been the MP there in 1945, would he have stopped the scheme? In the late 1930s he held the view that the best type of government for the UK at that point would have been a Labour-led coalition, within which some Conservatives and Liberals could have served.

(2) This compares with tax levels of 6s (30%) in 1919, and 5s (25%) in 1938. The UK's standard rate of income tax in 2021 is 20%: a level it was last at between 1926 and 1930.

(3) These remained far greater than the space standards used by the LCC when building its cottage estates in the 1920s and 1930s, which were enduringly popular. They are also significantly higher than those used by most private sector house-builders in recent years.

(4) Macmillan still built more local authority housing than anyone before, or since, peaking at 262,000 homes in both 1953 and 1954. By 1955 private house-building had recovered to something like its pre-war levels, and by 1959 there were, annually, more private sector homes being completed than local authority/new town homes. The rebooting of private house-building followed the abolition, in 1953-1954 of the complex system of post-1945 licences that had overseen private development. A 100 per cent tax on the profits of property development was abolished at the same time.

(5) Macmillan inherited two proposals for new towns, in Congleton and Mobberley. Both were in Conservative-held constituencies. (The MP for Congleton was Arthur Vere Harvey). He rejected both proposals in 1953-1954.

(6) Pre-1939 the UK imported the majority of its food. It had come close to being starved into submission by a German U-boat blockade in 1916-1917. Achieving as much agricultural self-sufficiency as possible was thus regarded as an important national requirement. Macmillan's comments should be seen in this context.

(7) Like Osborn the LCC architects' department (which employed 250 people alone on housing projects) had made a pilgrimage to Marseilles to look at Le Corbusier's masterpiece. Alton Estate, built 1951-1961, was the outcome. See: https://historicengland.org.uk/listing/the-list/list-entry/1466474

(8) See: http://midcenturymagazine.com/architecture/the-park-hill-estate-brutalist-icon/ Park Hill was built on a site previously occupied by back-to-back housing with shared outside lavatories.

(9) Density on Golden Lane Estate (79 homes per acre) is massively greater than anything planned or deemed acceptable by either Howard (who was born very close to the site) or Osborn. It is also approximately 40 times that found at Greenbelt, Maryland. Golden Lane, in the Cripplegate area, served as a prototype for the slightly later Barbican Estate. See: https://www.youtube.com/watch?v=AM2yw7hNyLI

(10) Whilst most of those exhibiting at *This Is Tomorrow* were from the UK, the show also had contributors from Italy, Russia, Hungary, the US, South Africa, Guyana and Ecuador.

(11) The Smithsons were employed in the LCC architects' department. The Exhibition is shown at https://www.youtube.com/watch?v=AY7oAPT7QXs and footage of their House of the Future can be seen at https://www.youtube.com/watch?v=CudemgNQqMs

(12) There were indeed plans to do just that. See *Basic Criteria for Moon Building*

John S. Rinehart *Journal of the British Interplanetary Society, Vol. 17,* September-October 1959 P126-129. Arthur C Clarke, a long-term member of the British Interplanetary Society, set the plot of his 1951 novel *The Sands of Mars* on a man-built city on Mars. The novel takes place in the 1990s, implying that the city itself had been built possibly a decade earlier.

(13) For more on this see: https://pasttenseblog.wordpress.com/2016/09/10/today-in-londons-housing-history-ivanhoe-hotel-squatted-bloomsbury-1946/ This notes, though, *"There were no actual evictions. The squatters mostly went to a 'rest centre' organised by the London County Council, from where they were eventually rehoused".* The brief squatting campaign in London at that time was organised by Ted Bramley, Communist LCC member for Stepney, Mile End.

(14) Figures taken from the *English Housing Survey 2015*

(15) There were builders who did this work, notably Day (Contractors) Ltd (run by a Mr Arthur Cattle) who built 1049 flats and houses on small sites, almost all in Islington, between 1955 and 1972. Of these 127 were purchased on completion by Islington, the remainder were sold privately, on long leases. Plots were purchased for very small sums from absent owners or from the local authority, in the latter case after they had been demolished and cleared. Properties were built to Ministry of Housing standards. As can be seen, the speed at which these homes were produced (approximately 60 a year) was far below that at which local authorities built. See *The Story of Day Flats in and around Islington* A Bosi 2001.

(16) The author is aware of instances, in the mid-1950s in Hackney, where households renting in properties requisitioned by the council were offered (and refused) the chance to buy them for £700, preferring instead a secure tenancy on the nearby Pembury Estate. In fact, as demonstrated in Colin Jones and Alan Murie *The Right to Buy* (2006), local authorities had always been obliged to sell certain types of property, and the notion that this began in 1980 via Margaret Thatcher is false.

(17) A process that continued down to the 1970s. A late example was the scheme developed by Essex County Council from 1972 on a ramshackle earlier "plotlands" site at South Woodham Ferrers. Very much in keeping with Howard's vision this created a low-density new town (in all but name) with separate shopping, employment and residential areas. In a very 1970s gesture, many of the new streets and roads in the development were named after characters in J R R Tolkien's *The Lord of the Rings.*

(18) See *Family Britain 1951-1957* David Kynaston p273-283 and p635-639 quoting various sources.

(19) Written as a riposte to Ivan Gottman's *Megalopolis: The Urbanized Northeastern Seaboard of the United States* (1961).

(20) See *The Letters of Lewis Mumford and Frederic J Osborn: A Transatlantic Dialogue 1938-1970* Ed Michael Hughes London (1971) Letter from Mumford to Osborn 3 July 1963.

11

DIVERGENT VIEWS

The consensus in the UK about housing, broadly a synthesis of the approaches taken by Bevan and Macmillan, seemed, by the mid-1950s, a solid and lasting feature of domestic politics. It was predicated on a commitment by the government (of whichever stripe) to provide sufficient housing for the population, and to raise sufficient money in taxes to enable this to be carried out.[1] What the public got from this approach was a mixture of garden cities in the guise of new towns, garden suburbs, overspill estates and urban flats, built by the combined might of the government, local government and the private sector. There was a huge role for the state, at all levels. It was a multi-track approach that worked well, with cheerleaders and detractors for all options.

One man with a foot in both camps was Michael Young, co-author of the 1945 Labour manifesto, who by the mid-1950s had switched to sociological research with a bias toward consumer protection. In 1957, he and his colleague Peter Willmott published *Family and Kinship in East London*. An astonishingly popular work, it ran to 14 editions, easily a record for a book of that type, became a standard text in planning, housing, family and sociology studies and was quoted from, approvingly, by government ministers. Its big message was that the mass housing programmes of the time were likely to end in failure, because the new homes, many of which were flats, were less popular than the houses that local people vacated. It also made a fair point about the breaking up of long-standing social networks when an area was demolished and the population moved.

In practical terms the book studied households and individuals from Bethnal Green that had moved to the LCC mini-new town estate at Debden, Essex, disguised as "Greenleigh" in the text. Based on interviews conducted with residents, Willmott and Young pointed out that there were fewer facilities (shops, public houses, cinemas) per capita in Debden than in Bethnal Green and that community cohesion generally was lower. This was despite a finding that *"Our couples left two or three damp rooms built in the last century for the 'industrious classes', and were suddenly transported to a spacious modern home".* [2] Noting that the LCC charged higher rents than the owners of most of the homes in Bethnal Green that their correspondents had vacated, they ended up arguing that maintaining multi-generation families close together was a good thing, and that the inner-city homes they vacated should be refurbished, rather than demolished, to continue that traditional sense of community. They also made the telling point about why this was not evident in Debden in the first place: *"One reason it is taking so long is that the estate is so strung out – the number of people per acre at Greenleigh being only one-fifth what it is in Bethnal Green – and low density does not encourage sociability."* [3]

None of this was a ringing endorsement of Howard's and Osborn's views about garden cities. But a lot of what Willmott and Young were saying was debatable, even at the time. To begin with, social networks everywhere were fraying by the mid 1950s, principally due to the impact of television (more people staying indoors in the evening) and to a lesser degree because of higher educational standards and an increase, generally, in social mobility. When young people upgraded from factory work to clerical or even managerial employment they often moved away from their original neighbourhood and acquired a different circle of friends. Secondly, moving from Bethnal Green to Debden was hardly an immense disruption. The LCC estate had been designed around a newly opened tube station on the Central Line, 27 minutes from Bethnal Green, and the area was served by three London Transport bus routes despite being outside the LCC boundaries. [4] Willmott and Young's preferred alternative – staying in London

E2 – was certainly feasible, but implied building even more homes in an area that was already noted for its density. It also ignored practicalities: many of the households who moved to Debden came out of properties where a grandparent was living in the living room, the mother and father had one bedroom and several children managed with whatever was left. The multi-generational household, with its overcrowding and lack of privacy might have sustained certain social networks, but it wasn't necessarily a healthy option.

In 1960 Willmott and Young followed up their earlier success with *Family and Class in a London Suburb*. As with their earlier book, this was based on sample interviews conducted in Bethnal Green and, in this case, the suburb of Wanstead and Woodford.[5] After examining family and community life, social mobility and social status, it endorsed the view that the traditional suburb was a friendly location. As with *Family and Kinship in East London* this wasn't what Osborn, his colleagues in the Town and Country Planning Association and most professionals particularly wanted to hear.[6] At the time Osborn noted, rather glumly, that Willmott and Young had *"started New Town blues"*,[7] even if his own views remained unchanged. Nor did he confine himself to the UK in proselytising these. The UK's policy of building new towns was widely studied, often in surprising places, with Osborn stating in 1958 *"...I have had a lot of correspondence with the USSR Ministry of Construction. They have fully adopted the Dispersal and Green Belt policy which they think they can operate more logically than Britain..."*

It isn't clear who Osborn was speaking to in this context – presumably not Nikolai Aleksandrovitch Dygai, Minister of Construction, Deputy Chairman of the Council of Ministers and Candidate Member of the Politburo – but more likely lower-ranking officials, asking generalised questions about the UK's policy of moving people out of its main urban centres. Unlike the episode half a century earlier when Lenin might have gone to, but almost certainly didn't go to, Letchworth, this contact actually happened. Why were the enquiries being made? Did the USSR really need advice from the Town and Country Planning Association? They didn't, and the most probable reason they were seeking such "advice" was to check that the USSR's dispersal policy, which was designed to preserve its population, and industrial capacity, in the event of a thermonuclear war, was consistent with anything the UK had, given its plethora of US bases. Certainly, Dygai's public announcements throughout this period were closely monitored by the CIA, notably at the 10 July 1962 meeting (in Moscow) of the World Congress for General Disarmament and Peace.[8] For his part, and despite this sudden swerve into geopolitics, Osborn remained consistent and continued to advocate the policies that had attracted him to Howard, Letchworth and Welwyn decades earlier. By 1961 – looking at future population predictions – he was suggesting that rather than have the population of London *"swell by two or three million"* government planners should build new garden cities further and further afield, to which both people and industry should be relocated.

Despite Willmott and Young's books, this was something that still commanded government support. Following in the path of Bevan and Macmillan came Keith Joseph, appointed Minister for Housing and Local Government by Macmillan on 13 July 1962 as part of a wide-ranging reshuffle of the government. Joseph had been elected MP for Leeds North East only six years previously, and his family ran the construction company Bovis (he himself had been its chair, though he resigned this position on becoming Minister) [9] and could be said to have done very well out of the post-war building boom. Bovis, like their competitors, were interested in diversifying away from building traditional homes with traditional materials. It was during Joseph's tenure that high-rise residential towers, often assembled from factory-manufactured components, became common. Part of the rationale for going down this route was economic: to produce more homes for less money during a time when taxation was being cut. Macmillan was aware of the ongoing importance of housing as a political issue and wanted an annual target of 400,000 new homes per annum by 1965, most of which were to be provided by local authorities and new town corporations.

To meet these objectives six new towns were established between 1961 and 1964: Skelmersdale, Telford, Redditch, Runcorn, Washington and Livingston. A further four new town-style developments that were not centrally directed by the government were also sanctioned: Cramlington, Killingworth, Daventry and Tamworth. The first of these, Cramlington, was private sector-led, an indication of how a move away from purely statist solutions was now deemed possible. A further example of this mixed market approach was Joseph's wish to increase the proportion of owner-occupied homes by offering first-time buyers help with mortgage deposits. Significantly, the four 'non-new town' new towns were all smaller and took longer to complete than state-run projects.[10]

The continued commitment by the government, and local councils, to a substantial programme of new towns and estates in what were formerly agricultural areas created other issues too. Whilst it was easy for the LCC in 1935 to plan Debden around a new tube station, replicating this type of access on the outskirts of a city elsewhere, proved problematic. In terms of public transport, particularly railways, a criticism can be made that the approach to providing this infrastructure for the post-1945 new towns was somewhat disjointed. Of the state-run new towns, Livingston, Skelmersdale and Washington remain (in 2021) inaccessible by rail[11] whilst five others, Cwmbran, Corby, Newton Aycliffe, Basildon and Telford all waited over 20 years for a train station, and Glenrothes (44 years) and Peterlee (56 years), even longer.[12] It does seem very chaotic today to be building what were effectively new cities without some kind of rail link. One clue as to why that occurred may be the axiomatic view held by many then that car ownership would always increase, and, indeed, that it was desirable that it should be maximised. Which is not to say that there weren't extravagant plans for an alternative: a monorail was intended to serve Washington, County Durham and in a burst of immense optimism a hovercraft service was considered too, linking various destinations (including Peterlee) between Newcastle and Middlesbrough. Neither was provided.[13]

Part of the reason for the increase in car ownership was also related to the low density of the new towns: the lower the density, and the greater the surrounding space, the further a household were from shops, schools or work and the harder it was not to have a car. This clearly couldn't have been envisaged by Howard in the 1890s when he first set out his proposals. But by the 1930s (and the blossoming car-orientated environment shown in Lewis Mumford's *The City*) it ought to have been clear to Osborn, and his followers, that low density would, of itself, contribute significantly toward an escalation in car ownership even if nothing else did. The virtues of slightly more congested traditional town centres should have been considered. That they weren't was noted by Mumford in 1964 when he commented to Osborn *"...for you there is only one tolerable density, and therefore only one type of ideal town: that which, though it has all the other desirable attributes of a genuine city, is laid out on the pattern of the best nineteenth-century suburbs..."*

As a definition of where Osborn's views stood then, this wasn't quite accurate. If anything, they were even more conservative than Mumford pointed out. Whilst it was true that low density remained his ideal, even where this applied Osborn was still capable of considerable criticism, noting about Cumbernauld in 1965 *"...and its skilful propagandists have done a lot of harm to the housing standards of the later new towns..."* Was this true? Eventually reaching a population of about 51,000, spread across 8 square miles (10 people per acre, or roughly an average of 3-4 homes per acre), Cumbernauld was well within, and even lower, than the standards set by Howard half a century earlier. What Osborn really disliked about it was the importation of modernist design quirks, notably an avant-garde shopping centre built of concrete that looked like nothing so much as a crashed space ship in the middle of a Scottish new town. It was linked to the surrounding residential areas by pedestrian pathways so that residents could walk safely to and from it without encountering any road traffic. However, this did not mean that Cumbernauld was expected by its designers to be a place where the motor car had a peripheral role. On the contrary. A giant motorway system was built to allow access to all parts of the development, and the residential areas were designed to accommodate 100% car ownership, something no town in the UK has ever achieved, with an abundance of lock-up garages and parking spaces being provided.

Cumbernauld was an early attempt to marry the concept of the new town with urban living whilst coping with the inexorable rise of road traffic. How much did Osborn understand this? The space standards were fine, and, if any criticism could be made, it would be that the abundance of concrete, and generally brutal appearance of the shopping centre, didn't wear well, not least because of the Scottish climate. Cumbernauld had a grand opening in May 1967 (via Princess Margaret and Lord Snowdon) and with its combination of wide dual carriageways and the UK's first indoor shopping mall, was much acclaimed, even being likened to a visionary work by Leonardo da Vinci. But it was also very American, and a pointer to what would come a little later in Milton Keynes. This is where Howardism led in practice, the creation of an environment where the car was king, and the irony – not foreseen by anyone – was that this was enabled on a massive scale in the UK by the provision of substantial state funding, something Howard had always tried to avoid.

To be fair, other countries followed this path too, even if none built as much as the UK. A 1967 study of Dublin, for instance, proposed surrounding the city with four low-density satellite towns, of 60,000 to 100,000 each, over a period of 18 years at a cost of £1bn. Furthermore, although the UK produced Cumbernauld, a kind of garden city-modernist hybrid, and increasingly embraced the private sector as a provider, it was in the US, nearly a century after Howard had first encountered low-density new towns, that its ultimate development would be most clearly seen.

Here, arguably the most thorough attempts at trying to devise a perfect environment for living and working were made by Walt Disney. By the late 1940s, with his studio awash from the profits generated by a string of hugely successful animation features, Disney's time was increasingly spent on trying to build a planned community. To this end he made an extensive study of the writings of both Howard and Le Corbusier.[14] Disneyland (built 1954-1955) was, of course, the most obvious example of his endeavours, but his interest in the subject was actually quite pronounced, and throughout the 1950s he promoted the use of various monorail and "people mover" designs as well as – like the Smithsons – dabbling in speculation about how mankind would evolve in the near future, with the advent of space flight.[15]

In housing, Disney's most widely seen product was the Monsanto House of the Future, a prototype of which appeared in Orlando, Florida in 1957. Designed by Marvin Goody and Richard Hamilton[16] and built almost entirely of plastic, this was a cross-shaped dwelling ("*Conventional plan is a T-shape*") that was elevated above ground level and perched on top of a broad column. The possibility of tailoring the design to individual requirements was recognised with an explanatory brochure proclaiming "*Futuristic models sprout wings where you need them*" and "'*Mansion' may look like this*". Each came with a car port. The interior of the standard model contained 1,250 square feet of living space, equivalent to most conventional 4-bedroom houses, and was packed, like the Smithsons' House of Tomorrow, with labour-saving gadgets. Being plastic throughout, most of the surfaces could be wiped clean. Lightweight, intended for mass-production and brightly coloured, this was pop-housing for the future, from the same people (Monsanto) who provided Agent Orange for use in Vietnam and later pioneered genetically modified crops. It seems that Disney intended to roll this, or something like this, out as part of his Experimental Prototype Community of Tomorrow (EPCOT), but none was ever built for commercial use. Nor did EPCOT ever come to fruition, despite the efforts made by Disney to build a massive ski resort at Mineral King, California, from 1966.[17]

All of Disney's plans were low density, depended on high levels of car use, and belonged best in a huge country with an abundance of space. Although he may have failed to build a major residential scheme, developments of this type were common throughout the US. Reston, Virginia where a new town took shape from 1964, was typical of these. Car-orientated, privately funded and just outside the Washington DC "beltway" this was intended to provide a self-

The striking, Le Corbusier-inspired Loughborough Estate, Brixton. Much admired by John Betjeman, it was one of thousands of new housing projects built after 1945 in inner-city areas.

Peterlee New Town, Durham. The abundance of funding for housing between 1945 and 1979 also allowed for experimentation in design.

Harold Macmillan
opens another house.
As Minister of Housing
and Local Government
between 1951 and 1954
nobody built more
homes than Macmillan.

Radical views of how we would shortly be living included the Monsanto House
of the Future, which could be visited at Disneyland, California from 1957.
Walt Disney was a great admirer of Ebenezer Howard.

Nowhere in the UK embraced the modernist ethos after 1945 more than T Dan Smith's Newcastle. This is Bewick Court, a residential tower built directly over a dual carriageway road cutting through the city centre.

Seifert's masterpiece: Centre Point. Not just an enormous office block, the scheme also provided residential flats, shops, community space and a new entrance to Tottenham Court Road Station on a very difficult, small site.

Goldfinger's masterpiece: Trellick Tower. Its initial problems would not have arisen if the GLC had agreed his plan for a concierge.

Ronan Point, Freemasons Road, London E16. Its partial collapse in 1968, due to poor workmanship and inadequate regulation, brought to the fore opponents of the postwar state commitment to social housing.

None of the criticisms made about modern housing and tower blocks was ever applied to the City of London's Barbican Estate, which remains a popular development.

After Ronan Point there was a move back to lower rise council housing. But there was still room for innovation via schemes like Robin Hood Gardens.

Milton Keynes: one of the last, and easily the most Americanised of the new towns. Popular with its residents, it continues to expand.

Michael Heseltine arrives in Liverpool.

Emerging economies plan their cities differently. This is Shenzhen, an hour's drive from Hong Kong.

Poundbury, Dorset. Much favoured by Prince Charles and typical of the kind of edge-of-town development found across the UK.

Selected parts of the UK, like North Acton here, are developing clusters of towers like the great cities of Asia as the twenty-first century progresses... but without any overall central planning.

contained urban environment for mainly well-to-do citizens. The architecture included some moderately high-rise residential blocks, but density, at 6 people per acre (roughly 1-2 homes), was absurdly low and beneath anything even Howard or Osborn would have recommended.[18]

The continued proliferation of out-of-town developments, all designed to be commutable from established urban areas, and the rapidity with which this trend occurred attracted the attention of leading US planners and theoreticians, notably the RAND Corporation, and the Hudson Institute. Both were strategic think-tanks that offered solutions to a range of issues affecting the US government, albeit many of these were primarily concerned with military matters. Herman Kahn was involved with both and with Anthony J Wiener authored *Crisis and Arms Control* in 1962. Five years later they followed this up with *The Year 2000: A Framework for Speculation on the Next Thirty-Three Years*, in which the huge expanse of residential, business and industrial development linking Boston, Massachusetts with Washington DC via New York City was noted and its massive future aggregation named, rather jokily, Boswash.[19] The remainder of their book predicted future technological developments in much the same way that Disney or the Smithsons might have done: computers, mobile phones, satellites in Earth orbit, space travel and so on. But not all of this was benign. Kahn, who worked for RAND from 1947 to 1961 before leaving to set up the Hudson Institute, was highly regarded for his studies of how the US could be best placed to survive a nuclear war. As with the dialogue between Osborn and the USSR Ministry of Construction, dispersing a country's population as widely as possible, rather than concentrating it in a couple of large easy targets such as "Boswash", was considered by political and military figures a much better option, and one they were happy to take advice about from experts. In Kahn's case, displayed most clearly in his work *On Thermonuclear War* (1960) concepts such as a Doomsday Machine and the use of mineshafts as long-term nuclear shelters for the select few are introduced. It was a key text in the preparation of Stanley Kubrick's 1963 film *Dr Strangelove*.[20]

In later years Kahn pondered topics such as over-population and a collapse of the world economy caused by various factors (pollution, food shortages, depletion of natural resources) and firmly discounted both, expecting, by the 1980s, cities on the Moon followed by colonisation across suitable bits of the solar system in the decades that followed. Like most nineteenth-century and early-to-mid-twentieth-century thinkers, he tended toward the boundlessly optimistic. A good comparator might be HG Wells. In this respect he was similar to Howard, even though – like his Soviet counterparts – he saw the usefulness of low-density, residential "dispersal" schemes in terms of enabling much of a country to survive a nuclear holocaust. It is an extraordinary quirk of history, given the fact that many of those to whom Howard pitched his ideas in the 1890s were religiously inclined progressives, pacifists and so on, that their application should have been sought for such destructive means.

* * * * * *

In the meantime, and pretty much divorced from speculation about the future, most people continued to live in long-established towns and cities. And, in so far as innovation and new ways of living were concerned, that is where noticeable changes occurred. The first supermarkets in the UK both appeared in London, in Manor Park (near a Cameron Corbett estate) and Croydon in 1948 and 1950 respectively. The providers were long-established purveyors of groceries, the Co-op and Sainsbury's, and their decision to embrace this form of high-volume retail was quite simple: the numbers of customers living in the immediate vicinity of their stores made them commercially viable. In contrast, new towns, with their lower density and dispersed populations, continued to opt for "parades" of traditional shops, as Bevan had so warmly endorsed several years earlier.

The spread of more and more Howard-Osborn type developments, whether new towns, large local authority estates or private sector schemes that aped both of these was not without its critics, and by the mid-1950s a backlash against "English Vernacular" architecture was underway. In June 1955, Ian Nairn, an early observer of how architecture and planning were rapidly changing the UK landscape, commented in the *Architectural Review* "*...By the end of the century Great Britain will consist of isolated oases of preserved monuments in a desert of wire, concrete roads, cosy plots and bungalows... Upon this new Britain the Review bestows a name in the hope that it will stick... SUBTOPIA...*" As with all predictions of this type, this was both unduly negative and only partly true. What did emerge was a symbiotic relationship between the two different housing models, with one (the new towns) sucking population from the other (the older towns/cities), to its advantage, thus creating a terrain in the abandoned areas where it was easier to build modernist avant-garde schemes, and cultural riches (clubs, galleries, arts cinemas, niche bookshops, small theatres and so on) thrived in low rent surroundings.[21] Much of the latter was helped on its way by the 1956 Housing Subsidies Act, which gave three times more government subsidy for a flat in a block up to 15 floors high, than it did for a house. It became better value for local authorities to build blocks of flats.

What emerged, from this possibility of a virtual *tabula rasa* in selected inner-city areas, was an imaginative and visually striking series of high-rise schemes, the most celebrated practitioners of which at the time were Richard Seifert and Erno Goldfinger. Both had a European background (Seifert, Swiss; Goldfinger, Hungarian), both were influenced by Gropius, the Bauhaus and Le Corbusier, both favoured high-density urban living and both came to public prominence around 1960, when spectacular, and very tall, buildings began to blossom across London: the Shell Centre, the Post Office Tower, the Empress State Building, Millbank Tower and the Hilton Hotel.[22]

Of the two Seifert was the most prolific, and in purely financial terms, the most successful. Working with the LCC to improve the cluttered five-way road junction at the southern end of Tottenham Court Road, he obtained planning permission for Centre Point, a mixed-use office-residential development, in 1960. When complete the GLC acquired the freehold, and the developer, Harry Hyams, was granted a lease for 150 years.[23] Regarded as *"a notable example of Le Corbusier style planning in London"* it was later listed on the basis of having *"the elegance of a Wren steeple"*. For Goldfinger it was *"...London's first pop-art skyscraper..."* and was certainly noted for its scale, juxtaposition with smaller, traditional buildings and how much Seifert got onto a small site, whatever notoriety it had as an empty building in later years. Seifert's practice followed it with Space House, in Covent Garden, another Hyams project[24] but in many ways his signature scheme was probably Tolworth Tower. Built in a low-density traditional UK suburb criss-crossed by arterial roads this was an immensely tall mixed-use retail-office development, with the ground floor occupied, unusually for the time, by a supermarket.[25] It really was, whatever one thought of the architecture, a very Americanised environment when it opened in 1963, and made a huge impact visually, and culturally, on its surroundings.

In the tradition of Gropius and William Morris, Goldfinger was an all-round designer, whose work included shop fronts, furniture and exhibition materials. He was commissioned by the LCC in 1963 to design two residential buildings, Balfron Tower and Carradale House on a cleared site adjoining the motorway-width northern approach road to the Blackwall Tunnel. They were a prelude to what remains his masterpiece, Trellick Tower, designed from 1966 and opened by the GLC in 1972. An immensely strong structure, with 217 dwellings over 31 floors, this was briefly the tallest residential building in Europe.[26] Both schemes were built with reinforced concrete, poured on site, and both – like the very first examples of social housing at Lower Road, Pentonville and Old Pancras Road over a century earlier – were built on marginal land. In this case, not long-hidden, culverted rivers or space left over after the building of a railway terminus, but demolished sites adjoining newly completed urban motorways.

Such opportunities became common after the publication in 1960 of the White Paper *Traffic in Towns*. This looked at the problems caused by increasing car ownership in an urban environment and proposed an immense motorway construction programme, around and through existing towns and cities, to accommodate this. For various reasons relatively few examples of these were built, and those that were usually ended up being less extensive than envisaged in the report. In London, the greatest example, and one which swept past Trellick Tower, was the Westway. This provided a motorway-width connection between central London and the A40, the main route from London to Oxford, south Wales, and central Wales. To achieve its objective, minimise demolition and save on costs, it was built at roof height between Edgware Road and White City, making it (at 2.7 miles) the longest continuous elevated structure in Europe. Even with minimal disruption, this required the acquisition of a wide corridor of land along the route. The compulsory purchase of affected properties began in 1962 and eventually 3,356 people were moved. Not everything acquired was demolished though; some remained standing and were either left derelict or let on a short-term basis. Finally opened in July 1970 by John Peyton, Minister for Transport and his junior minister Michael Heseltine, it cost £30m to build (roughly £500m in contemporary prices) of which 25% was met by the GLC and the remainder by the government. It certainly eased traffic congestion initially, but a longer-term legacy of its construction was the wasteland that remained beneath the elevated section for many years afterwards for which the government had neglected to have any plans.[27]

Outside of London the most famous exponent of remodelling traditional cities via a combination of motorway building, demolition and new high-rise housing was T Dan Smith, the powerful leader of Newcastle City Council.[28] Examples of such work within his "domain" included Trinity Square, Gateshead, a 1967 mixed-use scheme combining retail units and multi-storey car park (famed for its appearance in the 1971 film *Get Carter*) and Byker Wall, built from 1969. The latter, like Trellick Tower, was designed to adjoin an urban motorway, albeit one that, in this case, was never completed. Consisting of 620 maisonettes in one long sinuous block resembling a city wall, its architect Ralph Erskine had actually worked on schemes at Welwyn Garden City in the late 1930s, prior to embracing modernism in Sweden throughout the 1940s and 1950s.[29] The most striking example, though, of the architectural licence that reigned in Smith's Newcastle must surely be Bewick Court, a residential tower block in the city centre itself, built in 1970 by Taylor Woodrow, entirely on massive concrete supports above a dual carriageway-width main road. As an example of making the best use of scarce resources it could scarcely be bettered, floating as it does on air.

Almost every urban area in the UK had examples of modern, flatted council housing built during this period. Most were robust, long-serving and spacious, and many survive today, having given immense service to their local communities. Others were controversial even at the time. Just south of Goldfinger's Balfron Tower Alison and Peter Smithson were commissioned by the GLC to build a new estate on another marginal site directly alongside the motorway-width approach road to the Blackwell Tunnel. In their case this was land cleared by the demolition of Grosvenor Buildings, 500 pre-1900 dwellings that were now deemed unfit for human habitation. They replaced it with Robin Hood Gardens, their only complete estate, containing 213 "brutalist" flats, built using a significant amount of concrete. It is interesting to note in this instance how modernism actively reduced density in a kind of micro-example of London being remodelled to fit increasing numbers of motor vehicles as its population decreased. Throughout the 1960s, with significant funding available, there were many other examples of innovative projects: Kenneth Frampton's Corringham Building in 1962, Eric Lyons's Pitcairn House for the LCC in Hackney 1963 and Kate Macintosh's Dawson's Heights in Southwark, from 1964. The largest, though, would be the City of London Corporation's Barbican Estate. Built from 1965, by the same team that had completed the adjoining Golden Lane Estate a few years earlier, this was a large, dense, mixed-use development containing 2,000 homes. Ironically part of it was built across Fore Street – Ebenezer Howard's birthplace – and with a density of 57 homes per acre (nearly 37,000 per square mile) it was the polar opposite of what he would have wanted. The scheme included a trio of residential towers, 42 floors high. They were approved at a point when the spread of high-rise buildings across London caused some concern, and was even briefly banned by George Brown MP (Minister for Economic Affairs) in 1964, though an exception was made for both these and the new residence of the Household Cavalry at Hyde Park Barracks.[30]

* * * * * *

From the mid-1950s there was a move to save money and loosen some of the post-1945 regulations but, in comparison with what came later, funding remained abundant and optimism prevailed. Each year, large numbers of new homes were built, split evenly between those completed for local authorities and new towns, and those completed for private sale.[31]

There were other innovations too. The issues that had been raised, after 1951, by the retreat from Bevan's enhanced space standards were tidied up and codified by Sir Parker Morris, Chief Executive of the Metropolitan Borough of Westminster, in his report *Homes for Today and Tomorrow*. This concluded that council housing needed to be improved to match the rise in living standards and provided a set of arithmetical tables ("the Parker Morris Standards") specifying the size of future properties. These were adopted by Sir Keith Joseph in 1963, and were later made mandatory for all housing built in new towns (1967) and all council housing (1969).[32] The opportunity was also taken to bring much of the surviving late nineteenth- and early twentieth-century social housing within a state-funded and state-regulated framework. Many of the older "trusts" (Guinness, Samuel Lewis, William Sutton, Peabody and so on) were hardly developing new homes by the early 1960s as much of the earlier benefactions that they had relied on were spent. To address this, the 1964 Housing Act established the Housing Corporation, with powers to register, regulate and fund such bodies, most of which were now referred to as Housing Associations.[33] Finally, in recognition of how much London had increased as a geographical entity to include many of its suburbs, the London County Council gave way, in 1964, to the Greater London Council which expanded out into the surrounding counties and green belt as Charles Latham had wanted in 1947.

Today it may seem striking that Goldfinger and the Smithsons should have been commissioned to design and build entire social housing estates, for which they also designed elaborate windows, furniture and other fittings. This is to forget that both had participated in *This Is Tomorrow*, quite possibly the UK's finest ever exhibition of pop art, with its robots, jukeboxes, pictures of Marlon Brando and much else. And it is also to forget that this was a time when divisions between different branches of the arts were being discarded (something Morris and Gropius would have approved of) as part of completely recasting the type of environment people should live in. By the early 1960s, this approach had been taken a step further by Archigram, a collective that exhibited at the ICA in 1963. They envisaged a future in which the "Plug-in-City", a kind of "high-tech", lightweight, modular and disposable design, would be common and manufactured in such a way that it could be adapted to any environment. In appearance, parts of this looked not unlike proposals made by Vladimir Tatlin, another all-rounder (in his case an artist, architect, musician and clothes designer) whose 1919 *Monument to the Third International* was a spiral structure 1300 feet high containing within it 3 separate, rotating buildings resembling gigantic versions of the Post Office Tower restaurant. Tatlin's tower was never built, and nor was much of Archigram's output, but by the mid-1960s there were many design collectives that tried with varying degrees of success, during a time of considerable state funding, to mix architecture, design and other disciplines.[34]

The impact of building so many new homes in cities, new towns and suburbs produced collectively an immense rearranging of the UK population. Millions of people moved to a new location, often connected to their employment and, in many cases, enjoyed living in their first ever secure, purpose-built home. Between 1914 and 1970 the UK housing stock doubled and the proportion of households which rented from local authorities increased steadily, peaking at 32% in 1980. Despite political changes, and variations in emphasis, there was no indication that this wouldn't continue. In 1966, for instance, the GLC announced plans for two new towns of 40,000 people each as far away as Devonshire, and the highest ever number of housing completions, 415,000 and 426,000 respectively, occurred in 1967 and 1968.[35] Income tax remained at a rate high enough to pay for this, and much else besides.

It was a system that gave ordinary people a lot even if some of it wasn't perfect. In the popular culture of the time, new towns served as the backdrop to the long-running TV series Z-Cars and were affectionately portrayed in the films Here We Go Round the Mulberry Bush and The Garnett Saga, the plot of the latter centring on the family finally leaving the nineteenth century terraces of the deepest East End for a tower block maisonette in an unspecified location in the Home Counties.[36] Some criticism could be made that the new towns and estates lacked the level of closely spaced public facilities that characterised the older settlements, but they were mostly welcomed by the people who moved into them. In the depopulated (and depopulating) areas that they left behind the properties that survived were usually cheap to buy (or rent) and in some areas a new type of informal housing economy emerged. This took the form of large, old houses being converted into "bed-sitters" and, slightly later, of streets of empty properties that were due for redevelopment being reoccupied by bands of young cultural and political activists. Eventually, with local authorities planning extensive building and road-widening programmes, around 30,000 homes in London were awaiting demolition, only 1-2% of the total stock, but concentrated in certain areas. For many, this is where their experience of living, and making their way in the capital city began.

Throughout this period, it seemed that a consensus existed across political parties, supporting state-funded housing. And to some extent it did, as the figures for the number of new homes testify, but glimpses of a different language and a colder reality could even then be seen. The fictional Garnett, bounced out of his house and into a new estate, was a great admirer, as many were, of Enoch Powell. As early as November 1955, Powell, MP for Wolverhampton South West, spoke at some length in Parliament expounding his views on housing.[37] Starting with an attack on the Labour opposition, Powell claimed that their most recent manifesto (May 1955, *Forward with Labour: Labour's Policy for the Consideration of the Nation*) would inevitably lead to the nationalisation of all privately owned housing, because as Powell asserted *"One cannot leave uncontrolled one sector of a commodity—and that the minor sector—and purport to control all the rest"*. (What Labour had actually suggested, unsuccessfully, six months earlier was *"The failure of the Tory Rents and Repairs Acts has proved that the landlords will not repair those houses without steeper increases of rent than even a Tory Government would dare to permit. Labour will therefore ask local authorities to submit schemes for gradually taking over and modernising rent-controlled private property, subject to fair compensation. We shall help those who wish to do so to own their own homes. We shall give leaseholders an opportunity of purchasing the freeholds of their houses"*).[38] From here Powell moved on to claim *"The House ought to recall that the conception of subsidised housing, both after the First World War and the Second World War, has been that it is, in essence, temporary—to deal with conditions created by war"*, a statement for which there was no evidence at all; neither Christopher Addison in 1918 nor Aneurin Bevan in 1945 said they were only carrying out a few temporary measures. Finally, he gets to the point: *"We must, therefore, ask whether, in comparing the 1930s with today, the relationship between current building costs and wages has changed to the disadvantage of the tenant. We must ask whether the same people who in the 1930s were being built for by private enterprise, the people who were moving out of rented houses into houses built by private enterprise and sold on mortgage, are today less able to afford current costs either as rents or repayments on houses built to sell."*

What is being said here, and what Powell clearly believed, is that the housing market worked very well in the 1930s: the decade that enjoyed a private sector-led building boom. The 1930s were a time when things worked well for the lower middle classes, and upper working classes – people in secure employment who were careful with their money and saved a bit. From this (and ignoring how the rest of the country then lived) Powell extrapolates and asks the question: given how much living standards have now risen, why are we now doing something so different? Can't we just – shouldn't we – just revert to what we did in the 1930s and let the private builders do what they wish? Which is not to say that Powell wanted no social housing, or indeed wanted ribbon development all the way from London to his constituency. Rather, one imagines that he supported how social housing had been provided circa 1885, by privately funded companies and benefactors working in tandem with politicians like Joseph Chamberlain, a figure he greatly admired.

His arguments were selective, carefully constructed and had immense emotional appeal, creating as they did a fantasy of a recently vanished past and endorsing a kind of resentful victimhood in certain middle- and working-class quarters. They got him noticed politically. In December 1955 Prime Minister Anthony Eden appointed him junior housing minister to Duncan Sandys. Post-Suez, Harold Macmillan advanced him to the position of Financial Secretary to the Treasury. In the first of his theatrical denunciations, Powell resigned from this position, together with the Chancellor of the Exchequer Peter Thorneycroft MP, after just a year, with Thorneycroft stating by way of explanation *"For twelve years, we have been attempting to do more than our resources could manage, and in the process, we have been gravely weakening ourselves... I believe that there is an England which would prefer to face these facts and make the necessary decisions now. I believe that living within our resources is neither unfair nor unjust, nor, perhaps, in the long run even unpopular."* Decoded, this was a firm laying out of what some years later became the Conservative mainstream position: since 1945 we have been spending too much, and that reverting to a pre-1945 way of doing things was both better and more popular than people imagined.[39] Macmillan was having none of it. He speedily replaced them, and, though a modest cut in taxation followed in

1960, the state still collected enough money to keep public services at a good level.

This was the backdrop against which Young and Willmott issued their findings about Debden. Although they partially recanted, their arguments would be picked up and recycled opportunistically by those who, however they framed their views, disliked the post-1945 consensus. It was hard, of course, to see exactly what Young and Willmott were recommending as an alternative. Presumably something along the lines of what Osborn had long suggested: the government should just give the public what it wanted. Recent re-evaluations of *Family and Kinship in East London* have cast serious doubt on its value as an impartial work. To begin with, it isn't clear how many interviews they actually carried out, but it was certainly well below the threshold of a thousand, the level which statisticians accept as statistically significant. Critics have noted that their assertion that "the majority" of Debden residents wanted to return to Bethnal Green was based on replies supposedly made by 41 households, supposedly being the operative word as when the notes are read in full it is clear that the majority were not expressing a view that they actively wanted to move back to the East End.[40]

For those on the political right, questioning the level of public spending on housing, it helped no end that they could state that Young had been one of the co-authors of Labour's 1945 manifesto. Another straw in the wind came in 1958 when John Betjeman abandoned his prior enthusiasm for modernity and became secretary of the Victorian Society. Based in Bedford Park, the Society aimed to raise awareness of the many good points associated with Victorian architecture, and also to preserve buildings, monuments and streets that were facing destruction from the extensive redevelopments being carried out in UK towns and cities. They were particularly active on the issue of the Euston Arch, the immense 1837 entrance to Euston Station that resembled a Greek temple. In 1960, proposals were made to completely demolish and reconstruct Euston Station, and get rid of the Arch. Betjeman, the Victorian Society and others fought this vigorously, up to cabinet level, where it was considered twice on 17 and 26 October 1961. They lost and Macmillan won.[41] There was no sentiment it seemed for old buildings at government level, and none at all for anything associated with the smoky, dirty atmosphere of the early industrial revolution. The building of the new Euston commenced with its airy open concourse, clean, electric trains, adjoining office tower and much use of concrete.

Notes

(1) Again, in this respect note that the standard rate of income tax was 9s in the £ (45%) in 1955, falling to 7s 9d (38%) by 1960 before rising to 8s 3d (42%) in 1965. All were considerably greater than the amount levied today.

(2) See *Family and Kinship in East London* p126.

(3) See *Family and Kinship in East London* p153.

(4) The conversion of the LNER Liverpool Street-Leyton-Epping-Ongar service into an extension of the LT Central Line had been approved in 1935 by Herbert Morrison's LCC, and agreed by the government as a measure to help alleviate unemployment. The decision to locate a new estate at Debden dated from this time and was intended to ensure the viability of the railway line.

(5) The MP for the area then was Sir Winston Churchill. Today part of it is represented by Ian Duncan Smith. On the Central Line, it is approximately 9 minutes closer to Bethnal Green than Debden. Young had opened his Institute of Community Studies at 18 Victoria Park Square, London E2 in 1953, in a building originally used as a settlement by Oxford University theology graduates. It was less than a minute's walk from Bethnal Green tube station. Hence his focus on Bethnal Green, Debden and Wanstead.

(6) Though in this case at least one contemporary reviewer noted that the book's conclusions were not borne out by the data. See: https://www.journals.uchicago.edu/doi/abs/10.1086/223119

(7) Something he considered they had recanted by 1964.

(8) See *Daily Report, Foreign Radio Broadcasts, Issues 132-133* CIA. In this Dygai confirms *"...350 new flats are being built in Moscow every day. Last year alone half a million Muscovites moved into new flats"*. The main UK delegate at the conference was Canon Collins. For a full account of Osborne's dealings with the USSR see Appendix One.

(9) He kept his shares however.

(10) Throughout this period Parliament continued to exercise itself about proposals to increase the population of Stevenage from 80,000 to 140,000. See the February 1964 debates reported in Hansard about extending existing new towns. By this point Alec Douglas-Home was Prime Minister and Harold Wilson Leader of the Opposition. At the general election held that October, Labour gained Hitchin, the constituency containing Letchworth and Stevenage.

(11) The new developments waiting the longest for a rail service include Livingston (line closed 1948: nothing for 73 years), Skelmersdale (line closed 1956, 65 years), Daventry (line closed 1958), Killingworth (station closed 1958) and Washington (station closed 1963, the first such "Beeching" casualty).

(12) The Minister of Transport 1959-1964, with prime responsibility for introducing

cuts that were blamed on Beeching, was Ernest Marples MP. Like Joseph he had significant business interests outside Parliament, in his case 80% of the shares in the road building firm Ridgway.

(13) The extent to which car ownership was favoured above all else can be read in the deliberations of Washington Development Corporation (actually an area where car ownership was significantly lower than the national average) where a 1968 review proclaimed *"By constructing a road system that is based on a primary network of urban motorways capable of carrying the ultimate anticipated traffic volumes and of distributing the traffic generating activities evenly throughout the town, Washington New Town will set a pattern that is likely to be adopted by the rest of the world...The inhabitants of Washington are fortunate in that whilst other towns wrestle with the problem of traffic congestion, they will be the first to enjoy a road network without equal".*

(14) Disney and his team were also influenced by Victor Gruen's *Metropolis of Tomorrow* from his book *The Heart of Our Cities*. (An Austrian, Gruen became prominent in the US in the 1940s by designing shopping centres). Others that they studied included Clarence Perry's neighbourhood unit plan(s) for New York City (from the 1920s), Clarence Stein and Henry Wright's pedestrian-oriented plan for Radburn, New Jersey, the emerging UK plans for Milton Keynes as well as various American company towns and planned communities. For a discussion on the links between Howard and Disney see: https://scholarcommons.usf.edu/cgi/viewcontent.cgi?article=3345&context=etd

(15) Like many at the time Disney was a firm believer in the imminence of widespread space travel. See his 1955 film *Man in Space* at https://www.youtube.com/watch?v=WFXza9RH7-E This includes a prediction from Wernher von Braun that passenger services into space will be running in about ten years, ie, by 1965. Disney's obsession with developing a monorail as a viable means of terrestrial transport was equally unsuccessful. It remains, though, emblematic of a period when such optimistic thinking was taken for granted. For a satire of this, see the 1993 episode of *The Simpsons, Marge vs the Monorail*.

(16) Sadly, not the same Richard Hamilton of *Just What Is It That Makes Today's Homes So Different, So Appealing?*

(17) Announced on 19 September 1966 the plans for "Disney's Mineral King Ski Resort" in the valley were only finally stopped in 1978, after lengthy opposition by preservationists, when the valley became part of Sequoia National Park, following an Act of Congress. On EPCOT and Disney's approach to ideal urban development see: https://carolinaangles.com/2017/04/21/walt-disney-planner/

(18) Reston was planned by Robert E Simon as a private sector-led version of Greenbelt, Maryland. Like Howard's Letchworth and Welwyn schemes it was governed by an elaborate set of legal agreements and covenants. Like them too, it developed at a slower pace than anticipated and took many years to reach its intended population. Because of this, financial problems arose and Smith had been replaced as owner by Gulf Oil by 1967.

(19) However, this was not an original idea from Kahn and Wiener. For its genesis see *Visit to the World's Fair 2014* by Isaac Asimov in the *New York Times* of 16 August 1964 which can be viewed at https://archive.nytimes.com/www.nytimes.com/books/97/03/23/lifetimes/asi-v-fair.html

(20) So much so that Kahn commented about the film *"I liked the movie... Since Stanley lifted lines from On Thermonuclear War without change but out of context, I asked him 'Doesn't that entitle me to a royalty?' He pretended not to hear me at first, but when I asked him again, Stanley replied, in the firmest tone I've heard him use: 'It doesn't work that way.'"*

(21) Note in this respect the comments of Mumford in 1958 *"...in cities like New*

York, *the older parts are more and more dedicated to the under privileged minorities;
and in Washington, if the exodus continues, the core of the city will be simply one vast
Negro slum... Space, with country or suburban living, has always been an upper-class
privilege...*"

(22) All dating from between 1961 and 1963, though none was a residential building.
The London Hilton, in Park Lane and the Post Office Tower, with its famous
revolving restaurant, were particularly admired. Ironically, in 1962, Walter
Gropius designed his only significant London building 100 yards to the north of
the Hilton at 45 Park Lane. A small mixed-use scheme, the commercial element
was occupied for many years by the Bunny Club.

(23) The height of Centre Point was dictated by the cost of buying out the multitude of
landowners in the area, something that also led to a reduction in the residential
element of the scheme. Famously, Hyams kept Centre Point empty until 1975,
insisting it could only be let to a single tenant. He did agree, though, to its being
used as a film set for the 1967 Frank Sinatra spy film *The Naked Runner*, footage
of which (the only surviving images of how it looked when completed) can be
viewed at https://www.youtube.com/watch?v=zk3txHCx3yk. Remodelling busy
road junctions with an abundance of modern high-rise buildings was actively
pursued by the LCC throughout the 1950s. Goldfinger designed the DHSS
HQ at the Elephant and Castle (1963) and Gropius worked for several years,
unsuccessfully, on a projected redevelopment of Piccadilly Circus.

(24) Which like Centre Point remained empty until 1975, when Hyams finally let it
to the Civil Aviation Authority.

(25) The first tenant of which was Fine Fare. In another irony, the first Fine Fare
supermarket had opened in Welwyn Garden City in 1951, under the ownership
of Howardsgate Holdings, a company started by Ebenezer Howard.

(26) The rents for Balfron Tower and Trellick Tower were set at what was then quite
a high level, reflecting the view that these were prestigious addresses. A flat in
Balfron Tower cost £4 15s 6d (£4.77) per week in 1967, roughly 28% of average
earnings, then. Comparable figures today would be a rent of £165.85p.

(27) The extensive network of empty streets, awaiting demolition, along the Westway
route was used as the setting for the 1970 John Boorman film *Leo the Last* and
features in many other cinematic and TV works.

(28) Smith served on Newcastle City Council 1950-1965, and was Leader from 1959;
his influence persisted long after he had vacated the Civic Centre. He served
on the Buchanan Committee, which produced *Traffic in Towns*, alongside Oleg
Kerensky, an engineer and the son of Alexander whom Lenin ousted from power
in 1917. Another committee member was architect William Holford, who had
been on the team designing the new Brazilian capital of Brasilia in the 1950s.
Smith often stated that his ambition was to turn Newcastle into the Brasilia of
the north. Looked at today many of the findings in *Traffic in Towns* follow on
logically from the Abercrombie Plan.

(29) Smith too was much taken with Scandinavia, and oversaw the construction of
a new Civic Centre that was opened, in 1968, by King Olaf V of Norway. Its
Council Chamber was designed to be the seat of government for the proposed
regional parliament in the North East of England, something recommended, as
part of a division of the UK into 11 regions, by the 1968-1969 Redcliffe-Maud
Committee of 1969, of which Smith was also a member.

(30) Hyde Park Barracks, built by Sir Basil Spence from 1967, accommodates 514
officers and men and 273 horses in a residential tower over 300 feet high. It is
thought to be the only tower block in the world designed for horses, and includes
a special lift to transport them to and from their floors. One wonders if the

urban myths that proliferated from the late 1960s about some council tenants in tower blocks keeping horses on their balconies are possibly misremembered or garbled accounts of the arrangements made for the Household Cavalry.

(31) Between 1955 and 1970 5.48m new homes were completed (an average of 342,000 per year – considerably higher than today) of which 48.9% were for local authorities and new towns and 51.1% for private sale.

(32) A comprehensive account, by Julia Park, of how space standards have evolved in the UK can be read at http://housingspacestandards.co.uk/assets/space-standards_onscreen.pdf

(33) Similarly, the Act also allowed for the creation and registration of cooperatives. An early, and notable, development from one such body was 125 Park Road NW8, by Terry Farrell/Nicholas Grimshaw, built in 1968. Many of the newly created housing associations and cooperatives concentrated initially on buying and refurbishing neglected or abandoned pre-1919 housing in inner-city areas.

(34) At the extremities of which, but still arguably within the genre, one can locate The Fool, a Dutch collective which produced clothing, music, film sets, album sleeves and decorated the exterior of the Apple Boutique in Baker Street during its brief existence in 1967-1968. The early version of The Pink Floyd was not dissimilar, combining 2 architects (Roger Waters and Nick Mason), a musician (Rick Wright), an artist (Syd Barrett), an economics lecturer (Peter Jenner) and a lighting technician (Peter Wynne-Wilson). The main practitioners at Archigram actually had day jobs with Taylor Woodrow at one point. One of their more feasible early ideas was a tower of buildings made of containers, stacked one above the other. The art work for this, together with many variations by other practices, can be seen at https://www.treehugger.com/its-time-another-look-plug-housing-4851410 and resembles a Blake or Hamilton pop collage.

(35) The Minister of Housing at the time was Anthony Greenwood MP, whose father Arthur Greenwood had introduced subsidies for slum clearance whilst Minister for Health 1929-1931.

(36) *The Garnett Saga* was actually filmed at John Walsh Tower (built 1966) overlooking Epping Forest. An account of the history of this block, which echoes that of many similar buildings, can be read at https://architectsforsocialhousing. co.uk/2016/08/10/what-are-the-options-fred-wigg-john-walsh-towers/ New towns were not always portrayed as benign environments. The 1956 Philip King play *Serious Charge*, for instance, portrays teenage hooliganism, and Keith Waterhouse's 1961 comic novel *Jubb* features a seedy, predatory single man whose indecent ambitions are thwarted by bureaucratic local committees.

(37) See Hansard 21 November 1955.

(38) See http://www.labour-party.org.uk/manifestos/1955/1955-labour-manifesto. shtml

(39) On 1958 Thorneycroft later stated *"We probably made our stand too early"*. In terms of supposed golden eras in the past that could be invoked as periods of better government note that the standard rate of taxation stood at 4s 6d in the £ in 1938 (22.5%) and at only 1s 2d in the £ (6.5%) in 1914. Both were significantly lower than the 1958 figure of 8s 6d (42.5%).

(40) For a contemporary view see https://fabians.org.uk/family-and-kinship-in-east-london-revisited/ A study of how Young's views developed appeared in *The Guardian* on 25 April 2007 and can be read at https://www.theguardian. com/society/2007/apr/25/communities.britishidentityandsociety Young's background was originally in market research and no survey today of such a large population group would be based on such a tiny number of respondents: a minimum of 1,000 replies would be considered essential, this being likely

to produce data that is "statistically significant". Nor would those surveyed be asked such leading questions.

(41) See https://cabinetroom.wordpress.com/2015/06/12/a-doric-tragedy-demolishing-the-euston-arch/ JM Richards, editor of *Architectural Review* who was part of a delegation that visited Macmillan on this issue, implied afterwards that he thought the Prime Minister might have been asleep during their meeting: *"Macmillan listened – or I suppose he listened... he sat without moving with his eyes apparently closed. He asked no questions; in fact, he said nothing except that he would consider the matter."*

12

MISTAKES, DISASTERS
AND TRAGEDIES

At 5.45am on the morning of 16 May 1968, Ivy Hodge, the tenant of 90 Ronan Point, Freemasons Road, London E16, went to make a cup of tea in her kitchen. As she tried to light her gas stove an explosion occurred. It blew her across the room, and started a partial collapse of one corner of the 22-floor block. Fortunately, the building had just been completed and was not fully occupied, but 4 people were killed and 17 injured. Visually, the damage was both spectacular and terrifying and news of the disaster was quickly spread by radio, TV and newspaper. Images of the block, with one corner ripped out, flashed around the world. Psychologically, it was an enormously significant event and was quickly presented as a wake-up call to a country that had built so much modern housing – a sign that something, somewhere, was awry. In the years that followed, that interpretation was accepted by a great many people, and "Ronan Point" (the name itself being sufficient to conjure up both the image of the collapse, and the dreadful context in which it supposedly occurred) has passed into history as a prime example of a serious mistake made during the post-1945 period of high state spending. The block was referred to by many in unflattering terms, from the highest level down to popular historians like Alan and Veronica Palmer who note in *The Pimlico Chronology of British History* (1995) *"May 1968 Tower Block municipal housing discredited when new high-rise flats at Ronan Point, Newham, collapsed after a gas explosion"*.

Ronan Point was one of nine such blocks built along Freemasons Road from the mid-1960s. The area had previously been occupied by traditional streets of terraced houses, dating from the 1890s, housing a population that worked in the Royal Victoria and Albert Docks together with the adjoining industrial, commercial and transport businesses across Canning Town, Custom House and North Woolwich. Heavily damaged by aerial bombing between 1940 and 1944, many of the original houses were demolished after 1945 and replaced by prefabs until, in 1960, a comprehensive scheme to redevelop the area was agreed. Not all of this was high-rise: there were low-rise terraces of houses, smallish blocks of flats and maisonettes, and shops and garages too. The design wasn't particularly distinguished and was a modification (by Taylor Woodrow, the contractor) of the Larsen-Nielsen system developed in Denmark in 1948, and was one of many such adopted across Europe after 1945 to provide millions of urgently needed homes. Unlike traditional brick buildings, or even buildings based around a strong steel or concrete frame, Larsen-Nielsen involved constructing a terrace, block or tower from large concrete panels, cast in a factory, that were bolted together on site. The system was perfectly safe for 4 floors, and not recommended without modifications for buildings above 8 floors. As altered by Taylor Woodrow, Ronan Point was nearly three times as high.[1]

Via James Callaghan, Home Secretary, the government responded to the events of 16 May 1968 by arranging an enquiry, and announcing, through the Ministry of Housing in August, that it would "discourage" the building of any more tower blocks. This immediately struck a discordant note with many architects. Among these was Erno Goldfinger, at that point designing Trellick Tower for the GLC, who stated he was "appalled" by a "ridiculous attitude which will put us back 30 years". The report from Callaghan's enquiry arrived in November after it had deliberated for slightly less than six months. Produced by Hugh Griffiths QC, Sir Alfred Pugsley and Sir Owen Saunders, its findings were announced to Parliament by Lord Kennet on 6 November 1968: "The Tribunal find that this behaviour of the building was inherent in its design and was not due to faulty workmanship". In other words, the large panel system was wrong from the start and the Ronan

Point collapse was nothing to do with whether the block had been properly built. Rather curiously, the findings then went on to say that buildings of this type above 6 floors should be strengthened to make them safe, and that the use of gas for cooking and heating in such schemes should be phased out. By which they appeared to be admitting that large panel systems below 6 floors were fine (as Larsen-Nielsen had always stated) and that the practice, in the UK, of incoming tenants bringing their own, often elderly, gas cookers with them into new flats in high-rise buildings was not very safe.[2]

Suitably strengthened, Ronan Point survived and became fully tenanted. Today, one is struck at how insular the 1968 enquiry was. Had it looked abroad, say to Denmark, it would have found no problems with the Larsen-Nielsen system, which continues to function there, and elsewhere, to this day.[3] Equally, it was never clear how thorough any official discouragement of new tower blocks would be, and criticism of this type certainly didn't apply to the City of London's Barbican Estate. In truth, such was the impact of Ronan Point in popular consciousness, it probably didn't need to be. After 1970, most local authority architects opted for lower rise developments of a type that responded to the expectations of tenants. And tenants, in keeping with many politicians and opinion-formers, continued to have preferences that Osborn, Howard, Morris, Ruskin and many others would have endorsed: in an ideal world a house with a garden was better than a flat in the sky. Consequently, however much the local authority tried to "normalise" and improve Ronan Point, neither it, nor its sister blocks, became popular. In the mid-1980s, faced with high maintenance costs, resident demands and doubts about how resistant they might be to a serious fire, the London Borough of Newham decided to demolish them.

This was not arranged as a spectacular fun-for-all-the-family "blow down". Instead, the blocks were dismantled panel by panel and the quality of the workmanship examined. When this was done, cracks were found in the concrete that had been used for their construction and they were shown, in some cases, to be kept together by the weight of the panels pressing down, and across, on each other. Bolts and joints specified in the drawings had been left out by Taylor Woodrow. Not a great deal resulted from this. Given the deaths of four residents in 1986 one might have expected a police investigation, followed by arrests, court appearances and prison sentences. There was no appetite for this at official levels in the UK in 1968. Nobody at Taylor Woodrow was prosecuted or imprisoned. No one lost their pension. Instead, the site of each of the tower blocks was replaced by small terraces of "English vernacular" houses, often arranged at right angles, Radburn-style. They survive to this day. As do the original medium-rise blocks and terraces that accompanied Ronan Point, albeit massively depleted in numbers (as social housing) by post-1980 right-to-buy purchases. The lack of action in trying to establish effectively the cause of the Ronan Point tragedy, and ensure that justice was done is striking. But perhaps not surprising. *Construction News* noted, for instance, on 7 December 1990 that *"Taylor Woodrow tops the league in Conservative Party donations with £170,000 a year, according to figures released this week by the Labour Research Department".*[4] In fact, Taylor Woodrow, which first came to prominence developing London suburbs during the long building boom in the 1930s, had long been significant sponsors of the Conservative Party, along with many other house-builders. The idea that anyone in the Thatcher government, in 1986-1987, would have pushed for action against them, on an historic case, was extremely unlikely.

If the wheels of justice were permanently jammed on Ronan Point, they moved with somewhat greater speed when dealing with the business affairs of T Dan Smith. In a case strung out across nearly four years – and one that the state pursued with some tenacity – the former Leader of Newcastle City Council was charged with bribery in January 1970, acquitted in July 1971, arrested and charged with corruption in October 1973 and, after pleading guilty, sentenced to six years imprisonment in 1974. The allegations against him related to his connections to John Poulson, who ran a major architectural practice,[5] and Bovis, the building contractors owned by Sir Keith Joseph's family. These arose out of the nexus between development, house-building and politics – at both local and national level – that had arisen during the long post-1945 period of high spending on public housing and civic development. The overwhelming majority of local authorities, local councillors, planners and architects were honest and won contracts openly and fairly. But there were exceptions, and John Poulson was one of them.

Poulson started down the road that led to imprisonment in 1958 when his friend Herbert Butcher, National Liberal and Conservative MP for Holland and Boston, advised him to use lobbyists to get business. Lobbying was legal, albeit somewhat novel in the 1950s, and its effectiveness depended on the contacts available to whoever was doing it. In this respect, Butcher was lacking. By the 1950s the National Liberal group of MPs had been almost wholly subsumed within the Conservative Party and they had few members at local level who could open the appropriate doors. Fortunately, Bovis, who worked closely with Poulson's firm, had noted the enthusiasm displayed by T Dan Smith for major construction projects and recommended that he join Poulson as a lobbyist. He was appointed as such in February 1962, and his extensive local government connections were immediately put to use on Poulson's behalf.[6] A key figure in the Poulson-Smith network was Alderman Cunningham, a major player in trade union and local government circles across the North East. Cunningham held positions on a number of quangos and was subsequently judged to have improperly helped steer contracts in Poulson's direction. In fact, Poulson's firm designed an entire housing estate in Felling (Cunningham's home town) which Bovis built: Crowhall Tower and its surrounding maisonette blocks, all of which utilised the same Larsen-Neilsen system that was used at Ronan Point.[7] Construction of this began in 1966, the same year that Reginald Maudling MP, previously Chancellor of the Exchequer, accepted a directorship in Poulson's company.

The idea that there was something murky going on in local government, principally in "the north", seems to have taken root in public consciousness circa 1970, after the Ronan Point collapse.[8] And, in truth, Poulson routinely used bribery to win contracts. The extent of this became clear in early 1972 when, after Poulson had filed for bankruptcy, official hearings took place into how he had conducted his company's affairs.[9] In July that year Maudling, now Home Secretary with responsibility for the Police, resigned as Poulson's intricate web of dealings with local politicians, civil servants, lobbyists and MPs came into focus. Poulson was prosecuted, convicted and imprisoned, and Smith and Cunningham were dragged down in his wake. No legal proceedings were ever taken against Maudling, Joseph or any of Poulson's other significant political contacts.[10]

Given the shift in public attitudes toward modernist architecture, town centre redevelopment and high-rise residential schemes that occurred as a result of the coverage of both Ronan Point and the lengthy proceedings against Smith, Poulson and Cunningham, it is worth pointing out what type of buildings Poulson and his practice produced. Throughout the 1950s and 1960s they turned out libraries, rebuilt railway stations, swimming pools, hospitals, housing estates, office blocks, hotels and shopping centres. Some lasted, some were demolished. None was particularly outstanding and a few exhibited maintenance issues from early on in their existence. But most did what they were intended to do for a reasonable period of time, and some survive to this day. In short, his output was typical of the period.

The issue with Poulson was not specifically what he was developing (though there are many who excoriate what he erected, and prefer the buildings he replaced) but how he obtained contracts, and to a lesser degree, given how local authorities and similar organisations made decisions then, how much input local people had into such proposals. This was a logical point of view, but such things do not always prevail. By 1970, there was an audience for an alternative to state-funded full-on modernism and the media duly provided it. On television John Betjeman, by now a notable campaigner against demolition, made an early impact with *John Betjeman's London* (1967) before triumphing with *Metroland* (1973). This explored the evolution of London's outer suburbs and, in its own way, endorsed the type of popular low-density development – almost all of which was for private sale, to respectable middle-class buyers – that had been carried out by the Metropolitan Railway in the early years of the century. Betjeman was urbane, witty and poetic in his choice of language and music. For those wanting a more denunciatory tone, Ian Nairn provided it via his TV series *Nairn at Large* (1969), *Nairn's Journeys* (1971) and *Nairn Across Britain* (1972). In these extended travelogues, Nairn, often motoring to and from his destinations in a Morris Minor, frequently displays a curmudgeonly tone not always apparent in his writings.[11] The apogee of anti-developer feeling, though, was surely the 1973 paperback book *Goodbye London*.[12] Written by Christopher Booker and Candida Lycett Green (Betjeman's daughter), both of whom were contributors to *Private Eye* magazine, this listed virtually every significant building in London that was either abandoned, empty or threatened with demolition. Developers were named, with Seifert cast as a major villain. Illustrated with photographs of the main perpetrators (presumably so that campaigners and activists could recognise and accost them in the street) it also commented on their background and/or ethnicity: Sir Max Rayne ("son of Polish immigrant in rag trade"), Joe Levy ("son of a bookmaker"), C H Elsom ("son of Russian-Jewish tailor"). Some of the concerns raised by Booker and Lycett Green were reasonable, but the overall tone of the book was not, and it veered into unpleasant territory.[13]

Nor was this type of anti-modernist/anti-development sentiment restricted to middle-class sections of the media. The 1970s was notably a time when newspaper reports about council estates, and anything newsworthy that occurred on them, began to concentrate on their supposed failings. A depressing liturgy began to emerge, based on broken lifts that stank of urine, burnt-out cars that never got removed, vandalised entry doors, graffiti, broken glass and gangs that loitered... threatening the law-abiding and terrified tenants who were usually quoted (though usually not named) as stating that they couldn't wait to move out. The fact that most people didn't live in tower blocks, and that most council estates were well-managed low-rise developments was never mentioned, and it didn't help that this imagery matched much of the landscape portrayed in Stanley Kubrick's version of *A Clockwork Orange*. Filmed in 1970 and 1971, this was his follow-up to the hugely successful, and influential *2001: A Space Odyssey*. It featured key scenes shot at the then brand-new Thamesmead South Housing Estate, showing Alex and his gang in action in a gleaming, modern, concrete environment. A grim – and brilliant – cocktail of sex and violence, *A Clockwork Orange* was eventually withdrawn from distribution by Kubrick in 1973 in the midst of a sustained campaign to have it banned led by various local authorities, moralising activists and MPs.

The dramatic opportunities that the new urban terrain provided were also seized on by JG Ballard in his definitive trilogy of novels, *Crash* (1973), *Concrete Island* (1974) and *High Rise* (1975). The first of these was about how moral values and personal behaviour declined in a society where the motor car is allowed free rein. The second takes place on a battered, overgrown and demolished piece of miscellaneous land, surrounded by new urban motorways, a sort of inner-city atoll on which the survivor of a car crash finds himself marooned without prospect of escape.[14] The third is set in a massive Goldfinger- or Seifert-style residential block, an immense vertical utopia lovingly planned by a messianic architect in which everything that can go wrong, does go wrong. It ends with a brutal civil war breaking out amongst class-based groups of residents. Ironically, no one was more suburban than Ballard, who lived in Shepperton, Middlesex. His books, though, should not be seen as fantasies, but rather as careful observations of emerging modern trends, that drew from the same material that inspired Kubrick and Nairn.

The truth was that unashamed modernism was fading by the 1970s, and if architects wanted to press forward in that style, they increasingly needed to justify themselves. In 1970, the BBC came looking for Alison and Peter Smithson, showcasing them in a 30-minute documentary, *The Smithsons on Housing*.[15] Filmed when Robin Hood Gardens, their only housing estate, was under construction, the tone here is defensive and both are quick to stress how adventurous the GLC are when commissioning work, and how much they regret the levels of vandalism they see around them in London. (Mentioning in passing how little the UK is like Europe, where vandalism is much less of a problem). Above all they explain the rationale for Robin Hood Gardens: separating pedestrians, particularly children, from traffic whilst providing spacious, high-quality homes. It's all very logical, but the fact that this now required explanation is indicative of the changing times.

The Smithsons on Housing was directed by the experimental novelist BS Johnson, one of a number of TV productions he did at this time, and he seems an appropriate choice to record this for posterity. After its completion, the design by the Smithsons quickly became the butt of criticism. The extensive walkways that linked the flats had many blind spots, encouraging antisocial and even criminal activity, and the level of maintenance required to keep the fabric of the building in good order was higher than predicted. There is much validity in these claims and it was clearly a mistake by the Smithsons, given the UK's climate, to use so much unweathered concrete in the estate's construction. Poplar was not the south of France. (The south of France features in their film as something they were trying to emulate). By 1970, many architects building similar schemes were airing their concerns about resident security within a block, given how large individual buildings were becoming and how many people might be circulating, or loitering, within them. Trellick Tower, for instance, was intended by Goldfinger to have a concierge system but none was installed as the GLC did not wish to pay for such a measure. [16] Any block of that size in Europe would have one, and today many in the UK do too. This should also have been considered for Robin Hood Gardens, if not by the architects, then by the client. And if mounting maintenance costs in later years were an issue, the Smithsons, to be fair, could not have foreseen the spending cuts that would fall on local government, and housing, after 1979. Watching *The Smithsons on Housing* today, it is odd (and sad) to see a project like Robin Hood Gardens being explained, justified, and then built, on screen, with the Smithsons looking as they narrate their vision like avant-garde visitors from a future that never materialised.[17]

For all its anti-modernism, *Goodbye London* fails to mention either Trellick Tower or Robin Hood Gardens, though it is rather sniffy about the role (and power) of the GLC. In this it was following an emerging trend, already noted in the playing out of the Ronan Point disaster and the Poulson scandal: blame was now being pushed onto local councils and/or their architects. Both were deemed to be out of touch with what people really wanted and meddling in things they didn't fully understand. It was a point of view Howard and Osborn would have appreciated.

* * * * * *

For the moment, despite these warning signals, the new town programme continued to expand. During the Wilson and Heath years another batch were designated: Milton Keynes; Newtown, Powys; and Ballymena (all 1967); Northampton; Peterborough; and Warrington (1968); Londonderry (1969); and finally the rather vaguely named Central Lancashire (1970) notable for being the largest and based on a combination of Preston, Leyland and Chorley. The expansion into Northern Ireland, an area with much poor housing, was of note. More importantly it was clear that government planners were abandoning Howard's purist vision of the stand-alone, built-from-scratch, low-density city surrounded by a wide belt of surrounding countryside. The proposals for Northampton, Peterborough, Warrington and Central Lancashire were all based around existing, long-established settlements and consequently somewhat easier (and cheaper) to plan and build.

The one that wasn't, Milton Keynes, would turn out to be easily the most Americanised development ever undertaken in the UK. Plans unveiled for it in March 1970, showed a city built along the same US grid system that Howard had observed in Chicago 100 years earlier, with the caveat that absent the vast number of high-rise buildings characteristic of Chicago, this was more akin to

Los Angeles, Buckinghamshire. Free and unimpeded circulation of motor vehicles was prioritised, whilst a railway station, finally agreed in 1978, took until 1982 to arrive. Early proposals for a water bus service to London, along the Grand Union Canal, were dropped and a proposed monorail system – once again the transport of the future, albeit one that never quite arrives – was quickly abandoned.[18] But, even if it were the butt of many jibes, Milton Keynes, which enjoyed easy access (for car owners) to the M1, was successful, and popular with its residents.[19] Major employers, led by the Open University, relocated there and its population had reached 76,000 by 1976, passing 100,000 eight years later. It continues to grow today. Above all, and contrary to the ethos that dominated UK political discourse after 1979, Milton Keynes owed its success almost entirely to state planning, and an abundance of state funding. It could never have been built by Howard, given his rejection of this model, and if attempted today by the private sector would require either similar amounts of support, or comparable subsidies – possibly the same sort of exemption from taxes granted to the developers of Canary Wharf in the 1980s.

Originally, the intention had been that Milton Keynes should be even bigger, with a brand-new international airport, the largest ever built in the UK, sited ten miles south at Cublington. This was proposed by the Roskill Commission, which deliberated between 1968 and 1970 and issued its findings in January 1971. Alas, its findings were not unanimous: one member, Sir Colin Buchanan, issued a minority report, suggesting the airport be built instead at Foulness, an island in the outer Thames estuary, and the government eventually opted for this, via the Maplin Development Act (1973).[20] Nor was this intended to be solely an airport. The very pinnacle of state planning, it was to include the largest container port in Europe, an oil terminal and a new town for up to 600,000 people. The development would be connected to the rest of the UK via high-speed rail and motorway links. In 1973-1974, trial foundations were built. But the Labour Party was opposed to the scheme, and their Shadow Spokesman on the

Environment, Anthony Crosland MP, had already declared the project a *"mad plan for Heathograd in South-east Essex"*. In February 1974 when Heath failed to win an election and was replaced as Prime Minister by Wilson, a review was announced. Maplin/ Foulness was duly cancelled later the same year, and the last, and largest government-led new town project faded away.[21]

Yes, of course Maplin would have been expensive, and taken time and resources, but it was at least an honest attempt to plan in a meaningful way for the future. Its scale was also an admission, by its proponents, that the UK had fallen behind its European and global rivals and needed to catch up. What replaced it was piecemeal. It is hard to imagine Aneurin Bevan in 1945 taking the same view about either the NHS or public housing, both of which were also expensive, long-term commitments designed to improve the UK far into the future. It is also interesting to see Crosland using a comparison with the Soviet Union to debunk the scheme, echoing the attacks made 25 years earlier on his own colleague Lewis Silkin in reference to Stevenage. There was certainly a sense by the late 1960s, particularly in the Labour Party, that housing had been tackled effectively as an issue. In October 1969, the post of Minister of Housing ceased to be a cabinet position. When Edward Heath became Prime Minister in June 1970, this was restored, with Peter Walker MP taking the role. Four months later Heath created an immense new ministry, adding housing to transport, public buildings and works as he established the Department of the Environment. Walker was appointed to run that too, the first such political position of its type anywhere in the world, but housing was now just one of several junior ministries within a larger organisation and had lost its unique identity and status.

Such a move was typical of Heath's ambition. He was aware, for instance, that many regions within the UK were falling behind London and the South East in terms of growth and that there was an over-centralisation of power in Whitehall. In 1972, he addressed this by creating six new metropolitan county councils: Greater Manchester, Merseyside, South Yorkshire, Tyne and

Wear, West Midlands and West Yorkshire. All were existing, highly urbanised areas and they became active from 1 January 1974 exercising almost unlimited borrowing powers. Part of the rationale for their creation lay in a desire to disperse government work, and departments, from London. They were also intended to address the inner-city blight that often arose when traditional towns and cities were depopulated by the construction of new towns and suburbs on their fringes. There was certainly much to be done in that respect, and action was not restricted to long-term problems. In London, for instance, criticism of Centre Point lying empty continued, with Lena Jeger MP commenting in Parliament in 1973 *"Centre Point is a symbol of a society in which those who make money are more blessed than those who earn money"*. The building was duly squatted, had its name appropriated by a homelessness charity (and newly registered housing association) and became the subject of unrealistic compulsory purchase proposals. Hyams eventually found a tenant for his tower and the protests faded away, but they were symbolic of people wanting real, and perceived, local issues addressed. Typical of this, in London, were the start made to redeveloping redundant and abandoned waterside areas like St Katharine's Docks and the switch, partly as a reaction against tower blocks, to "more human" housing estates, such as the Brunswick Centre, and the Whittington Estate.[22] Both of these were medium-rise developments in Camden involving a lot of concrete, rather like the Smithsons' Robin Hood Gardens, and there were many similar projects that appeared as the decade saw itself out.

* * * * * *

The culminative impact of high spending on public housing by successive governments was certainly noticed by the public, even if they didn't like every manifestation of this largesse. By 1970, the majority of UK households had either bought or were buying their own home. Renting from a private landlord, once commonplace across the working and middle classes, had become unusual and something only a minority did. The remainder rented from local authorities, or new town corporations, with the percentage that did so rising slowly each year as the private rented sector crumbled. With a continuing commitment, by both the political parties, to full employment, a sound manufacturing economy and state planning, there seemed no reason why this shouldn't continue.

Being an adult member of the public during the 1970s might have had drawbacks, but it also meant living at a time when safety nets existed, training and education were accessible and affordable, and destitution could be avoided. And with politicians in Westminster focussing on a more community-based approach to the UK's beleaguered and knocked-about cities, there were openings and opportunities to be had. The continued decline in the population of urban areas, as existing residents moved out to the ever-expanding suburbs and new towns, led to many municipal housing departments advertising "hard to let" properties: usually unfashionable pre-war flats, or small bedsit/1-bed apartments in newly built tower blocks that were often allocated to anybody on their waiting list who wanted one. It was better than leaving them empty.

Similarly, a great many of the wide-ranging proposals launched by the larger local authorities (the GLC, and after 1974, Heath's new Metropolitan County Councils) involved compulsory purchase orders and slow, phase-by-phase, systematic redevelopment. Inhabitable properties were often left empty for extended periods, during which time they might be squatted and then licensed as "short-life" homes by whoever owned them to whoever was living in them. Some curious figures could be found in these. At one point Astrid Proll (late of the Baader-Meinhof Gang) and more recently employed by Hackney Council, was living in a feminist housing cooperative in Broadway Market whilst the GLC sorted out its plans for that area. She remembers this period in *Goodbye to London: Radical Art and Politics in the 70's* which strikes a somewhat different tone to the similarly titled work by Brooker and Lycett Green.[23]

But the political weather was changing, even if few realised it at the time. A shift in attitudes was taking place, propelled by the right wing of the Conservative Party, and it selected public housing as an early battleground. Broadly, the stance taken by Powell and Thorneycroft in 1958 was attracting adherents. In 1965, Powell contested the Conservative Party leadership, finishing bottom with only 14 supporters, albeit some of these would later exercise immense influence.[24] Following Heath's significant 1966 electoral defeat there were plenty within the Conservative Party open to the idea of a change in direction and Heath, despite quickly sacking Powell after his appalling 1968 *"rivers of blood"* speech, duly trimmed toward them.[25] In June 1970, the Conservatives won a general election on a manifesto that, by the standards of the time was considered to be quite right wing. It stated, inter alia, that the government would reduce taxation, reduce the size of the state, increase home ownership and, most significantly *"... encourage local authorities to sell council houses to those of their tenants who wish to buy them. Thus, many council-house tenants of today will become the owners of their own homes tomorrow. As a result, more money will be immediately available for the local authorities to provide housing for the aged, for the disabled, and for those on the housing lists... Our policies for encouraging home ownership will also mean that more council house tenants can move into homes of their own, thus releasing their council houses for those in need..."* [26]

Heath was as good as his word. The standard rate of income tax was reduced to 7s 9d (38.75%) in 1970 and then cut further to 30% in 1973, a level that was beginning to creep below that levied in many other comparable European economies. And legislation was passed giving any local authority that wished to do so the power to sell a council home to its tenant, if the tenant asked to buy it. There was no compulsion on the local authority to do this. Any council that had, say, lengthy waiting lists could decline to participate in the scheme, and there was no discount for the buyer. Sales were at full market value, and the tenant had to agree to use the property as their main residence post-purchase. Most importantly, the money raised from sales had to be recycled, by the local authority, into providing replacement social housing. In practice, most of the sales were made by Conservative-run local authorities, many in rural or suburban areas, and many Labour councils didn't participate in the scheme.

This was a shift, but, in housing terms, the essentials of the post-war settlement remained in place. There was a laudable commitment to helping the homeless. The network of existing new towns carried on expanding and, whilst a higher percentage of the homes in these areas were now for sale than in previous years, there was still an abundance of state funding and a considerable amount of state planning.[27] Heath, as his manifesto made clear, was determined to achieve growth in the UK. After UK unemployment rose by 75% in the opening 18 months of his premiership, edging in early 1972 dangerously close to the totemic figure of a million, he abandoned the liberal economic approach that had been brokered with the pro-Powell group a few years earlier and reverted to the standard post-1945 Keynesian methods of managing the economy. Heath, like many in Parliament then, had been a young man in the 1930s and didn't subscribe to the view that it had been an era of unbridled prosperity to which the country should revert.

The upshot of the Heath U-turn was an increasing schism within his own party. By 1973, the core of the right-wing opposition to him had coalesced around the Selsdon Group, the President of which was Nicholas Ridley, an early supporter of Powell. Members of this were required to subscribe to the Selsdon Declaration, something not widely known to the public, and a requirement that suggested their views had a kind of formal, semi-religious standing. Indeed, if one takes Ridley's concluding remarks at their inaugural meeting seriously, it is clear that they were based on the libertarian, free-market and pro-business opinions of William Boetcker, a prominent US Presbyterian clergyman (and anti-union evangelist), circa 1915, even if on the day Ridley misattributed them to Abraham Lincoln. Both Ridley's remarks and the Selsdon Declaration itself were expressions of the type of political direction this group wished to take. As was to be expected amongst the generalisations about lower taxes, less regulation and a smaller role for the state, it was not obvious – then – what they might actually *do*, if they obtained power.[28] Another reasonable view might have been that they were saying not much more than the right had been saying for about 30 years, without, to that point, significantly changing too much of the post-1945 arrangements. Their opportunity to demonstrate exactly what they meant came sooner than expected. In early 1974 Heath called and failed to win an election, and then lost another, by a wider margin, later the same year. The Selsdon Group, and other like-minded colleagues moved against him. They demanded a review of how the Conservative Party elected its leader, making it easier for a contest to be held against Heath. After this had been granted Heath, thinking he might beat off a challenge, called a leadership election. He lost, and Margaret Thatcher, the candidate backed by the Selsdon Group, won.[29]

For the moment, this seemed less significant than would be the case in later years. In 1975, Harold Wilson was Prime Minister of a Labour government which put the standard rate of income tax back to 35%, trimming it only slightly to 34% (1977) and 33% (1978) both of which were, more or less, within the parameters levied by other western European economies. In housing, both Wilson and Callaghan retained Heath's Department of the Environment and treated it as an appropriately senior position: the post of Secretary of State was held by Anthony Crosland and then by Peter Shore, both regarded as significant figures.[30] Beneath them a Ministry of Housing continued to do its work, with the position of Minister of Housing occupied by Reg Freeson MP for the entire duration of the 1974-1979 Labour government.

During Freeson's tenure funding for new housing remained at a high level and the new towns continued to expand. Most notably his period in office continued the shift toward regenerating urban areas with the passing of the Community Land Act (1975) and the Home Purchase Assistance and Housing Corporation Guarantee Act (1978). The latter, in particular, enabled a growing number of small housing associations, and housing cooperatives, to function on a proper basis with their own staff, premises and development programmes. In terms of the number of properties these actually built, or renovated, their output was relatively limited, but their concentration in particular inner-city areas made a significant visual impact as well as providing much needed accommodation.

Both these pieces of legislation paled in significance, though, when compared to the 1977 Housing (Homeless Persons) Act. Passed under a Labour government, and endorsed by a Labour housing minister, this was actually sponsored by a Liberal MP, Stephen Ross.[31] Prior to its arrival local authorities had dealt with the homeless by maintaining waiting lists, to which people could apply, with the local authorities being obliged to give a reasonable preference to the various categories of persons on their lists when allocating housing. In an era when up to 200,000 new local authority homes were being completed annually (and 100% of their funding met by the state) the argument that additional legislation was needed to give "rights" to the homeless may appear – today – to be rather strange. But there were problems: some local authorities built relatively little housing and could not (or would not) meet the needs of genuinely homeless households within their area, whilst other local authorities, despite building a great deal of housing, could not meet the demands placed upon them in anything approaching a reasonable period of time. Ross's Act created a statutory entitlement for the homeless to be housed, either temporarily or permanently, by the local authority to whom they had applied. It gave, in practice, their cases greater priority than those of other persons who for the moment had accommodation of some type where they could remain. The impact of this was immense, particularly after 1979 when state funding for new housing diminished. Effectively, it reversed the lettings policies of every local authority in the UK. Up until 1977 most new council housing had either been let to existing tenants of other council properties in the same area, who were moved into better, improved properties, or was offered to whichever households had registered for the longest periods of time on their waiting list. After 1977 a high proportion of all new lettings went instead to people who were considered to be immediately homeless and/

or destitute. Clearly not foreseen by Ross, Freeson and the Act's many supporters this was the start of treating council housing as housing of the last resort, rather than a facility to which all could have access.

Notes

(1) Specifically, Taylor Woodrow modified the unreinforced H2 joints and adapted the design, pushing it up to 22 floors.

(2) On the enquiry see: https://api.parliament.uk/historic-hansard/lords/1968/nov/06/ronan-point-flats-inquiry-report Sir Alfred Pugsley was a structural engineer with expertise in aircraft design and suspension bridges and Sir Owen Saunders was a mathematician.

(3) The use of large panel systems to build significant amounts of public housing was extremely widespread. As well as the eastern bloc, where it was commonplace, Sweden adopted the system when implementing its 1965-1974 "Million Programme". Proportionally, this saw Sweden building three and half times the amount of state funded housing provided by the UK during the same period, which certainly puts into context how significant (and adventurous) the UK programme really was. Most of the examples of panel-system housing built outside the UK tended to be low or medium rise, though, and there were no examples abroad of spectacular Ronan Point type collapses.

(4) Quoted at https://www.constructionnews.co.uk/archive/07dec90-uk-tory-cash-donors-have-taylor-woodrow-at-head-of-list-06-12-1990

(5) And, for those who wish to make the comparison, like Le Corbusier, Poulson was not a qualified architect.

(6) As to how he got noticed in the first place, it helped Smith that he had been named Man of the Year by *The Architects' Journal* in 1960. It is worth stressing that councillors were not paid at this time: payment of attendance allowances was only introduced in 1972, by Heath, as part of his local government reforms.

(7) Four of the low-rise maisonette blocks were demolished in 1987 owing to their poor state of repair and unpopularity with tenants. At the time of writing two maisonette blocks and the high-rise block Crowhall Towers remain. Poulson provided Cunningham with holidays abroad and a (non-existent) job for his wife.

(8) Note in this context the rather odd timing behind the production of the film *Get Carter* which was filmed from July to September 1970. The novel on which this was based was optioned prior to publication, and the action was switched from Scunthorpe to Newcastle. The cast of characters includes a seedy amoral Mr Big (played by John Osborne) who dominates the area and a key scene has the anti-hero (played by Michael Caine) defenestrating one of the villains from the top of Owen Luder's brutalist car park in the centre of Gateshead after an attempt has been made at bribery.

(9) Poulson had managed by this point to get himself appointed as a Commissioner of Taxes, despite his own tax affairs being in considerable disarray. The Inland Revenue were eventually awarded a judgement against him in November 1968, and Poulson was removed from control of his companies just over a year later.

(10) Maudling had resigned his role with Poulson in 1969, after the Inland Revenue's successful action and prior to the removal of Poulson from control of his

companies. Poulson had paid him £5,000 per annum, approximately £140,000 today. Other MPs on the Poulson payroll were Albert Roberts (Labour, Normanton 1951-1983) who received £2,500/£70,000 pa and John Cordle (Conservative, 1959-1977) who received £1,000/£28,000 pa. Cordle was – eventually – forced to resign because of his dealings with Poulson.

(11) For all that, Nairn was quite measured in his comments about Owen Luder, the architect responsible for the much-derided Tricorn Shopping Centre in Portsmouth and Eros House, Catford. The latter was opposite another Luder scheme, the Catford Centre, built in expectation that the Fleet Line tube would be extended to south-east London. It has yet to arrive, though current plans might see the Bakerloo Line pass nearby quite soon.

(12) On brutal town centre schemes Sandbrook in *White Heat: A History of Britain in the Swinging Sixties* (2006) notes p624-626 that over 500 had appeared by 1965. This equates to about 25 proposals a year from 1945, which in a heavily populated and highly urbanised country, at a time of high state funding and post-war recovery, doesn't actually seem that excessive. Specific mention is made of the 1954 plan from Pilkington Glass to roof over 83 acres of Soho (roughly 13% of the area) with six high-rise residential blocks perched on top of this. As expected, it was never built but demonstrates the ambition, and avant-garde nature of many such plans at that time.

(13) Booker, who died in July 2019 was latterly a pronounced Eurosceptic and climate change denier.

(14) Technically, a site like this is known as a SLOAP (Site Left Over After Planning). There were many such miscellaneous parcels of land scattered around UK inner-cities from the 1960s, some taking decades to redevelop. Ballard would have seen many of these on his daily journey to work along the Westway via Trellick Tower.

(15) This can be watched at www.youtube.com/watch?v=UH5thwHTYNk

(16) On Goldfinger and his failure to get agreement for a concierge at Trellick Tower see *Erno Goldfinger: The Life of an Architect* by Nigel Warburton (2003). It is possible that the 1967 change of political control at GLC affected the approach made to Trellick Tower. The addition of large swathes of suburban London when the LCC was replaced in 1964 resulted in Labour losing control of the expanded body after 33 years and not returning to office until 1973.

(17) Particularly Alison Smithson who appears in the latter half of the film in a silvery glittery top. Peter Smithson makes do with a silver tie. They may have been emulating the garb worn at Grope Fest, which celebrated on 19 May 1970 the July 1969 death of Walter Gropius. The press coverage of this mentions men in silver ties and guests in shimmering silver robes. See: *The New York Times* 20 May 1970 at https://www.nytimes.com/1970/05/20/archives/gropefest-honors-gropius.html The article also states that those assembled were entertained by two rock bands and a nude revue. Which seems extraordinary until one considers that in his early life Gropius was the partner of Alma Mahler and, with Freud, Schnitzler and others, part of the avant-garde cultural life of pre-1914 Vienna.

(18) One wonders why the water bus service was ever considered a viable option. Milton Keynes is approximately 60 miles from London via the Grand Union Canal, which skirts the development rather than passing through its centre. The locks along the route are of limited width and any water bus would have been a narrow vessel akin to a long boat, capable of no more than 5-10 mph, implying a journey time of 6-12 hours.

(19) For a typical example of the mockery inflicted on Milton Keynes, listen to The Style Council's 1985 hit single *Come to Milton Keynes*.

(20) The Roskill Commission also included Alan Walters an economist who later helped justify the policies pursued by the Thatcher governments. There was considerable criticism of the cost benefit analysis that was used to identify Cublington as the original site. Heath, who had sat, as a civil servant, on the committee that oversaw the plans for the expansion of Heathrow in the late 1940s was a strong supporter of Foulness.

(21) As well as cancelling Foulness, the incoming Labour government also cancelled the Channel Tunnel rail link, Anthony Crosland claiming *"it is out of the question that the Government should approve or finance an investment of this magnitude"* and added into the mix a referendum on membership of the European Union. Interest in Foulness was briefly revived in 1979 by the then Conservative-led GLC and Essex County Council and finally died a few years later when Alan Walters persuaded the government that the project was too costly. For a detailed account of this see: https://researchbriefings.files.parliament.uk/documents/SN04920/SN04920.pdf

(22) The redevelopment of St Katharine's Docks, a GLC project, was undertaken by Taylor Woodrow, without mishap. The Brunswick Centre was originally a mixed-use, private-sector scheme, the residential portion of which was eventually leased by the council. Whittington Estate was designed by Peter Tabori, a Hungarian émigré and protégé of Erno Goldfinger.

(23) Similarly, the author encountered Andy "Thunderclap" Newman in "short-life" housing in south London in 2013, 44 years after he had enjoyed an enormous worldwide hit record with *Something in the Air*.

(24) Among Powell's backers in 1965 were Nicholas Ridley (Secretary of State for the Environment 1986-1989), John Biffen (Lord President of the Council 1982-1983, Lord Privy Seal 1983-1987), Michael Alison (Principal Private Secretary to Margaret Thatcher 1983-1987) and Harold Gurden (an early member of the Monday Club, and a keen advocate that council tenants should have a right to buy their properties). It is thought that Geoffrey Howe (Chancellor of the Exchequer 1979-1983, Foreign Secretary 1983-1989) may also have supported Powell.

(25) The right were clearly on the march when Powell unveiled his notions of what an ideal Conservative government budget would look like, at Morecambe in October 1968. This called for a reduction of the standard rate of tax to 21%, mass privatisation and the ending of all "housing and rent subsidies" except for those "who could not afford their own housing" (ie, ending future council house-building and reducing council housing to housing of the last resort). Under a Powell government the UK would have quickly returned to the house-building arrangements of circa 1880: private house-builders, building for rent and sale and a few isolated charities providing dwellings for the thrifty and well-to-do working classes.

(26) The 1970 Conservative Party manifesto is at http://www.conservativemanifesto.com/1970/1970-conservative-manifesto.shtml Containing much that seemed radical then, it reads now like an ongoing massive compromise: lurking behind each section, the comments in which are inevitably caveated, can be glimpsed nastier ideas waiting for their time.

(27) Stonehouse, in Lanarkshire, was designated a new town in 1973. Due to take Glasgow's overspill it was de-designated in 1976, only a few days after its first residents had moved in, and never built. Its cancellation reflected a change in government thinking: the UK should stop dispersing its population and industry from traditional urban areas and concentrate resources on these instead.

(28) Ridley's speech at Selsdon on 19 September 1973 is at: https://www.

margaretthatcher.org/document/110861 The Selsdon Group met, and were named after, the Selsdon Park Hotel where Heath's shadow cabinet had formulated their election manifesto in early 1970. Boetcker, a kind of prototype motivational speaker, made remarks frequently attributed to Abraham Lincoln, and Ridley is not alone in making this mistake.

(29) Both Enoch Powell and Keith Joseph prepared the way for Heath's eventual ousting. Powell stood down from his UK constituency in February 1974, announced that he would be voting Labour and urged his supporters to do likewise. In October 1974 he re-entered Parliament as an Ulster Unionist MP, also urging his British supporters to vote Labour. In both elections he gave as his reasons for doing so that Heath had taken the UK into the EEC without a mandate (which was untrue) and had reneged on his manifesto ie, Heath had not implemented the policies agreed at Selsdon in 1970. Joseph gave a speech on 19 October 1974, shortly after Heath's second electoral defeat, firmly putting the record straight about his own views and calling inter alia for a smaller state, lower taxes and compulsory birth control for those *of low education and... low educational attainment* to save the nation as it *moves toward degeneration*. The speech can be read at https://www.margaretthatcher.org/document/101830

(30) So much so that both contested, albeit without success, the Labour Party Leadership, Crosland in March 1976 and Shore in November 1980.

(31) Ross was able to pass his Act due to the Liberal-Labour pact that functioned during a period when the Labour Party lacked a majority, between March 1977 and September 1978. Des Wilson, a founder member of the housing charity Shelter, was a key figure advising the Liberal Party on their policies at this time. Legislation giving the homeless (and those threatened with homelessness) statutory rights had regularly been sought, without success, particularly after the huge success of the November 1966 BBC TV play *Cathy Come Home*. This was because both the main political parties were committed to the provision of state housing, and, indeed, building unprecedented amounts of it at that time and for many years thereafter. Would Labour have passed Ross's Act if it had enjoyed a majority in the House of Commons?

13

THE GOVERNMENT WITHDRAWS
AND THE PRIVATE SECTOR PREVAILS

The defeat of James Callaghan in the 1979 UK general election is correctly considered to mark the end of an era in post-war British political arrangements. Even the date itself looms like a tombstone over subsequent events. Many of the important democratic and bureaucratic structures that had existed up until that point – some, like the GLC and its predecessor body the LCC, for the best part of a century – were either scaled back or abolished in the years that followed. In many areas state funding gradually retreated back to levels last seen in the inter-war period. And the standard rate of taxation was cut, by governments of both political persuasions, finally reaching the levels suggested by Enoch Powell in his 1968 "budget", under Gordon Brown in 2008. Decade by decade the UK slowly but surely distanced itself from how other major western, socio-democratic, European economies conducted their affairs.

Public housing, and the central role the government had in providing this was an early casualty. The first year of the Thatcher administration saw the new government take statutory powers that allowed it to regulate local authority spending and borrowing. By November 1980, these powers had been strengthened further via the setting of strict limits on local authority capital expenditure. This produced a rapid (and permanent) reduction in the number of homes built by councils. In 1978, 114,000 council houses had been completed. By 1982, the figure was below 50,000; by 1991 below 10,000; and by 1999 it was statistically insignificant. The days of UK local authorities building large, ambitious new housing projects where homes could be rented at a reasonably low and affordable price were over.[1]

Visually and emotionally, though, the most enduring and immediate legacy of the early Thatcher years was the speedy recasting of Heath's rules about the sale of council homes to their tenants. Implemented in August 1980 this created a "Right to Buy" (RTB) which no local authority could gainsay. Unlike Heath's earlier version it discounted the value of the properties sold and placed the capital receipts firmly beyond the control of the council that was selling them.

Making RTB a statutory requirement had been planned prior to 1979 as a popular electoral tactic, but according to Michael Heseltine today, the intention (certainly from himself) was to release 75% of the capital receipts raised from the sales back to the local authorities to fund the construction of replacement housing. Nothing like this ever happened, and the arrangements he thought he had made with the Treasury never came to fruition. Instead, post-1983 RTB receipts were increasingly switched to fund tax cuts, something that he now cites as his greatest regret from his years in office.[2]

But even allowing for Heseltine's decent and socially scrupulous attempts to make the revised RTB rules work, one had to ask why the policy was needed at all. In 1981, the average RTB valuation (the value the property was assessed at, prior to the discount being applied) was £19,557. Assuming it was a house, and was sold with the then maximum discount of 50%, this produced a sales price of £9,778.50p.

At that time there were many areas, even in London, where an existing, non-council home could be bought for that amount, which was well within the means of many council tenants. All of which calls into question why the people buying their council homes didn't just buy their own home somewhere else, possibly with some financial assistance from the government. Or, for that matter, if the government really wanted to attract people of limited means to home ownership, why it simply didn't introduce a low-cost home ownership programme targeted at such households.[3]

One of the saddest aspects of the RTB as implemented after 1980 was the number of people who purchased "non-standard" properties: houses and flats built from large concrete panels, prefabs and so on. None of these was "mortgageable" by most building societies and banks because they were regarded (correctly in most cases) as temporary housing that was only ever expected to have a limited lifespan. Nevertheless, many were purchased and the tenants concerned often used their savings to do so. In the years that followed they found that they couldn't sell them on and, if they were a leaseholder, that they were obliged to pay for major repairs as and when these were carried out by the local council.

Whatever one thinks about such matters, it does appear clear today that in the eyes of its keenest advocates (Heseltine excepted) the real purpose of the RTB policy was to dramatically reduce the scale of council housing and even, eventually, to get to the point where it could be abolished.[4] Politically of course, RTB was a huge success and as every commentator notes it was one of the defining characteristics of the Thatcher era. At a very basic level – having a place that you owned, getting to a point where you didn't have to pay either rent or a mortgage, having the freedom to sell and move on, if you wished – it chimed with the aspirations of the Chartists' National Land Company over a century and a half earlier, or even with Jesse Collings's *three acres and a cow*. It was a dream of liberty.[5]

Returning to the Department of Environment in 1979, much of Heseltine's energies – the revised Right to Buy notwithstanding – were taken up with proposals for dealing with the continued decline of London's docks.[6] He did that by the relatively straightforward approach of establishing the London Docklands Development Corporation (LDDC), a body that operated in exactly the same way as those set up by Attlee, Macmillan and Wilson to build the new towns after 1945. It took over the ownership of the docks that still functioned and exercised planning, compulsory purchase and land acquisition powers across eight square miles. Repeating the approach taken by the GLC, and the Heath government in the late

1960s and early 1970s in regenerating the St Katharine's Docks, it worked extensively with private house-builders, construction companies and major employers on quickly redeveloping the area, parts of which had by then been derelict for between 15 and 20 years.

Much of the housing built under the auspices of the LDDC, at least in its earlier stages, was conventional, low-rise and very typical "English vernacular" in style, as anyone visiting parts of the former Surrey Docks or Beckton today can see. The abundance of ornamental trees, shrubs, planted areas, grass verges and footpaths are much more like Milton Keynes than London. The homes provided here were almost entirely for private sale, with much of it designated as economically priced (and sized) "starter homes".

Partly this was down to the house-builders: this was what they built, more or less, wherever they built it. But, part of it was also down to anti-high-rise views that had taken hold since Ronan Point, and which were reinforced by much of the thinking on housing throughout the 1980s. During the final throes of Callaghan's government, a White Paper, *Policy for the Inner Cities*, established a budget for dealing with specific areas where targeted investment was required. Most of this money became available from 1979, and was retained by the incoming Conservative administration.[7]

This funding extended beyond bricks-and-mortar initiatives into community consultation and area-based studies led by organisations like the Priority Estates Project which duly began studying various post-war estates and lobbying for changes in how they were managed and maintained. Along with this, and mining some of the same ground explored in the 1950s by Young and Willmott in Debden, came the academic, Alice Coleman, whose 1985 book *Utopia on Trial* quickly became a seminal text.

Studying the vandalism and crime that was so widely reported about public housing by the early 1980s, she argued that much of this was caused by design features within the estates and blocks themselves – windy hidden corners, anonymous stairwells, poor lighting and so on. Her solution was to build fewer such estates and more houses, the kind of give-people-what-they-want approach that Osborn had voiced throughout the 1940s and 1950s. Coming from a person with her credentials, though, this constituted something of an official imprimatur for the anti-high-rise/high-density view.[8]

Another factor in determining what the early stages of the LDDC's programme looked like was that Heseltine and the new government wanted to make an immediate impact in these areas. The money designated pre-1979 by Peter Shore for spending on the "Urban Programme" in the former docklands was welcome but would never have been enough to transform the area quickly, and nor could anything at all have been done with any great speed without the existence of a Development Corporation. Hence the appropriation of these powers and their use in at least the early stages of large-scale, tried-and-tested, private-housing designs. And within some of the former docklands this worked quite well and was popular.

The problem arose with the scale of the task the LDDC had taken on. The various development corporations that Heseltine set up in the early 1980s would eventually be allocated £3.5bn, but more than half of this ended up being spent in London. Nor was it just a case of counting how much cash the government was providing. In 1982, a Docklands Enterprise Zone was set up, within which anyone developing anything could claim 100% of their construction costs against tax and enjoy an exemption from paying business rates for 10 years on any non-residential building they erected. The indirect subsidies were, therefore, enormous.[9]

Nowhere would this approach be more evident than at Canary Wharf, a demolished 81-acre site in the centre of the abandoned West India Docks. Here, from 1988, an immense (by UK standards) complex of high-rise offices, steel-clad and over 800-feet high, was built. The developer was Paul Reichmann who demanded, and got, an undertaking that the Jubilee Line would be extended to serve his scheme before he started building.[10] The end result looked uncannily similar to his 1983 scheme at Brookfield Place, New York and was much disliked by both Margaret Thatcher and Prince Charles but for most people working in housing, town planning, property and architecture its completion represented a release from nearly two decades of having anything above 5-6 floors frowned on and regarded as problematic. High-rise was back, initially as offices, but quickly, and increasingly thereafter, as housing.

By the time Canary Wharf was being feted (or damned) as the embodiment of everything the LDDC represented, Heseltine had given way at the Department of the Environment to Nicholas Ridley, whose period in office brought about a sharp downsizing of the UK's commitment to social housing and local government. The regional government structures established by Heath were abolished in 1986, along with the GLC, and by the end of the decade Ridley had also overseen the winding up of 9 separate new town development corporations, far more than any of his predecessors or successors.

The disappearance of these bodies said a great deal about UK governance in the 1980s and 1990s. Why did they go? After all, the speed at which the new towns built their housing (almost all of which was popular and stood the test of time), their provision of high levels of employment, shopping, social welfare and educational facilities, mostly provided rapidly and to a standard not previously seen by ordinary people, and the integrated way that these were delivered, were clearly much to be admired. One argument for their demise, though, was their democracy deficit: no one voted for their membership, or had that much control over their decisions even allowing for the working relationships they gradually achieved with some of the local authorities in their areas. Significantly, some County Councils actively disliked them, and had always done so, as can be seen by the fracas over Stevenage in 1947.

It had been the intention that a development corporation would be abolished whenever it was felt that it had reached the targets set for its area. Indeed, three (Crawley and Hemel Hempstead in 1962; Hatfield, 1966) went early. For rather different reasons, the government pulled out of the four in Northern Ireland (Antrim, Ballymena, Craigavon and Derry) in 1973. When a development corporation ended, its housing was usually transferred to the local

authority and its assets reverted to the ownership of the New Towns
Commission, for onward disposal if required. But this had been
on the understanding that the housing would remain intact, and
even continue to be increased, by the local authority concerned,
and the integrated planning of the area would continue, with high
levels of government funding.

After 1979 what occurred was an abrupt ending of development
corporations, in some cases before they had reached their targets,
and much of the housing was quickly sold via the revised RTB
regulations soon after its transfer to the appropriate local authority.
Nor, by the early 1980s, did the host local authorities retain the
spending powers that their predecessor development corporations
had enjoyed.[11] This was a state of affairs that would have appalled
Osborn and Morrison. But would it have annoyed Howard?
After all, Howard wanted nothing to do with state funding and
envisaged, whatever the intricacies of his ownership model, an
almost entirely private sector-led execution of his theories. His
ideal, of low-density housing, built on greenfield sites for private
sale by private companies, chimed very neatly with what occurred
during the Thatcher-era, even if in design terms it failed to match
his exquisite vision.[12]

The demise of the new towns took place alongside other
significant changes introduced by Ridley. Firstly, to speed purchases
on their way, he increased the RTB discount for council house
sales to 70%. Then, from 1988, he reduced funding for housing
associations – by that point the only organisations building social
housing in appreciable numbers – by ending the 100% grant
funding they could claim against their schemes. Instead, they
were obliged to seek "mixed funding" by borrowing privately or
using their reserves when developing, with the state portion cut,
on average, to around 67%.

In some cases where a housing association had significant
reserves (as did some of the older trusts) there was a case for
restricting funding. Cutting grant levels had nothing to do with
this, though, as the regulatory body (the Housing Corporation)
had always had the power to refuse funding to any housing

association that had unusually high reserves. What Ridley established by doing this was the principle of gradually cutting funding for social housing, and easing its providers back to an era in which the state had less involvement in such enterprises, much as the Conservative governments of the 1920s had tried (unsuccessfully) to roll back the gains made by Addison and Wheatley. His crowning achievement, though, was the passing of legislation that allowed local authorities to transfer their council housing to another landlord, typically a housing association, or indeed, for the Secretary of State to dictate that such a course of action was desirable. As it happens, the latter option quickly proved unworkable after a series of raucous residents' meetings, in 1987-1988, including one at the former LCC Boundary Estate. Ridley quickly retreated to a compromise position: there had to be a ballot where tenants could accept or reject a transfer proposal. With this agreed, and with local authorities finding their social housing diminishing via the Right to Buy, as well as being in a position where they could no longer build new homes, large-scale stock transfers began, the first occurring in Chiltern District Council in December 1988.[13]

These were huge changes and reversed, in less than a decade, the consensus on funding and management arrangements for public housing that had been built up, step by step, in the UK between the 1880s and the 1960s. It was a truly radical programme and chimed neatly with Enoch Powell's comments on housing in 1955 as well as his 1968 projected budget for a model Conservative government. When finally implemented it took place against a backdrop of spending and borrowing limits being imposed on local authorities, rising unemployment and cuts in the standard rate of income tax: to 29% in 1986, 27% a year later and finally to 25% by 1988, a level last levied in 1938.[14]

* * * * * *

After 1990, the rate of change was less frenetic and the climate gentler. John Major replaced Margaret Thatcher as Prime Minister and Heseltine returned as Secretary of State for the Environment, moving upwards a couple of years later to the position of Deputy Prime Minister. Within the Department of the Environment the housing portfolio was assigned to Sir George Young, who remained in post until 1994, as the new government pursued various inner-city regeneration schemes.

The most significant of these was City Challenge, regarded by Heseltine today as his finest accomplishment. Launched in 1991-1992, it was a programme targeted at local authorities that clearly exhibited signs of considerable blight, disadvantage and need. These authorities were invited to bid for government funding, made available for a period of five years, to improve a specific area – such as a town centre – where these problems were concentrated. They were required to involve residents, businesses and voluntary bodies in drawing up the proposals that they put to the government, and in particular needed to show how much inward (or "matching") investment from private sources their schemes would generate. Bids were judged on whether they met accepted local needs, their general outputs (homes built, jobs created, adults trained, and so on) and, most importantly, the "gearing" between the money the government supplied and how much additional investment came from the private and voluntary sectors. The greater the leverage, the more likely the government was to approve the bid. Funding was administered by a discrete local body, separate from the local council (although it included some locally elected members) which included representatives from businesses, other government agencies (the police, the NHS), voluntary groups and the wider public as well as the officials responsible for running the scheme. Thus were the criticisms aimed at earlier regeneration bodies, such as the new town corporations, and the LDDC, answered.

City Challenge provided a democratic balance that had previously been lacking within such bodies, with no one group of representatives able to outvote any of the others and the government retaining the power to suspend or deny funding if the agreed plans were amended without its approval. What Major, Heseltine and Young were doing here was carrying on – within the constraints set by their own party – the government-directed policies of the 1940s, 1950s and 1960s in a way that provided for greater accountability, resident involvement, and, given each programme only lasted for 5 years, maximum impact.

City Challenge was not a housing programme, but the provision of new homes played a considerable part within it. In particular, the demolition of selected 1960s estates, usually built from large concrete panels or similar materials, was a common factor to successful bids. They were replaced with new mixed-tenure developments, often built to a comparable or higher density, the physical implementation of which highlighted one of the problems created by the post-1980 Right to Buy sales: leasehold properties had to be "bought back" slowly and expensively (and often with the threat of compulsory purchase) before any redevelopment could commence. The need to do this greatly increased the price of estate redevelopments and slowed down such programmes hugely, in some cases causing further blight as they did so.[15]

None of these redevelopments was carried out by local councils acting on their own and almost no new council housing was provided by them. By 1992, council house-building was insignificant as a source of new homes and remains very low today despite some local authorities venturing back, very expensively, into new build.

Major, Heseltine and Young knew this and, acting within the antipathy to council housing within their own party, opted instead to provide new social housing via housing associations. They boosted spending accordingly and 26,500 new housing association homes were being built annually by 1992, with the number climbing, very slowly, to around 35,000 per annum today. Within the limits it set, City Challenge was a success, and a model that might have been usefully continued by the politicians who came after John Major.

By 1994, Heseltine was planning Thames Gateway as a follow-up. Hugely ambitious, the aim was to build a million new homes on abandoned industrial land in the Thames estuary, in a programme that was intended, Heseltine stated in 2020, to *"recreate the urban initiatives that had run from 1979 to 1983"*, though its lineage clearly stretched back in many ways to Heath's plans for south Essex in the early 1970s. Alas, Thames Gateway moved very slowly, and as events would transpire, failed to emerge from its chrysalis. The government's well documented problems with a minority of its own MPs about Europe restricted the amount of time available for complex projects. Added to which, by 1995, Heseltine was increasingly taken up with his duties as Deputy Prime Minister and Sir George Young no longer Minister for Housing. Momentum was being lost and John Major's period as Prime Minister and leader of a heavily divided party came to an end a couple of years later. The end of an 18-year spell of Conservative control was much celebrated in many quarters at the time. Political judgements are typically arrived at via a heavy dose of rough justice, but even allowing for this, it was unfair to rope in the relatively centrist government of Major and Heseltine with the longer, earlier and somewhat more caustic Thatcher period. Judging the legacy left by such a lengthy period of one-party government, though, one cannot help but concentrate on the assumptions that had underpinned the direction of travel.

Firstly, for many on the political right it was taken as axiomatic that, within housing, construction and planning, the private sector had been hampered by an excess of regulation and red tape. It was held that, if this were altered, a revival in private house-building would inevitably follow which would meet natural demand. In fact, post-1945, the private sector had enjoyed its most successful years when the state played a major role in planning the economy: it built 221,000 homes in 1964 (when Keith Joseph was Minister for Housing) and 226,000 in 1968 (under Anthony Greenwood). After 1979, the private sector only once came near this (in 1988 when it completed 207,000 homes) and frequently built at only half this level. To put it another way, in the period between 1964 and 1980 (a greatly maligned era) house-building had averaged 318,000 completions annually. Between 1981 and 1990, it slipped to 184,000 per annum, slightly higher than the inter-war period, and, by the 1990s, it was averaging only 138,000 a year, a return to pre-1914 levels.[16] Obviously, the figures wobbled about a bit, depending on overall economic circumstances, but after the mid-1980s the UK failed to build enough homes for its population. The truth was the private sector couldn't pick up the slack of the state. It had never done so. Nor could it reverse the policies set by the state, particularly when cutting income tax remained a central policy: the standard rate declining to 24% in 1996 and 23% by 1997. And, even though spending on housing association new build increased, by 1995 overall spending on public sector housing in the UK had halved in real terms, compared with 1980. Despite Heseltine's initiatives, the numbers of new homes being built declined sharply.[17]

Secondly, in the absence of new towns and new housing estates, what the private sector provided from the 1980s onwards were a lot of low-density suburban schemes, often sprawling on the edge of existing towns. In appearance these were a seamless continuum of "English vernacular", consisting of low-rise, often semi-detached houses and small, discreet blocks of flats. They usually came with a lot of surrounding landscaping (the maintenance of which was paid for via a service charge levied on local residents) and the properties themselves were smaller than those built previously thanks to the abolition of the Parker Morris standards in 1980.

Some might consider that the apogee of this style arrived in 1987, on the outskirts of Dorchester. Here, on land owned by the Duchy of Cornwall, Prince Charles began building Poundbury. Promoted as a carefully designed, self-contained, community-orientated town, even though it was, strictly speaking, a suburb of a long-established urban area, a great deal more thought went into this than other private sector-led projects of the time. Driehaus Prize-winner Léon Krier was hired to design the scheme, construction of which finally started in 1993.[18] Built in a variety of styles – Queen Anne, Georgian, imitation mid-nineteenth century cottage but most definitely not modern and never brutal – it covers less than a square mile and will eventually house around 6,000 people. Reminding one of a larger and more ambitious Portmeirion, it isn't unique and there are other places like it, particularly Seaside, Florida, used in 1997 as the setting for *The Truman Show*. Together these are referred to as the "New Urbanism", and are popular with some people. If they demonstrated anything, it was that their aesthetic is valued even if they aren't really much like old towns. It is interesting to note that, in the current debate about the beauty and appearance of new homes, these characteristics count for more than affordability. Ultimately, though with a proposed density of about 12,000-12,500 people per square mile (about 19 per acre, equating to an average of 4-5 homes per acre, a figure beneath those contemplated by Frederic Osborn), one thing is certain. Given the challenges faced through population growth, migration, food production and climate change, Poundbury and its cousins cannot and should not be the future of housing provision in the UK or anywhere else.[19]

* * * * * *

The election of a Labour government in 1997 was felt at the time to represent the beginning of a new era. It was expected, in housing, planning and regeneration circles, that the best of the Heseltine-Major initiatives would be continued, expanded and buttressed by substantial additional funding, with the state well to the fore in directing activities. Fresh programmes were anticipated too, dealing with all the difficulties caused by the post-1979 deindustrialisation of the economy. In fact, what emerged was far from being a change of direction. Rather like Heath in 1970, Blair created a super ministry, the Department of Environment, Transport and Regions, with John Prescott installed as Secretary of State, and, like Heseltine, doubling as Deputy Prime Minister. Rebranded the Department of Transport, Local Government and Regions in 2001, by 2005 it had been split up, with the housing section represented by the Secretary of State for Communities and Local Government. Housing itself remained a junior position, overseen by nine separate ministers during the thirteen years Labour were in office. The implication appeared to be that building homes was just one of many things with which local councils had an involvement, and wasn't a specific priority. There was a slight shift from 2007 when Blair's successor, Gordon Brown, allowed the Minister of State for Housing and Planning to attend cabinet meetings. But it remained a low-level portfolio.

Underscoring this lack of change, whilst certain government functions including housing were eventually devolved (after endorsement by referenda) to Scotland and Wales, the establishment of the Greater London Authority in 2000 was not accompanied by any attempt to resurrect the role of the GLC in this area. New Labour was not interested in fleets of Morrison-style estates, built to house the needy.[20] Indeed, the early Blair years saw the winding up of the London Docklands Development Corporation (1998) and the demise of the Commission for New Towns, which were formally abolished after paying back £80m to the Treasury in 1999 in respect of various outstanding loans. The option of rebooting either of these – to, say, build new towns or implement the stalled Thames Gateway project – was not taken. What emerged instead was New Deal for Communities. This dropped the competitive bidding between local authorities that had marked City Challenge in favour of inviting local authorities where deprivation was judged to exist to submit proposals for their area, the funding of which would then be negotiated with them. New Deal for Communities was not time-limited to five years either: a much longer period was allowed with the possibility of an exit strategy from the scheme that left in place some type of community investment organisation for the funding of ongoing projects well into the future.

By 1999, there were 39 NDC areas in operation between Bristol and Newcastle, with 10 of these in London. Some were focused on housing estates, but the majority were centred on neighbourhoods within local authorities.[21] Compared with City Challenge, the visual impact of the spending was less obvious as much of it went instead on training initiatives, childcare, literacy schemes or improving policing. Things which in other countries would be dealt with, as a matter of course, by far more adequately resourced local government, and, in fact, had been delivered by local government in the UK when it had the means to do so. For reasons that were never clear, neither Blair nor Brown were keen on re-establishing the type of regional government units that Heath had favoured. Nor were they interested in raising taxes – locally or nationally – back to the level where services of this type could be provided on a continual basis, somewhat more comprehensively.

Also observable during the Blair-Brown years was a tendency by the UK to simply copy US policy. Initiatives such as Underserved Markets, the Hope VI programme and Business Improvement Districts were all trialled in the UK. None of them achieved a great deal.[22] These attempts to pick a winner from across the Atlantic neglected to take into account the astonishing de-urbanisation of US cities (such as Detroit), a process that had been greatly accelerated by an extraordinary scale of private sector-led house-building, suburbanisation and car dependency.[23] To many this was an elementary consideration, and the UK's persistence in implementing schemes that were devised in another country with markedly different characteristics was one of the odd features of the 1997-2010 Labour governments. It was, though, intellectually consistent with Howard's adoption, a century earlier, of a US model for his original garden city proposal.

Finally, in 2000, after it had been in abeyance for a couple of years, Thames Gateway was formally launched. It was deemed necessary that this required not one, but two separate development corporations: London Thames Gateway Development Corporation and Thurrock Thames Gateway Development Corporation. Both had the same powers exercised by their predecessor bodies, but neither had either the funds or the borrowing facilities available to implement its projects within a reasonable timescale. More to the point, the membership of both differed considerably from that of the earlier corporations and Heseltine's City Challenge bodies. Instead of a balance between different interests (business, community, political and voluntary) both contained a great many councillors representing the various local authorities they covered, proportionally far more than had been the case previously. Because of this, and because too of an overly cautious approach to consultation, getting agreement over a credible business plan proved difficult, and, incredibly, no overall masterplan for the Thames Gateway area ever appeared.[24] When interviewed in 2020, Aman Dalvi (Chief Executive of London Thames Gateway, 2002-2010) compared his experience unfavourably to his prior dealings with City Challenge bodies, noting *"Heseltine's plans did work – but only as long as he was in power"*. He also observed that funding was minuscule compared to amounts available when he had worked at the Housing Corporation in the early 1990s, and also much more difficult to access: *"it was like trying to extract teeth without anaesthetic"*.

This was New Labour's attempt at a major initiative and, compared with the new towns of the 1940s, 1950s, 1960s and 1970s, and compared even with City Challenge in the 1990s, it failed utterly. In 2010, both development corporations came to the end of their intended life.[25] Neither was retained. Whatever they still had left to do, most of which would have happened anyway, was delegated to the local authorities across their areas to continue with in a piecemeal fashion. Much of the land holdings that had been assigned to them went to the Greater London Authority, and a good portion of this in and around Stratford was developed for use as the 2012 Olympic Park. Heseltine today is very clear about what went wrong, stating when interviewed that the Labour government generally had insufficient commitment to its development corporations and that Blair in particular made no serious effort at making them work.

* * * * * *

The Conservatives returned to power in 2010, initially leading a coalition government, later with an outright majority. Eric Pickles held the position of Secretary of State for Communities and Local Government between 2010 and 2015 and remains at the time of writing the last figure in UK politics to have held a portfolio overseeing housing and planning for a significant number of years. Like his predecessor Prescott he did not affect the UK's direction of travel which remained focussed on a private sector house-building model with a preference for low-density suburban options.

Gordon Brown's practice of having the junior housing minister attend cabinet meetings was discontinued, and in a further sign that the new administration had very specific ideas about what type of homes the government ought to be providing, the new Chancellor of the Exchequer abolished funding for "social rent", the type of rented housing local authorities (and housing associations) had been building since their inception. What would be provided in its place was low-cost home ownership and "sub-market" rent, the latter, in an echo of what the various nineteenth century industrial dwellings companies provided, typically set at 80 per cent of market rents, so that in areas of high demand (such as London) they were always significantly higher, and therefore less affordable, than equivalent social rents.

Looking further afield, and continuing with its cost-cutting approach, by 2011 the new government had wound up all the New Deal for Community schemes established by Blair and Brown in 1998-1999. In place of these came, eventually, a package of proposals from Heseltine, now in the House of Lords and operating as an "urban regeneration Czar". Known as "Plan H" these were intended to stimulate economic growth outside London, with an emphasis on decentralising control from Whitehall. Significant funds for this were announced in 2013, but little transpired as Cameron and his successors were hamstrung by the need to spend most of their time dealing with Brexit and its ongoing consequences.

Heseltine also tried to reboot the Thames Gateway initiative, persuading Chancellor of the Exchequer George Osborne it was unfinished business, which indeed it was. In this he was partially successful, as Osborne announced in March 2014 "a brand-new garden city" at Ebbsfleet, Kent.[26] To achieve this, he established the Ebbsfleet Development Corporation, under government control, with funding of £300m. There was no question of this being spent, as had been the case with the new towns, on local authority-style housing. Instead, the role of the Ebbsfleet Development Corporation was to coordinate development by various private house-builders (a minority of whom might be "Registered Providers", as housing associations were now called) and to act as the planning authority within its designated area. Up to 15,000 new homes would be built, and comparisons were made with the Stockholm suburb of Hammarby, an exemplary high-density scheme with many built-in environmental features.

Some people opposed this. Architect Richard Rogers, who had advised the Blair-Brown government in the late 1990s, commented *"They shouldn't be building down there. East London still has masses of brownfield land, so why are we building 15 miles out? This is not a sustainable option"* whilst Councillor Derek Hunnisett (Dartford, Conservative) noted *"We are looking for a higher quality than the normal and what we are getting is the norm – standard off-the-peg stuff"*. Both points of view were (and are) fair: Ebbsfleet is a conventional house-builder scheme, slotted in on vacant land near Ebbsfleet International railway station. Covering approximately 2,100 acres, its average density of 7-8 homes per acre was well within the parameters Frederic Osborn had recommended from the 1930s through to the 1970s. What the critics didn't address, though, was why something they would have been happier with hadn't happened during the Blair-Brown years. And indeed, why a clutch of development corporations, specifically to build new towns, hadn't been launched by John Prescott and instructed to develop schemes in line with Rogers's recommendations in his 1999 report *Towards an Urban Renaissance*. Ebbsfleet continues to emerge and has survived the dramatic post-2015 political changes in the UK. Currently, its non-housing targets include the construction of London Resort, a massive theme park consisting of water features, theatres, live music venues, cinemas, restaurants and hotels, as well as a training academy for the entertainment and hospitality sector, a new country park and a large science and education facility. In 2021, the Johnson government designated this as vital national infrastructure, allowing the developers to bypass local planning authorities. Some of the attractions on the site will be licensed by Hollywood-based Paramount Pictures and marketed by them as a rival to Disneyland.[27]

Unlike Ebbsfleet both George Osborne and Heseltine failed to survive the 2016 transition from Cameron to May. The vicissitudes of that government are well known, but within housing May and her Chancellor of the Exchequer Philip Hammond did at least reintroduce funding for social rent, assisting greatly the provision of slightly more affordable housing for those renting from Registered Providers.[28] Further signs of change occurred in 2019 when Boris Johnson reinstated the attendance of the housing minister at cabinet, and again in 2021 with the rebranding of the Secretary of State for Communities and Local Government as the Secretary of State for Levelling-Up, Housing and Communities. The new incumbent, Michael Gove (the sixth in as many years) becomes the first holder of the housing brief to attend full cabinet, and exercise voting rights, in 52 years.[29]

* * * * * *

Any account of the political and economic travails affecting housing in recent decades needs to comment on house price inflation, a phenomenon closely intertwined with rocketing increases in the value of land over the same period. Most people who own, have owned or would wish to own property have some experience of this. The scale of the problem, though, is only partially understood and many do not realise that in historical terms this is actually quite a recent phenomenon.

In his 1981 autobiography *A Better Class of Person*, playwright and actor John Osborne comments about how, in what was then the recent past, he heard an actor at a party state that he had bought a house in Finlay Street, London SW6 (where Osborne lived in the 1930s) for £15,000, a figure Osborne found amazing. The implication was that the transaction happened at some point in the mid-1970s, when £15,000 was approximately 3.5-3.75 times "average" annual earnings. For Osborne, who would have had memories of such properties being sold pre-war for maybe £200-

£300, this was incredible. Today (2021) the website www.rightmove. co.uk proudly advises that *"Properties in Finlay Street had an overall average price of £2,136,667 over the last year... Overall, sold prices in Finlay Street over the last year were similar to the previous year and 10% down on the 2014 peak of £2,366,238"*. All of which means that if you want to buy in Finlay Street now, the purchase price would be about 69 times average annual earnings. In the same book, Osborne also remarks that in the mid-1930s his grandmother lived in a semi-detached mock-Tudor house in Stoneleigh, near Epsom, Surrey. He states *"At this time, houses in places like Stoneleigh cost something in the region of £300 to £600 to buy, but many were rented"*. [30] In other words, circa 1935, you could buy a 3-bed semi, at the lower end of this scale, for twice average annual earnings. This earnings to property ratio held good until at least the beginning of the 1970s, when it was still possible to buy a new, or newish, home in an outer London suburb like Chessington, for about £3,000.

What caused this startling divergence of prices from earnings was the political desire to expand personal borrowing. Credit of any type – mortgages, hire purchase, bank loans – had traditionally been heavily regulated, and even frowned on, within the UK economy. In the last 40-50 years, though, it has become increasingly available and for much of the time, by historical standards, scarcely regulated at all. The OECD report today that UK household debt (the 11th highest in the world) is 142% of net disposable income.[31] According to the IMF, it is the equivalent to 87% of Gross Domestic Product. The IMF also note that, using this reckoning, it rose from 30% in 1980 to a peak of 94% by 2010. The International Institute of Finance paints an even starker picture, noting that the UK has comfortably the worst levels of household debt in the "mature markets", at 84% of GDP against only 58% within the Euro area and a level that exceeds even the US. (The UK also boasts the highest levels of financial services debt).[32]

All of which suggests that the "official" way of managing the UK economy, whatever some third parties might claim, is a kind of bust-boom model based on easy credit. Anyone who has lived through the last 40 or so years will have experienced a bust (1979), followed by a boom (1982), another bust (1988), a long boom (1993), a grim bust (2007) and, as far as house prices and personal debt are concerned, another boom (2013). How great the next bust might be, and how long it will last, is a matter of conjecture. The rapid rise in private house prices and land values that has occurred throughout this period escalated at some speed after the 1992 opening of the Land Registry to public enquiries, after which the appearance of all this data on the internet, by the late 1990s, led to a boom in land trading.[33]

As the first quarter of the twenty-first century draws to a close, the UK's house-builders have reverted to an almost pre-1914 model, or if not quite that, something John Osborne would have recognised during his childhood. They sell most of their product, but an increasing amount is now being rented out, via buy-to-let landlords. Within England, private home owners now account for 60% of all households, with the private rented sector at 21%. In another echo of the pre-1914 era, the latter category is now bigger than the number of housing association and local authority tenants combined at 11% and 8% respectively. Social housing rents have also reverted, with their emphasis on sub-market renting, to levels that would have been familiar to those running the Victorian and Edwardian "dwelling companies".

Despite all these changes the commercial house-builders have continued with their traditional model: they build mainly in the suburbs or on "greenfield" sites, and they build mainly low-rise, low-density schemes of a type that are popular with the public. Sometimes they build in inner-urban or town centre areas too, and when they do, they build high-density blocks, some of which are architecturally quite striking. They have always done this, and they are very good at it. But they will never, by themselves, meet housing demand. (They never have). Aman Dalvi commented, about his experience in Thames Gateway, which counted in a lot of already existing private housing schemes as part of its "outputs" *"The house builders just did what they had always done. They were not particularly interested unless they felt they couldn't sell their homes, at which point they would ask for infrastructure improvements"*. For him, and indeed for many people hoping something dramatic might still emerge in Thames Gateway, the problem was that the government treated the house-builders as the main driving force rather than the Development Corporation itself, or indeed any of the larger housing associations. Philosophically, within much of the UK's political class, the expectation is still that the private sector should lead any programme, providing whatever social housing is deemed necessary via legal agreements with local authorities and the registered providers that operate in their area. For most people, in most places, this remains the face of house-building in the UK today.

But there are alternatives. This is clearly evident in east London where astonishing population increases have occurred in the last 40 years – 71% in Newham and 129% in Tower Hamlets – as the redevelopment of the area that was started by the London Docklands Development Corporation continues to rumble on.[34] At Canary Wharf, Reichmann's pioneering offices are now circled by 18 residential towers, all of them between 350 and 700 feet high, looking like the offspring of an adjoining matriarch. Much of what they contain will consist of uber-expensive apartments, and some will be purchased by overseas buyers. But the scale is impressive. The same approach has given birth to other clusters of large towers elsewhere: in Croydon, North Acton and Stratford. [35] These and a few others like them are the only equivalent the UK has to the great towering cities of Asia. There are other plans elsewhere too. The Peabody Trust aim to complete Thamesmead, whilst on the opposite side of the Thames an abundance of new neighbourhoods, blocks and "quarters" continues to march across Newham. The juxtaposition of so many carefully designed and elegant buildings together with the attention now given to providing transport links and environmental sustainability makes one hope that a new form of architecture has arrived and taken root in the UK. One that can meet the demands of the future without worsening the condition of our world still further.

Notes

(1) There has been a small resurgence in council house-building in recent years – about 8,500 are included in the 2021-2026 Greater London Assembly programme – but it is nothing like the level formerly seen.

(2) A point made by him when interviewed for this book.

(3) For more on this see Beckett *Promised You a Miracle: Why 1980-1982 Made Modern Britain* p226. The author recollects being advised in Hackney in the mid-1980s that the average purchase price of ex-local authority maisonettes in Fellows Court E2 was around £6,000.

(4) It is worth noting in this respect the comments of Enoch Powell in 1962 *"The council house system today is morally and socially damaging. I think we ought to do something about this nuisance"*. Quoted in Beckett p220 and elsewhere.

(5) It seems ironic, given Margaret Thatcher's close identification with the RTB, that the famous picture of her celebrating the sale of a council house to its new owner dates from 1978 – before she was PM. See *The Guardian* 6 April 2014 at https://www.theguardian.com/society/2014/apr/06/margaret-thatcher-britains-obsession-property-right-to-buy Disputes continue about whether the Labour Party ought to have had its own RTB policy pre-1979. Rarely discussed is whether any other countries do this, and if they do, how the policy is managed.

(6) The majority of which had shut by 1979: East India Docks (1967), St Katharine's Dock (1968, sold to the GLC), London Docks (1969, sold to the London Borough of Tower Hamlets) and the Surrey Docks (1971). The West India Docks and the Royal Docks both closed in 1981.

(7) See Hansard 8 November 1977 where the Secretary of State for the Environment, Peter Shore, comments *"In my previous statement of 6th April I announced the Government's decision to increase the Urban Programme, to assist the inner cities in grant-aided expenditure, from the existing level of £30 million to £125 million in 1979. Five partnership areas were then announced—in Liverpool, Birmingham, Manchester/ Salford and, in London, Lambeth and Docklands—and on 24th October I made provisional allocations to them of £50 million a year for a three-year period from the starting date. I also told the House on 6th April that we would be giving further consideration to the case put by other authorities for assistance with their urban problems"*. One of the subsequent criticisms of City Challenge funding in 1992 was that it amounted to less – in terms of government money – per annum than the Urban Programme scheme it replaced. However, this does not take into account matching non-government funding that it attracted.

(8) Coleman, who carried out a Land Use Survey of the UK in the 1960s, didn't really consider in detail the impact on housing management of the Housing (Homeless Persons) Act 1977 and its higher volume of statutorily homeless households, the accelerated right to buy and how that impacted (visually, in particular) on people's attitude to their surroundings, spending cuts, the tripling of unemployment in the early 1980s and so on. Or even minor technical changes: there were no spray cans in the 1940s and 1950s, and therefore much less graffiti. One wonders why the Barbican Estate, which exhibits many of the problems she identifies, works so well.

(9) See *The Guardian* 7 March 1999.

(10) At the point Reichmann agreed to participate in Canary Wharf his net worth was cited as being $10 billion, making him one of the richest individuals in the world. By 1992, however, he had run out of cash and his business collapsed.

See his obituary at https://www.nytimes.com/2013/10/26/business/paul-reichmann-who-helped-develop-the-world-financial-center-dies-at-83 html This notes *"Mr. Reichmann took enormous business risks. He bet that each new development project could exceed the size of the previous one and still attract enough tenants to produce a windfall"* A colleague, Andrew Sarlos, likened him to *"a gambler, like being a heroin addict – he cannot stop,"* whilst in an article in Institutional Investor in 2000 Reichmann himself was quoted as stating *"You don't get the returns if you don't take the risk".* An interesting remark given his refusal to start Canary Wharf without the Jubilee Line.

(11) Also lost was the collective memory and associated database within the new towns as they gradually disappeared. At its peak Milton Keynes Development Corporation employed 1200 people.

(12) The winding up dates of those not already mentioned were as follows: Corby, Harlow, Stevenage (1980), Bracknell (1982), Northampton, Redditch, Skelmersdale (1985), Basildon, Central Lancashire (1986), Aycliffe, Cwmbran, Peterborough, Peterlee, Washington (1988), Runcorn, Warrington (1989), Telford (1991), Milton Keynes (1992), Glenrothes (1995), Cumbernauld, Irvine, East Kilbride (1996) and Livingston (1997). The hugely popular film *Gregory's Girl* was shot at Cumbernauld in 1980, whilst it was still being developed.

(13) As a result of this, by 2008, 1.5m council homes had been transferred and a third of local authorities had completely eliminated their involvement with social housing. Ironically, such transfers slowed down RTB sales (incoming tenants post-transfer were not able to exercise this right) and also increased the building of new social housing on transferred ancillary land. Whether Ridley envisaged this is not clear.

(14) On this see *Thatcher's Progress: From Social Democracy to Market Liberalism Through an English New Town* Guy Ortolano 2019 which argues how extensive the changes implemented by Thatcher were. Home ownership had never been suppressed pre-1979, even in the new towns. At Milton Keynes in 1979 41% of the development corporation programme were houses for sale. What did get suppressed was housing for rent, which had sunk to nil by 1990.

(15) A good example of this being the redevelopment of the Aylesbury Estate in Southwark.

(16) See English Housing Survey 2015 at www.designingbuildings.co.uk

(17) The Greater London Assembly *Planning for London's Growth* (2002) has council completions at 20,000-25,000 annually until 1978. Below 10,000 by 1982, they were no longer significant by 1987. Housing association completions were collected as part of private housing until 1975 after which they were shown as being around 1,500-2,500 annually, rising to 5,000 by 1993. The private sector built around 8,000-9,000 annually year on year, decade on decade. During the high point of the LDDC (roughly 1987-1995) the private sector increased to 11,000-14,000. Once funding for council housing ended, insufficient homes were built in London.

(18) Krier, from Luxembourg, originally worked at Sir James Stirling's modernist practice. The first sign of his revolt against this came in 1977 when he devised an unimplemented scheme for Blundell Corner in Hull which envisaged a neo-classical redevelopment of the area. Prior to being appointed to masterplan Poundbury he published *Albert Speer: Architect 1932-1942* which attempts to reappraise Speer's legacy.

(19) The favourite architect of the Prince of Wales appears to be Quinlan Terry, who designed a castle for the Barclay brothers in the Channel Islands, and was appointed, by the Qatar Investment Authority, to redesign the Chelsea Barracks

scheme after criticism from HRH. Terry's son is an architect too and has worked on Poundbury.

(20) The GLA got a regulatory role, though. In 2011 it reintroduced Parker Morris-type space standards, following on from similar action in 2008 by English Partnerships, a government agency that held a great deal of former new town and development corporation land.

(21) One of these covered the Aylesbury Estate in Southwark. A 10-year plan, it didn't start until 2009. New Deal for Communities boards had a far higher ratio of local community representatives than City Challenge, often up to as many as half the membership.

(22) For a critique of this pro-US approach see *Regeneration and Renewal* 4 November 2005 *Lost in Translation* by Ben Walker and 1 December 2006 *Hope Springs Eternal* by Joey Gardiner. At the time *Regeneration and Renewal* magazine was one of a stable of publications run by the Haymarket Press, Michael Heseltine's company. In January 2002 the author attended a dining club in Hackney (Socialist Piecrust) where the keynote speaker was Lord Falconer, at that point Minister for Housing, Planning and Regeneration. Falconer had flown into London that day from Los Angeles, where he had been on a fact-finding visit to study urban renewal.

(23) On the scale of collapse within US cities see the article *Requiem for a Dream* in *The Telegraph Magazine* 5 July 2008. The key work on this topic remains Jane Jacobs's 1961 book *The Life and Death of American Cities*. Jacobs cites Greenwich Village (population 23,000; density 79,000 per square mile) as an ideal example of a neighbourhood.

(24) Conversation with Aman Dalvi 19 August 2020. The London Borough of Bexley stopped construction of a new bridge between North Woolwich and Thamesmead, which had originally featured in the Abercrombie Plan. In previous development corporations an individual local authority would never have been able to block a major scheme.

(25) Mention should be made of the increasing housing role afforded to the Mayor of London from 2000, and in particular the introduction by them of viability assessments that seek to increase affordable housing provision within large private sector schemes. This is welcome, but as with the building of new council homes in limited numbers, is no substitute for the spending and planning powers that were once enjoyed at regional government level.

(26) In fact, Ebbsfleet had been identified as a major redevelopment site as far back as 1996, this being one of the reasons for opening Ebbsfleet International Station in the area in 2007.

(27) The Cameron government also set up the Old Oak and Park Royal Development Corporation to oversee the development of redundant railway land and adjoining industrial estates in west London. This too is unlike an NDC, although in this case day-to-day management is devolved to the Mayor of London.

(28) In this context it may be relevant that Hammond had previously been a director of the Castlemead Group, a medium- sized developer. See https://www.castlemead-ltd.co.uk/residential/

(29) Since 1997 there have been 11 cabinet ministers with overall responsibility for housing and 18 junior ministers. In terms of a modest change for the better we should note that the GLA Housing Budget 2020-2021 increases grant per unit for social rent from £70,000 to £160,000-£180,000 per unit. (Very approximately a grant rate of 54% ie, less than that available between 1988 and 2002). Outside London, Homes for England pay about £60,000.

(30) See John Osborne: *A Better Class of Person* 1981 p17 and p39.

(31) See https://data.oecd.org/hha/household-debt.htm

(32) See https://www.iif.com/Portals/0/Files/content/Global%20Debt%20Monitor_January2020_vf.pdf It is worth commenting that throughout the UK's period as a major oil production nation there was, effectively, bipartisan agreement on not establishing a Sovereign Wealth Fund. Instead of being used to plan industrial expansion and significant regeneration, oil revenues were largely used to subsidise tax cuts.

(33) Pre-1992 enquiries to the Land Registry about land ownership could only be made via a solicitor. Post-1992, there were a vast number made by members of the public seeking information about plots of land in their area, or even the precise particulars of their own homes.

(34) A victim of which was the Smithsons' Robin Hood Gardens which was demolished after only 45 years due to repair costs of £77,000 per unit. Which is not that much, actually, for a bespoke high-profile development. The truth was that land in that location was simply too valuable, and the mythologies, about how dreadful the council housing of the 1960s and 1970s had been, too powerful to resist. It is being replaced by 1500 new homes (costing £200,000 each) of which 561 are for rent, 189 for shared ownership and 750 for private sale. The area has been rebranded "Blackwall Reach". On population growth, most UK cities outside London have increased too, but at a much lower rate: Newcastle is only 16% over the same period.

(35) Croydon started early down this road: Seifert, clearly a man before his time, developed two major high-rise office schemes there in 1970. One of these, in Addiscombe Road, survives and has been converted into residential use.

14

WHAT NEXT?

Anyone flying across the UK on a clear day looks down on a country where towns and villages are close together, divided by narrow slivers of woodland or farm land and connected by a substantial network of roads and railways. Compared to driving through France or Spain, where human settlements are further apart, any casual observer would consider the UK, and particularly England, as a place with a great liking for suburbs and low-density development.

And indeed, it is, with the kind of housing readily facilitated by the house-builders, large and small. Today, a century and a half after Ebenezer Howard returned from the US, the type of detached private homes that he would have recognised from his visits to Chicago and New York are still being planned and built in the UK. This is no accident: the house-builders, who jog along completing something between 100,000 and 150,000 homes per year, every year, decade after decade, are well-connected politically and much in favour of more "garden cities" being built. As are the CBI and the CPRE.[1]

The popularity of this type of development is recognised too by politicians. Around the time that George Osborne was announcing funding for Ebbsfleet, proposals were unveiled for a similar scheme at Bicester, where it was to be bolted on, so to speak, to an existing urban area. A close inspection of the plans for this reveal something quite similar to a 1960s or 1970s new town: new homes, greenery, new shops, other employment, new transport links... but minus the pre-1979 "statist" elements, and definitely no council housing.[2] By 2015, Osborne was announcing plans for something akin to this in North Essex as well as a rebooting and expansion of Didcot. Then in 2016 came the "Black Country Garden City" (45,000 new homes, scattered across various defunct ex-industrial sites in the West Midlands), followed a year later by a whole set of mini "garden villages", of between 1,500 and 10,000 new homes and a selection of larger "garden towns".[3]

The locations for the former include Warwickshire, Oxfordshire (2,200 homes over 531 acres at Eynsham, an average of only 4 per acre), Northamptonshire, Devon, Hampshire, Cornwall, Essex, Lincolnshire, Merseyside, Surrey (at Runnymede, by house-builder Crest Nicholson whose HQ is in the same area), Lancashire, Derbyshire, Cumbria and Cheshire. The garden towns are to be newly designed expansions of Aylesbury, Taunton and Harlow, Essex. All in all, there are about 50 such projects that will, supposedly, provide 400,000 new homes, an average of about 8,000 per scheme. But at the time of writing less than 5% have been built and many have yet to be granted a detailed planning consent. At this rate of progress, it would take 40-50 years to complete the programme. And, of course, it is only a tiny proportion of the new homes the UK actually needs.

Ironically, in addition to the chunks of land owned by private house-builders that underpin many of these schemes, a great deal else of what is being committed is either state, or local state, property. Much of this has been recycled through several variations of ownership since the New Town Commission became dormant and then defunct in the 1980s: English Partnerships and the Homes and Communities Agency were two such "successor" organisations, both now disbanded. Thus do the land acquisition policies, pursued from the 1940s through to the 1970s, continue to affect us. From time to time, further land is added into this pot, often being ex-MOD, ex-NHS or similar, from recently decommissioned sites.[4]

Relatively few government-owned sites exist within most cities, though. Here, the inflated prices demanded by landowners, and the reduced amount of state funding available for development have driven residential building remorselessly upwards. Hence the clustering of tall towers found in the most expensive areas, within which an increasing number of properties are now rented out to buy-to-let landlords. This "model" works for neither local house-builders nor local would-be home owners. Nor does it function efficiently as a means of providing social housing. What might remedy this state of affairs would be some way of limiting the price of land, as suggested by Lord Reith in 1941 and Churchill in 1945. There are few major politicians in the UK today who would advocate this. In the absence of such controls, what works in practical terms, as far as most people are concerned, is the continuing construction, in modest numbers, of low-density, out-of-town developments built for private sale: the traditional suburb/garden city/new town approach still built to a template that would be recognised by Ebenezer Howard.

The question must be asked, though, just how sustainable is this in the twenty-first century?

Before weighing up the great strategic issues of our age, it is worth pointing out that even at a basic, practical level, low-density development comes with many hidden costs. The most obvious of these is the expenditure required on regular maintenance of the colossal amounts of communal open space they contain, over and above private gardens and public park areas. The abundance of grass verges, planted areas, bushes, ornamental trees, traffic islands, immense roundabouts and roads that either proceed down heavily wooded cuttings or along similar embankments, all become unsightly eyesores if neglected. Strewn with carrier bags, crushed drink cartons, tins, bottles, blown out tyres, shopping trolleys and miscellaneous bits of furniture, glass, plastic, wood and metal, many increasingly are.[5]

Looking at the various garden cities, garden suburbs and new towns today, Letchworth remains well-kept because of Howard's heritage fund and associated governance mechanisms. Its neighbour Welwyn, though, is decidedly tatty as are most of the post-war developments, reduced after the sale of most of their income-generating assets to being just large residential areas

managed by cash-strapped local authorities. One solution might
be to reboot Howard's governance structures and apply them
everywhere. But would this work? Most people do not wish to pay
service charges on the scale that would now be required, nor do
they want to live in some king of gigantic housing cooperative.
Put simply, the problem is the design: because less taxes (local or
national) are raised from low-density developments, the cost of
providing infrastructure and services is disproportionately greater
than the cost of doing so in a high-density community.[6]

But this isn't just a case of adopting a different style of
architecture. In a future where global warming has made parts
of the planet uninhabitable and has led to significant amounts of
migration, coupled with population rises elsewhere, why would
building anything, anywhere, at about 5% of possible urban
density make any sense? Consider the facts. Currently the UK
has a population density of 724 people per square mile, one of
the highest in Europe. There are various estimates available about
how much higher it will go. One prediction has the population
at 75 million by 2040.[7] To have enough homes for that many
people, the UK needs to build 115,000 per annum over and above
what it currently does. In other words, it needs to provide an extra
2.3m extra homes, by 2040 – 1.9m more than are set to emerge
from all the new "garden villages", "garden towns" and similar
projects currently being prepared. None of this takes into account
either the complications caused by an ageing population and the
demand that creates in turn for a bigger, younger workforce, or
for that matter, changes in the size of households. Nor does it
consider the possible abandonment of settlements in low-lying
coastal areas should sea levels rise.[8]

Where would we want this extraordinary volume of new
housing to be provided? Considering the wider environmental
issues we face, expanding cul-de-sacs, low-rise blocks and semi-
detached houses further across woodland and farmland is surely
the worst approach. We need to be planting more trees – on quite
some scale – to maximise carbon capture. And with the likely
population increases the UK faces, we should be raising food

production to match this, rather than relying on buying what other countries export. Is it time, therefore, to change the way we plan and build new homes? Yes, and fortunately, any exercise that looks critically at where they are to be located, and how new, high-density, socially and ecologically viable towns and cities can be provided, doesn't need to start from scratch and reinvent the wheel.

One option would be to look closely at Hammarby, the development of which supposedly influenced Ebbsfleet. Located just south of Stockholm city centre, Hammarby is clearly part of an existing urban area and was originally intended as the Olympic village for Stockholm's bid for the 2004 games. The bid failed, but the area was built out anyway as an eco-town. Covering 66.5 acres it houses about 25,000 people: at a density of 376 per acre (roughly 90 homes per acre) it is about 20 times that of the proposed UK garden villages. Unlike the latter it also benefits from being within an existing city, with residents able to travel to and from work using public transport, bicycles and carpools rather than there being any requirement to own their own vehicle. Something like this is appearing on the site of the UK's Olympic village at Stratford, and more developments of this type, built to the same Hammarby-style template, could and should follow.[9]

If a completely new city were required, then Shenzhen, formerly a village on the Chinese-Hong Kong border, could be considered as a prototype. With a population of almost 20m, and a density 50% greater than that found in London, it features a vast number of high-rise residential buildings, massive amounts of public transport infrastructure, extensive business, industrial, tourist and leisure areas, all within a carefully designed and maintained public realm. Images of the city at night resemble the world of Philip K Dick's *Blade Runner*, as reimagined by Le Corbusier. But this is somewhere real. And if the Earth needs new cities, better this, surely, than cul-de-sacs of semi-detached houses stretching to the horizon.

As it happens, the UK probably doesn't need additional cities. We just need to make better use of those we already have. Leaving aside Poundbury and its brethren, typical UK house-builder schemes feature a traditional mixture of terraced, semi-detached and detached houses interspersed with occasional blocks of low-rise flats. In most places, these don't even create the type of streetscape produced by Archibald Cameron Corbett pre-1914, dipping way below this in density terms.[10] Nor is architecture the only problem. Housing in the UK costs too much. Far too many people today spend too much of their income on keeping a roof over their head. To be precise, as noted by the OECD, 25% of UK households now spend more than 40% of their income on housing, the highest level in the world.[11]

The policies followed by governments from both the UK's main political parties in the last 40 years have led the country to this position. We have been living through a period which has seen the UK evolve from a manufacturing economy with post-industrial features, into a financialised, globalised economy with a self-restraining feeble state. Aside from housing, and its many issues, there has been an economic restructuring occurring within all our major cities. Assuming one wants to change this (and some don't, or at any rate don't see housing and town planning as a primary issue of concern) we have to consider how to address the failures of the past whilst also planning in a sustainable way for the future.

During the UK's deliberate journey away from high levels of state provision, particularly spending on housing, there have been many who have made a positive contribution, despite having to navigate these difficulties. Of all the architects, politicians and planners, though, none has been more consistent in this field, or wielded as much influence during that time as Michael Heseltine. When he was interviewed for this book in October 2020 both his experience and continuing commitment to urban renewal and improved housing were apparent. We spoke by telephone during the first lengthy pandemic lockdown, ranging over a career that stretched from the immense optimism of the UK in the 1960s (when he was better known, to some, as a magazine publisher), through the political battles of the 1970s and 1980s to his triumph in the 1990s with City Challenge and his brief Indian summer under David Cameron and George Osborne.

How would he tackle today's problems? Without hesitation he answered *"...I'd create a land register with every site on it. I would compel land owners – and most of the bigger ones are government departments – to release their land by starting with a legal presumption that it was available for purchase, and transferring control of the land to a central body, a sort of roving Development Corporation, responsible for its disposal. I'd also face down the issues raised about the green belt, much of which is actually quite poor-quality land. I'd have an arrangement where for every acre of green belt developed, 10 acres of "brownfield" land elsewhere would have to be "greened". People would understand that. For private sites, and land that wasn't being properly used I'd use Compulsory Purchase Order powers. Government-owned land is the key here..."* Having set out an unashamedly "statist" position, he then underscored this with *"...Government has an absolutely crucial role – there is no conceivable way you can get any progress without it. Reform of local government is also required..."*

And what would he build? Whilst agreeing that the UK was a small country with a high population, he favoured a mixed approach *"...I'm a great believer in creating free-standing towns – attractive places where people want to live. To do that we need to clear more land and also do a lot of land assembly. You're really talking about having another Land Commission, of the sort that operated under Sir Henry Wells when the New Towns were being built in the 1960s... I think we need to do both – build traditional towns and go up in height. We also need to industrialise housing production..."* The latter point was particularly intriguing, with its implication that the state would have an industrial strategy directed at tackling shortages across the economy, in this case within housing. A far cry from where we have been in the last couple of decades.

Finally, he acknowledged the critical issue of affordability, stating *"...To produce council housing you need government subsidy... which can only come with government commitment... The private sector does a fantastic job, but the private sector is there to make a profit. You can't make a profit out of social housing..."* After a couple of decades of bipartisan agreement about the primacy of the private sector and the importance of endlessly expanding home ownership it was refreshing to hear such a thorough counter-argument being made: one, incidentally, that many Prime Ministers and Chancellors of the Exchequer, stretching back over 100 years would have automatically accepted.

Today, we live at a time when the future of the planet is more to the fore in the minds of most people than at any time since the peak years of the nuclear stand-off between east and west. With regular reminders appearing on news bulletins about unusual weather, the spread of arid conditions, storm damage and flooding, the market – if one could put it that way – for "green" policies has never been greater. Accordingly, all the major political parties ensure that their manifestos feature significant commentaries and commitments on environmental matters. Some of this might be implemented. Whether it will be sufficient or not is a moot point, and we should perhaps judge such remarks against the policies proposed by the Green Party, support for whom has never been higher. Today they participate in government in Scotland (and Ireland), so how would they organise housing provision nationally, were they to get the chance?

In July 2021 I contacted Councillor Carla Denyer, representing Clifton Down in Bristol for the Green Party whilst doubling as their national housing spokesperson. She replied to a detailed set of questions within 3 weeks, which, given she became Joint Leader of the Green Party 24 days after responding, said much for her commitment and organisation. Like Heseltine she favoured a greater role for the state, and, like him, she would, for the main, build in existing cities and towns, commenting "...*Higher density urban living is more sustainable in terms of carbon footprint and also helps sustain local high streets, bus routes and other facilities by providing the critical mass of customers. I want to see a future where most people live in a '15-minute neighbourhood'...*" There were other areas too where the Green Party approach overlapped with Heseltine's statist model: they wanted a housing market where people have real choices (ie, genuinely affordable housing and a balanced mixture of tenure) and significantly increased funding to enable all of their proposals to come to fruition.

Where they were different was in the scale and scope of the regulatory framework that the Green Party would erect. Firstly, they would introduce rent controls, implement a licensing scheme for all private landlords and put the local housing market across the UK under local authority regulation.[12] Next, they would adopt, presumably at national level, a statutory provision for affordable housing, irrespective of what has been paid for land, (echoes here of Reith and Churchill) and would end RTB discounts in England.[13] They would allow local authorities to borrow to build, as had been the case pre-1979, and they would reboot non-local authority affordable housing, including an enhanced role for housing cooperatives. Thirdly, they would improve the building regulations and the regulatory framework within which private developers operated.[14] Finally, they would instigate a massive national emergency retrofit programme – across all tenures and ownerships – to ensure that every home in the UK was environmentally compliant. Most radically of all, though, was a pledge to hold down house prices by ending tax breaks, with the policing of this being given to the Bank of England as a duty.[15]

None of the above ought to surprise anyone. Considering the UK's housing journey over the last century and a half, it is clear from studying the evidence that, if we wish to build sufficient homes, ensure that they are truly affordable and produced in a way that both respects the environment and takes into account all the important social factors governing their location, then the state, and only the state, must have a major role in deciding, funding and implementing this. It is clear that the private sector cannot do this by itself. Leave them to build their 100,000 to 150,000 units per annum (subject to location and improved regulation) and instead reboot local authority housing, on a massive scale! And, as part of this, reconsider the role and functions of housing associations. Today, many of these, after 20 years of mergers, re-brandings, further mergers and further re-brandings, are effectively large corporate businesses. Most are also somewhat remote[16] and have little in common with the sharply focussed community-based organisations they once were when founded in the 1960s and 1970s. Having non-local authority social housing providers is a good thing: if nothing else, it provides the public with a choice of social landlords within their area. But do we need such entities to be so immense? It might be better, surely, if they were more localised in function and able, once more, to tackle specific problems rather than just act as the recipients of whatever amounts of social housing local house-builders were amenable to providing on their traditional low-density schemes.

There are many challenges bearing down upon us. The way we build our housing in the future, and who we build it for, will determine if we can survive and indeed thrive despite these. This book argues that we should put aside the way we have conducted the political economy of the UK in recent decades, so that we can make the best-informed choices about how to proceed. It is time to provide for all, plan strategically, and accept the cost that entails. Our children and grandchildren must not look back and wonder why we failed.

Notes

(1) On the CPRE and garden cities see: https://www.cpre.org.uk/stories/garden-cities-for-the-21st-century/
(2) For more on Bicester see *The Financial Times* 1 December 2014 at https://www.ft.com/content/5e815bc6-798a-11e4-9e81-00144feabdc0
(3) On the Black Country Garden City see the brochure at: https://www.blackcountrylep.co.uk/upload/files/GardenCity/bcgc_brochure_FINAL.pdf
(4) For new garden city proposals see: https://www.housinglin.org.uk/_assets/Resources/Housing/OtherOrganisation/New_towns_report.pdf This argues for more of them and shows how much ex-new town development corporation land is owned by Homes for England, the latest quango to inherit that role. It also argues for a continuation of the Letchworth community investment model. On the issue of whether private house-builders buy and hoard land, the 2019 Bellway Homes Annual Report says that they started 13,000 homes that year and had enough land in reserve to last about 3 years if they ceased buying. (Enough for 42,000 homes). They recorded an annual profit before tax of £663m.
(5) Impenetrable roundabouts seem to be something of a haven for the destitute, some of whom have resided there for many years. Frequent news reports appear about their use by the homeless: https://www.bbc.co.uk/news/av/uk-england-tyne-39411937 (Sunderland), https://www.leeds-live.co.uk/news/leeds-news/man-living-armley-gyratory-roundabout-15010718 (Armley Gyratory), https://

www.examinerlive.co.uk/news/local-news/homeless-man-camped-roundabout-hopes-19283919 (Scarborough) and https://www.westerntelegraph.co.uk/news/18907128.community-pays-tribute-kilgettys-mini-man-lived-outdoors-half-life/ (Kilgetty, Pembrokeshire). In something like a cross between Clive King's 1963 children's novel *Stig of the Dump* and JG Ballard's 1974 *Concrete Island*, the Wolverhampton Ring Road was home for nearly 50 years for Jozef Stawinoga, thought at one time to be a Nazi war criminal. See: https://en.wikipedia.org/wiki/J%C3%B3zef_Stawinoga

(6) The Goldsmith Street scheme in Norwich, built as council housing by Norwich City Council, provides an example of a dense, low-rise, energy-efficient scheme: 93 homes over 4.5 acres (roughly 17 per acre). It is built to *passivhaus* standards, a concept developed in Europe from the early 1990s. Not all such schemes are low-rise. China has the largest project of this type. See: https://www.treehugger.com/chinese-city-has-largest-passive-house-project-world-4856144 Spain has the tallest such building, in Bilbao. See: https://prismpub.com/bolueta-in-bilbao-spain-is-now-the-tallest-passive-house-building-in-the-world/

(7) On the rising population of the UK see: https://blogs.lse.ac.uk/brexit/2019/07/01/what-the-uk-population-will-look-like-by-2061-under-hard-soft-or-no-brexit-scenarios/ In Europe, the Netherlands (1,060 per sq ml) and Belgium (983 per sq ml) exceed the current UK level with Germany somewhat lower at 608 per sq ml. Population density in the US is 91 per sq ml. (12.5% that of the UK).

(8) In terms of comparisons with neighbouring countries, the IPPR think tank compared the UK with Germany at: https://www.ippr.org/publications/german-model-homes It found that, allowing for population differences, the UK builds, year on year, about 14% less housing than Germany. Ireland, on the other hand, built 21,686 "affordable" homes in 2020, which pro-rata to the population size is vastly in excess of the UK output. See: https://www.gov.ie/en/publication/a5cb1-construction-activity-starts/

(9) The UK's Olympic Village, the Stratford Olympic Park, is almost the same size as Hammarby and was developed by the Olympic Delivery Authority, established by the Blair government in 2006. Unlike the New Deal for Communities schemes, this was very much a route one development corporation. Unlike in Sweden, its assets have subsequently been sold to the Qatari Sovereign Wealth Fund. Other parts of the area continue to be developed by the London Legacy Development Corporation, under the jurisdiction of the Mayor of London. Scandinavia hosts many innovative architects, notably Jan Gehl (Danish, and an advocate of car-free areas within cities from the early 1970s) and Finn Williams (a UK national, now City Architect in Malmo).

(10) One example of this might be the redevelopment of Regent Quay, Sittingbourne. A 26-acre former industrial site, the northern section of this contains 102 homes on 9.5 acres. Most of these are 4-bedroom houses, and all but 4 are for private sale. In appearance – garages excepted – many resemble pre-1914 garden suburb/garden city properties. Which is not a specific criticism (after all, these are popular and they sell) but rather an indication of how deeply embedded this type of aspirational housing is.

(11) Evidence of this can be seen at: https://assets.publishing.service.gov.uk/government/uploads/system/uploads/attachment_data/file/898397/2018-19_EHS_Housing_costs_and_affordability.pdf and also at https://www.oecd.org/els/family/HC1-2-Housing-costs-over-income.pdf

(12) Rent controls are common across Europe. See: https://www.iut.nu/wp-content/uploads/2021/04/b017e9d8-ccda-4974-b4ab-e455010aa32d-1.pdf They also exist in selected areas within the US, but have no equivalent in the UK.

(13) With the advent of devolved government, the RTB has been abolished in Scotland and Wales, and similar is expected to happen in Northern Ireland. In an example of "English exceptionalism" no one else operates an RTB discount of the type available to English council tenants. Some countries (Denmark, Sweden, Belgium) allow no sales of social rented properties at all, others allow a sale "to sitting tenants", approximately the same policy that the UK had pre-1972. See: https://www.europarl.europa.eu/RegData/etudes/note/join/2013/492469/ IPOL-EMPL_NT(2013)492469_EN.pdf

(14) A topical issue once again following the disastrous fire at Grenfell Tower, and the subsequent discovery of inadequately regulated and inspected practices in building construction: in this case the use of cladding as an integral part of a buildings structure. In another legacy of the Thatcher era, (and an echo of the root cause of the earlier Ronan Point collapse) the UK's building regulations have been greatly reduced since the 1980s, as have the numbers of staff at local authorities with a duty to enforce them.

(15) This might seem odd to some people, but compared to other national banks, the Bank of England has few, if any, duties outside of managing the UK's currency. In comparison, the US Federal Reserve is expected to assist the economy in maintaining maximum employment, the Bank of France is in charge of the economic education of the public and assists businesses of various sizes in obtaining credit, the Reserve Bank of Australia is responsible for the maintenance of full employment and "the economic prosperity and welfare of the people" whilst De Nederlandsche Bank may – subject to Royal Decree – "perform other tasks in the public interest". The Bank of England could do with a bit more work.

(16) In every sense as a great many now shelter behind call centres in business parks located on the fringe of urban areas.

APPENDIX

(When Osborn went to Moscow)

Like most European countries the Soviet Union suffered significant damage in the Second World War. Much of the western section of the country was devastated by extensive battle damage and, after 1945, urgent steps were taken to replace the housing that had been lost and to provide new homes for a rising population. The Soviets did so by building immense high-rise developments, usually located on the fringe of existing cities, together with specially planned new settlements, often with a military, industrial or strategic purpose, dispersed in the interior of the country. The architecture adopted for these made copious use of factory-manufactured materials that were rapidly assembled on site.

However, they also reached out, particularly after the death of Stalin in 1953 and the rapid elevation thereafter of Nikita Khrushchev. As noted in Chapter 11, Frederic Osborn wrote to Lewis Mumford *"...I have had a lot of correspondence with the USSR Ministry of Construction. They have fully adopted the Dispersal and Green Belt policy which they think they can operate more logically than Britain..."*[1]. This followed an approach made to Osborn by the USSR earlier that year *"to advise on the organisation and design of a prototype new town"*. A trip to Poland and the USSR followed (in May-June) after which Osborn began working on how best to advise the Soviets. On 1 July he wrote to HW Wells, of Chesterton's Surveyors[2], stressing *"we wouldn't want to send a team that would simply carry Continental ideas to Russia as if they were British ideas"*, by which one would suppose that he was emphasising that Le Corbusier-style schemes ought to be avoided and classic UK vernacular, with possibly a few low-rise blocks of flats, recommended instead.

This is at odds – possibly – with what TASS reported in a press release dated 8 July 1958. Here, Osborn is quoted as stating *"The scale of housing construction in the Soviet Union is truly striking"*, notes that rent levels in the Soviet Union are exceptionally low in comparison with England and concludes by praising the Moscow suburb of Cheremushki. The last is a misspelling, the suburb mentioned actually being Cheryomushki. If Osborn liked what he saw there, he was breaking the habits of a lifetime. From 1956 the district was used as the site for a massive prefabricated housing project, culminating a couple of years later with a design competition in which seven different Soviet architectural practices were asked to provide a model block of high-rise, high-density flats. Built almost exclusively from concrete panels assembled on site, the winner (a block designated K7) was selected for mass production and construction across the USSR, being replicated thereafter in hundreds of thousands of locations. It was nothing like Letchworth, albeit Cheryomushki also contained a great deal of open space, health centres, nurseries, schools, cinemas, libraries and theatres. In fact, at about the time Osborn came to visit, the location was the centre of the largest prefabricated housing construction project in the world, and many others came too to see how the future was emerging on the outskirts of Moscow.[3]

The TASS press release kicked off media interest in the UK with *The Daily Telegraph* running an article on new housing estates in Moscow (15 July 1958) after which the Royal Seed Establishment wrote to Osborn (23 July 1958) advising *"it is not normal practice to apply artificial watering to grass sown in Russia, but that is largely due to the fact that it is allowed to grow too long"*. Further correspondence in a similar vein followed with Ransomes, Sims and Jefferies, of Ipswich[4] sending Osborn a lawnmower catalogue, because, it would appear *"Our attention has been drawn to recent articles in the press referring to your efforts to interest the Russians in finer strains of grass and better lawns"*. What was this fetish about grass cutting and lawn maintenance about, and why did Osborn and others think the Russians couldn't manage this effectively?

Finally, a brief for what was required arrived from the Soviet Union.[5] Dated 21 August 1958 (and with a note explaining it was only received on 7 October) it specified, inter alia:

- Up-to-date methods of planning and building
- High technical level of industrial methods of production
- Experimental housing region in the south west part of Moscow
- 4 km from Moscow University
- Could be used as an example and implemented elsewhere in the USSR

All of which confirms that what Osborn was being asked to take part in was the competition to build a high-density, high-rise block of flats, rather than an idyllic UK-type new town. A briefing from the Town and Country Planning Association (24 October 1958) followed, confirming that the project was for a neighbourhood for 20,000 people on about 200 acres. (Which implied about 100 people per acre; say 20-25 homes per acre, about three times the amount Osborn usually recommended). In the days that followed a lot of information was provided to a Mr A Petrusevitch, listed as a Counsellor at the USSR Embassy, London, with Osborn confirming on 3 November 1958 that this included details of Peterlee and Newton Aycliffe.

At which point the Foreign Office got involved. Osborn gave details of a tour of Yugoslavia and Poland that the Town and Country Planning Association had undertaken and explained to a Mr Brimelow (4 November) that the Soviet Union, under the auspices of V Kucherenko, Chairman of Gosstroy, was considering commissioning a British town planner.[6] In the end nothing transpired from any of this. After a letter from Frederick Gibberd (5 November 1958) which made the point "I was concerned to find the neighbourhood is such a large one: it seems to me more like a new town" the correspondence in File DE/FJO/G22 (Planning Project in Moscow) held in the Hertfordshire County Council archives ceases. The Soviet Union weren't really looking for a Howard-Osborn type suburb at all. There were no UK entrants for their design competition. Cheryomushki emerged as a large-scale, flatted urban scheme using much prefabricated housing, and was used by Shostakovich as the setting for his 1959 comic opera *Moscow, Cheryomushki*, a farce about housing shortages and inept bureaucracy.[7] The area, which in the 1980s was briefly renamed in honour of Leonid Brezhnev, is much changed today, with a great deal of the 1950s housing demolished, but continues to thrive and expand. The HQ of Gazprom (the Russian state-owned gas monopoly) is based there, in a new high-rise office building.

Why did the Soviet Union contact Osborn in 1958? Was it inspired by a dim memory, somewhere in the mind of an elderly Bolshevik, of the Tolstoyan church in Southgate Road pre-1914 and its connection to Letchworth? Or did they just want to find out, for strategic planning reasons, how the UK was dispersing its population? Or a combination of both? Given how much the Howard-Osborn model for housing development owed to the US, this episode, and Lenin's much earlier supposed visit to Letchworth, are striking reminders of how their projects continued to be viewed as "progressive" in leftist, non-capitalist circles.

Notes

(1) Correspondence dated 1 August 1958.
(2) A long-established firm of London surveyors owned by the Chesterton family, one of whose members was the writer GK Chesterton, and another the English fascist AK Chesterton. Henry Weston Wells was a partner there from 1934 and later Chief Estates Officer of the Ministry of Town and Country Planning (and therefore one of the chief architects of the 1947 Town and Country Planning Act). He served on innumerable committees during the post-war expansion of British housing, and in 1965 was elected President of the Royal Institution of Chartered Surveyors.
(3) For more on this period of Soviet town planning see: https://www.calvertjournal.com/features/show/4235/soviet-mass-housing-novye-cheryomushki-belyayevo-suburbs
(4) Gardening equipment manufacturers, by appointment to the Crown.
(5) And written in very poor English, Sacha Baron Cohen/Borat style. Didn't the USSR have any decent translators?
(6) Kucherenko, a middle-ranking functionary, is referenced in the journal of AM Puzanov, Soviet Ambassador to North Korea, copies of which (marked Top Secret)

can be found at https://digitalarchive.wilsoncenter.org/document/119471.
pdf?v=d2173d3d8950c64e1e2b1c795ca0750b (Presumably his communications
were being intercepted by the CIA). In these Kucherenko is thanked for
providing construction materials to the regime of Kim Il Sung, at a reception
hosted by the Chinese Embassy as part of The Great Leap Forward. Gosstroy
was the Soviet State Committee for Construction.

(7) In one scene of which, prefiguring Ronan Point, a young architect who has
moved into a new flat finds that one of the walls collapses.

INDEX